1986

ADVANCED
UNIX
PROGRAMMING

ADVANCED
UNIX
PROGRAMMING

Marc J. Rochkind

Advanced Programming Institute, Ltd.
Boulder, Colorado

PRENTICE-HALL, INC., Englewood Cliffs, New Jersey 07632

Library of Congress Cataloging in Publication Data

Rochkind, Marc J.   (date)
   Advanced UNIX programming.

   Bibliography: p.
   Includes index.
      1. UNIX (Computer operating system) 2. Electronic
digital computers—Programming. I. Title.
QA76.76.063R63 1985   001.64′2   85-9267
ISBN   0-13-011818-4
ISBN   0-13-011800-1 (pbk.)

Editorial/production supervision: *Lisa Schulz*
Interior design: *Jayne Conte*
Cover design: *Lundgren Graphics, Ltd.*
Manufacturing buyer: *Gordon Osbourne*
Indexer: *Ian Tucker*

UNIX is a trademark of AT&T Bell Laboratories

Prentice-Hall Software Series,
Brian W. Kernighan, Advisor.

© 1985 by **Prentice-Hall, Inc.,** Englewood Cliffs, New Jersey 07632

The author and publisher of this book have used their best efforts in preparing this book. These efforts include the development, research, and testing of the theories and programs to determine their effectiveness. The author and publisher make no warranty of any kind, expressed or implied, with regard to these programs or the documentation contained in this book. The author and publisher shall not be liable in any event for incidental or consequential damages in connection with, or arising out of, the furnishing, performance, or use of these programs.

Printed in the United States of America

10 9 8 7 6 5 4 3 2 1

ISBN 0-13-011818-4
ISBN 0-13-011800-1 {PBK.} 01

Prentice-Hall International (UK) Limited, *London*
Prentice-Hall of Australia Pty. Limited, *Sydney*
Prentice-Hall Canada Inc., *Toronto*
Prentice-Hall Hispanoamericana, S.A., *Mexico*
Prentice-Hall of India Private Limited, *New Delhi*
Prentice-Hall of Japan, Inc., *Tokyo*
Prentice-Hall of Southeast Asia Pte. Ltd., *Singapore*
Editora Prentice-Hall do Brasil, Ltda., *Rio de Janeiro*
Whitehall Books Limited, *Wellington, New Zealand*

In memory of my mother, Eva Brooks Rochkind

The example programs in this book are available in computer-readable form. For ordering information, write to:

Advanced Programming Institute
3080 Valmont Road, Suite 220
Boulder, CO 80301

CONTENTS

PREFACE xi

Chapter 1 FUNDAMENTAL CONCEPTS *1*
1.1   INTRODUCTION *1*
1.2   FILES *1*
    1.2.1   Ordinary Files 2
    1.2.2   Directories 2
    1.2.3   Special Files 3
1.3   PROGRAMS AND PROCESSES *4*
1.4   SIGNALS *5*
1.5   PROCESS-IDS AND PROCESS GROUPS *6*
1.6   PERMISSIONS *7*
1.7   OTHER PROCESS ATTRIBUTES *9*
1.8   INTERPROCESS COMMUNICATION *10*
1.9   USING SYSTEM CALLS *12*
1.10 PROGRAMMING CONVENTIONS *14*
1.11 PORTABILITY *16*

Chapter 2 BASIC FILE I/O *18*
2.1   INTRODUCTION *18*
2.2   FILE DESCRIPTORS *19*
2.3   creat SYSTEM CALL *20*

2.4   unlink SYSTEM CALL *21*
2.5   IMPLEMENTING SEMAPHORES WITH FILES *21*
2.6   open SYSTEM CALL *24*
2.7   write SYSTEM CALL *28*
2.8   read SYSTEM CALL *31*
2.9   close SYSTEM CALL *31*
2.10 BUFFERED I/O *32*
2.11 lseek SYSTEM CALL *37*
2.12 PORTABILITY *40*

Chapter 3 ADVANCED FILE I/O 42
3.1   INTRODUCTION *42*
3.2   I/O ON DIRECTORIES *42*
3.3   I/O ON DISK SPECIAL FILES *45*
3.4   DATES AND TIMES *49*
3.5   FILE MODES *53*
3.6   link SYSTEM CALL *54*
3.7   access SYSTEM CALL *57*
3.8   mknod SYSTEM CALL *58*
3.9   chmod SYSTEM CALL *60*
3.10 chown SYSTEM CALL *60*
3.11 utime SYSTEM CALL *61*
3.12 stat AND fstat SYSTEM CALLS *62*
3.13 fcntl SYSTEM CALL *70*
3.14 PORTABILITY *72*

Chapter 4 TERMINAL I/O 74
4.1   INTRODUCTION *74*
4.2   NORMAL TERMINAL I/O *75*
4.3   NONBLOCKING TERMINAL I/O *78*
4.4   ioctl SYSTEM CALL *82*
      4.4.1 Basic ioctl Usage 83
      4.4.2 Speed, Character Size, and Parity 84
      4.4.3 Character Mapping 84
      4.4.4 Delays and Tabs 85
      4.4.5 Flow Control 85
      4.4.6 Control Characters 85
      4.4.7 Echo 87
      4.4.8 Punctual Input 86
4.5   RAW TERMINAL I/O *88*
4.6   OTHER SPECIAL FILES *89*
4.7   PORTABILITY *90*

Chapter 5 PROCESSES *93*
5.1 INTRODUCTION *93*
5.2 ENVIRONMENT *93*
5.3 exec SYSTEM CALLS *101*
5.4 fork SYSTEM CALL *110*
5.5 exit SYSTEM CALL *113*
5.6 wait SYSTEM CALL *114*
5.7 SYSTEM CALLS TO GET IDS *117*
5.8 setuid AND setgid SYSTEM CALLS *118*
5.9 setpgrp SYSTEM CALL *118*
5.10 chdir SYSTEM CALL *119*
5.11 chroot SYSTEM CALL *119*
5.12 nice SYSTEM CALL *120*
5.13 PORTABILITY *121*

Chapter 6 BASIC INTERPROCESS COMMUNICATION *123*
6.1 INTRODUCTION *123*
6.2 pipe SYSTEM CALL *124*
6.3 dup SYSTEM CALL *129*
6.4 A REAL SHELL *132*
6.5 BIDIRECTIONAL PIPES *146*
6.6 PORTABILITY *154*

Chapter 7 ADVANCED INTERPROCESS COMMUNICATION *156*
7.1 INTRODUCTION *156*
7.2 DATABASE MANAGEMENT SYSTEM ISSUES *157*
7.3 FIFOS, OR NAMED PIPES *159*
7.4 IMPLEMENTING MESSAGES WITH FIFOS *160*
7.5 MESSAGE SYSTEM CALLS (SYSTEM V) *182*
7.6 SEMAPHORES *185*
    7.6.1 Basic Semaphore Usage 185
    7.6.2 Implementing Semaphores With Messages 187
    7.6.3 Semaphores in System V 188
    7.6.4 Semaphores in Xenix 3 190
7.7 SHARED MEMORY *192*
    7.7.1 Basic Shared Memory Usage 192
    7.7.2 Shared Memory in System V 193
    7.7.3 Shared Memory in Xenix 3 198
7.8 RECORD LOCKING IN XENIX 3 *203*
7.9 PORTABILITY *206*

Chapter 8 SIGNALS *208*
8.1   INTRODUCTION *208*
8.2   TYPES OF SIGNALS *209*
8.3   signal SYSTEM CALL *212*
8.4   GLOBAL JUMPS *217*
8.5   kill SYSTEM CALL *219*
8.6   pause SYSTEM CALL *220*
8.7   alarm SYSTEM CALL *220*
8.8   PORTABILITY *225*

Chapter 9 MISCELLANEOUS SYSTEM CALLS 227
9.1   INTRODUCTION *227*
9.2   ulimit SYSTEM CALL *227*
9.3   brk AND sbrk SYSTEM CALLS *228*
9.4   umask SYSTEM CALL *230*
9.5   ustat SYSTEM CALL *231*
9.6   uname SYSTEM CALL *232*
9.7   sync SYSTEM CALL *233*
9.8   profil SYSTEM CALL *234*
9.9   ptrace SYSTEM CALL *234*
9.10 times SYSTEM CALL *235*
9.11 time SYSTEM CALL *237*
9.12 stime SYSTEM CALL *237*
9.13 plock SYSTEM CALL (SYSTEM V) *238*
9.14 mount SYSTEM CALL *238*
9.15 umount SYSTEM CALL *239*
9.16 acct SYSTEM CALL *240*
9.17 sys3b SYSTEM CALL (SYSTEM V) *240*
9.18 PORTABILITY *240*

Appendix A SYSTEM V PROCESS ATTRIBUTES *242*

Appendix B STANDARD SUBROUTINES *245*

BIBLIOGRAPHY *255*

INDEX *257*

PREFACE

The subject of this book is UNIX system calls—the interface between the UNIX kernel and the user programs that run on top of it. Those who interact only with commands, like the shell, text editors, and other application programs, may have little need to know much about system calls, but a thorough knowledge of them is essential for UNIX programmers. System calls are the *only* way to access kernel facilities such as the file system, the multitasking mechanisms, and the interprocess communication primitives.

System calls define what UNIX is. Everything else—subroutines and commands—is built on this foundation. While the novelty of many of these higher-level programs has been responsible for much of UNIX's renown, they could as well have been programmed on any modern operating system. When one describes UNIX as elegant, simple, efficient, reliable, and portable, one is referring not to the commands (some of which are none of these things), but to the kernel.

How hard is it to learn UNIX system calls? When I first started programming UNIX, in 1973, it wasn't very hard at all. UNIX—and its programmer's manual—was only a fraction of its present size and complexity. There weren't any programming examples in the manual, but all of the source code was on-line and it was easy to read through programs like the shell or the editor to see how system calls worked. Perhaps most important, there were more experienced people around to ask for help. Even Dennis Ritchie and Ken Thompson, the inventors of UNIX, took time out to help me.

Today's aspiring UNIX programmers have a tougher challenge than I did.

UNIX is now so widely dispersed that an expert is unlikely to be nearby. Most computers running UNIX are licensed for the object code only, so the source code for commands is unavailable. There are twice as many system calls now as there were in 1973, and the quality of the manual has deteriorated markedly from the days when Ritchie and Thompson did all the system call write-ups. It's now full of grotesque paragraphs like this:

> *If the set-user-ID mode bit of the new process file is set (see chmod(2)), exec sets the effective user ID of the new process to the owner ID of the new process file. Similarly, if the set-group-ID mode bit of the new process file is set, the effective group ID of the new process is set to the group ID of the new process file. The real user ID and the real group ID of the new process remain the same as those of the calling process.*

As an old-timer I understood what this meant when I first saw it, but a new-comer is sure to be completely baffled. And until now, there's been nowhere to turn.

This book's goal is to allow any experienced programmer to learn UNIX system calls as easily as I did, and then to use them wisely and portably. It's packed with examples—over 3500 lines of C code. Instead of just tactics (*how* the system calls are used), I've tried also to include strategies (*why* and *when* they're used). And there's lots of informal advice as well, based on my experiences programming UNIX over the past dozen years.

There are many versions of UNIX these days, five of which are most important:

1. System V, the newest AT&T offering. Its system calls are a superset of those in System III.

2. System III, which preceded System V (System IV wasn't released).

3. Version 7, the last release to come from the Bell Laboratories research organization (in 1979). While no longer in distribution itself, this version has formed the basis for many UNIX derivatives which are in distribution. It's probably the best understood AT&T version because most UNIX books are about Version 7.

4. Berkeley 4.2BSD from the University of California, an extensive modification of Version 7. Many of its system calls appear to be a blend of Version 7 and System III, but there are dozens of differences. Over 60 system calls have been added.

5. Xenix, a product of Microsoft Corporation. The newest version, based on System III, is called Xenix 3 in this book. Although Xenix is only one of many competing commercial systems, I've singled it out for special emphasis because it's the most popular microcomputer version, and—of paramount importance—it's supported by IBM on the Personal Computer AT. That almost guarantees that more computers will run Xenix 3 than will run all other versions combined.

It's desirable to write UNIX programs that can run on all of these five versions. Unless I've noted otherwise, everything in this book applies to System III, System V, and Xenix 3—and to the numerous brand names (such as PC/IX and UniPlus) that are repackagings of one of them.[1] All system calls in those three versions have been included, except for a few insignificant system calls in Xenix 3. I've also given hints for writing programs that can be ported to Version 7 and Berkeley 4.2 BSD. I haven't included the 60 or so system calls unique to 4.2 BSD, but most of what is in this book will work on that version. Insofar as non-AT&T-based systems such as Idris, Coherent, and Regulus are accurate clones of UNIX, this book applies to them too, but I've not included specific information about them. In any event, this book will help you learn how to program any version of UNIX—it's easy to pick up the details once you know the concepts.

You'll want to keep your UNIX manual nearby while reading this book. That way you can check for differences between what I've presented and the way your particular system works. In addition, it allows you to familiarize yourself with the organization and wording of the manual. In the long run the manual will be your primary reference, so you need to come to terms with it sooner or later anyhow.

A UNIX industry organization called /usr/group has proposed a UNIX standard that includes specifications for system calls. It's essentially a subset of System III (and hence also of System V and Xenix 3), with the addition of one system call, l o c k f (for record locking). But it's too incomplete to help very much with portability—the committee was only able to agree on that which was already uniform across the various versions. Specifically, it omits details of terminal I/O and newer interprocess communication mechanisms such as messages, semaphores, and shared memory. There are references to and comments on the standard throughout this book.

This is an "advanced" UNIX book. You should already be familiar with UNIX, at least as a user, and you should know the C programming language (you'll know it even better when you finish this book). Chapter 1 is a refresher that summarizes the facilities of the kernel and introduces terminology I'll be using throughout. If you find yourself unprepared for Chap. 1, start with one or two of the books I've recommended in the Bibliography.

I've organized the system calls into functional groups. Chapters 2 through 4 describe system calls for I/O on files and terminals. Chapter 5 is about processes (multitasking) and Chaps. 6 and 7 are about communication between processes. Chapter 8 is about signals. I've put system calls that didn't fit anywhere else in Chap. 9. Appendix A is a complete list of process attributes, and Appendix B summarizes the standard subroutines used in the examples. I've included it for those readers who wish to read in bed or on a plane and don't have their UNIX manual with them.

I've assumed that many readers will read this book out of sequence, especially

---

[1]The proliferation of names isn't because these systems are so different, but simply because UNIX resellers are prohibited from using AT&T's trade-mark.

those who are already UNIX programmers. There are numerous cross-references to help you find your way around. For those who want to study UNIX more methodically, I've arranged the presentation into a sequence that minimizes references to subjects that haven't yet been introduced. I haven't been able to totally eliminate these, however, so sequential readers will occasionally find themselves using the cross-references too. But in all cases the peeking ahead may be deferred on first reading without impacting your ability to follow the material. A careful reading of Chap. 1 when you start will help considerably.

This book makes a good supplementary text in an upper-level or graduate course in operating systems. Along with the theoretical principles, it's valuable for students to see how things are done in real life. Naturally, most of what UNIX does is grubbier than what the textbooks propose, but a few things about UNIX—such as its magnificent blend of simplicity and power—are hard to capture when speaking in generalities. You need to see the details to appreciate the contributions of UNIX to operating-system technology.

I've included some exercises at the end of Chaps. 2 through 9, almost all of which require some UNIX programming. With a few exceptions, these should take only a few hours to do, provided a UNIX system is readily accessible and response time is adequate. It's best if these programs are reviewed in code-walk-through sessions (after debugging and testing). UNIX is rich enough so that two programmers are likely to come up with vastly different solutions to the same problem. Sharing these solutions is at least as valuable as arriving at one.

Although I am the sole author of this book, I didn't figure UNIX out by myself. Over the years I've been tutored by many of my colleagues at Bell Laboratories, especially Bill Burnette, Rudd Canaday, Don Carter, Ted Dolotta, Alan Glasser, Rich Graveman, Dick Haight, Evan Ivie, Paul Jensen, John Linderman, Terry Lyons, John Mashey, Dennis Ritchie, Bill Roome, Ken Thompson, Larry Wehr, and Peter Weinberger. None of these people had anything directly to do with this book; the opinions—and the inevitable mistakes—are all mine. But they originated many of the techniques and strategies that I've passed on.

Brian Kernighan, who also could be on the previous list, was involved with this book from the start. He carefully reviewed my original proposal and outline, helped me secure a contract with Prentice-Hall, and reviewed the final manuscript.

Microsoft Corporation graciously provided a complete set of documentation for Xenix 3. Thanks to their help, I've been able to include up-to-date information that will be of great benefit to the legions of programmers who will be using the IBM Personal Computer AT.

I wrote all the text and tested most of the programs under PC/IX, a version of System III ported to the Personal Computer XT for IBM by Interactive Systems Corporation. Brian Lucas and his colleagues deserve praise for the most efficient, reliable, and best-documented UNIX system I have ever used. Its performance on the $5000 XT is astonishing.

I'd like to thank Patricia Henry, my editor, and her staff at Prentice-Hall for their hard work in getting this book published smoothly and quickly. They've been a pleasure to work with.

Finally, thanks go to Dennis Ritchie and Ken Thompson, who showed a generation of programmers that complexity is avoidable. Dozens of other people have contributed to UNIX over the years, but Dennis's and Ken's solid foundation and clearly articulated philosophy have kept it still the most elegant operating system around.

Marc J. Rochkind
Boulder, Colorado
November 1984

ADVANCED
UNIX
PROGRAMMING

1 FUNDAMENTAL CONCEPTS

1.1 INTRODUCTION

This chapter takes you on a whirlwind tour of the facilities provided by the UNIX kernel. We won't deal very much with the user programs (commands) that normally come with UNIX, such as ls, ed, and sh. A discussion of these is well outside the scope of this book. And we won't say much about the internals of the kernel (such as how the file system is implemented) either.

This tour is meant to be a refresher. We'll use terms, such as *process*, before defining them, because we assume you already know roughly what they mean. If too much sounds new to you, you may want to become more familiar with UNIX before proceeding. (If you don't know what a process is, you definitely need to get more familiar with UNIX!) A good book to read is *The UNIX Programming Environment*, by Kernighan and Pike. The Bibliography lists some alternatives that may also serve your needs. We'll assume you know how to program in C; if not, there are many books on C too.[1]

1.2 FILES

There are three kinds of UNIX files: ordinary files, directories, and special files.

---

[1]We'll refer from time to time to Brian W. Kernighan and Dennis M. Ritchie, *The C Programming Language* (Englewood Cliffs, N. J.: Prentice-Hall, Inc.), 1978. This is the definitive reference on C.

1.2.1 Ordinary Files

Ordinary files contain bytes of data, organized into a linear array. Any byte or sequence of bytes may be read or written. Reads and writes start at a byte location specified by the *file pointer*, which can be set to any value (even beyond the end of the file). Ordinary files are stored on disk.

It isn't possible to insert bytes into the middle of a file (spreading the file apart), or to delete bytes from the middle (closing the gap). As bytes are written onto the end of a file, it gets bigger, one byte at a time. A file can be truncated to a length of zero bytes, but it can't be shrunk to any intermediate size.[2] When any of these impossible operations is required—in text editing, for example—one just writes a completely new file. This is safer, too.

Two or more processes can read and write the same file concurrently. The results depend on the order in which the individual I/O requests occur, and are in general unpredictable. Until quite recently, UNIX provided no efficient mechanism to control concurrent access, although there have always been inefficient mechanisms (see Sec. 2.5). Some versions of UNIX now provide file locking and semaphores (see Chap. 7).

Ordinary files don't have names, they have numbers called *i-numbers*. An i-number is an index into an array of *i-nodes*, kept at the front of each region of disk that contains a UNIX file system. Each i-node contains important information about one file. Interestingly, this information *does not* include either the name or the data bytes. It *does* include the following: type of file (ordinary, directory, or special); number of links (to be explained shortly); owner's user and group ID; three sets of access permissions, for the owner, the group, and others; size in bytes; time of last access, last modification, and status change (when the i-node itself was last modified); and, of course, pointers to disk blocks containing the file's contents.

1.2.2 Directories

Since it's inconvenient to refer to files by i-number, *directories* are provided to allow names to be used. In practice, a directory is almost always used to access a file. I-numbers are used only when patching the file system after it's been damaged.

Each directory consists of a two-column table, with a name in one column and its corresponding i-number in the other column. A name/i-node pair is called a *link*. When the UNIX kernel is told to access a file by name, it automatically looks in a directory to find the i-number. Then it gets the corresponding i-node, which contains more information about the file (such as who can access it). If the data itself is to be accessed, the i-node tells where to find it on the disk.

Directories are actually stored as ordinary files, but they are tagged as directories in the i-node. Therefore, the i-node corresponding to a particular name in a directory could be the i-node of another directory. This allows users to arrange their

---

[2]This can be done in Xenix 3 with the c h s i z e system call.

files into the hierarchical structure for which UNIX is so well known. A *path* such as memo / july / smith instructs the kernel to get the i-node of the *current directory* to locate its data bytes, find memo among those data bytes, take the corresponding i-number, get that i-node to locate the memo directory's data bytes, find july among those, take the corresponding i-number, get the i-node to locate the july directory's data bytes, find smith, and, finally, take the corresponding i-node, the one associated with memo / july / smith.

In following a *relative path* (one that starts with the current directory), how does the kernel know where to start? It simply keeps track of the i-number of the current directory for each process. When a process changes its current directory, it must supply a path to the new directory. That path leads to an i-number, which then is saved as the i-number of the new current directory.

An *absolute path* begins with a / and starts with the *root* directory. The kernel simply reserves i-number 2 for the root directory. This is established when a file system is first constructed. There is a system call to change a process's root directory (to an i-number other than 2), but this is very rarely done.

Because the two-column structure of directories is used directly by the kernel (a rare case of the kernel caring about the contents of files), and because an invalid directory could easily destroy an entire UNIX system, a program (even if run by the superuser) cannot write into a directory, although it can read one if it has appropriate permission. Instead, a program modifies a directory by using a special set of system calls. After all, the only legal actions are to add or remove a link.

It is possible for two or more links, in the same or different directories, to refer to the same i-number. This means that the same file may have more than one name. There is no ambiguity when accessing a file by a given path, since only one i-number will be found. It might have been found via another path too, but that's irrelevant. When a link is removed from a directory, however, it isn't immediately clear whether the i-node and the associated data bytes can be thrown away too. That is why the i-node contains a link count. Removing a link to an i-node merely decrements the link count; when the count reaches zero, the kernel discards the file.

There is no structural reason why there can't be multiple links to directories as well as to ordinary files. But this complicates the programming of commands that scan the entire file system, so the kernel outlaws it.

1.2.3 Special Files

A *special file* is either some type of *device* (such as a tape drive or communications line) or a *FIFO* (first-in-first-out queue), which is a mechanism used to pass data between processes. We'll review device special files here and FIFOs in Sec. 1.8.

There are two kinds of device special files: block and character. *Block special files* follow a particular model: The device contains an array of fixed-size blocks (usually 512 bytes each), and a pool of kernel *buffers* are used as a cache to speed up I/O. *Character special files* don't have to follow any rules at all. They might do I/O in very small chunks (characters) or very big chunks (disk tracks).

The same physical device could have both block and character special files and, in fact, this is usually true for disks. Ordinary files and directories are accessed by the file system via a block special file, to gain the benefits of the buffer cache. Sometimes, primarily in database applications, more direct access is needed. A database manager can bypass the file system entirely and use a character special file to access the disk (but not the same area that's being used by the file system). Most UNIX systems have a character special file for this purpose that can directly transfer data between a process's address space and the disk using *DMA* (direct memory access), which results in orders-of-magnitude better performance. Better error detection is another benefit, since the buffer cache doesn't get in the way.

A special file has an i-node, but there aren't any data bytes on disk for the i-node to point to. Instead, that part of the i-node contains a *device number*. This is an index into a table used by the kernel to find a collection of subroutines called a *device driver*.

When a system call is executed to perform an operation on a special file, the appropriate device driver subroutine is invoked. What happens then is entirely up to the designer of the device driver; since the driver runs in the kernel, and not as a user process, it can access—and perhaps modify—any part of the kernel, any user process, and any registers or memory of the computer itself (such as segmentation registers). It is relatively easy to add new device drivers to the kernel, so this provides a hook with which to do many things besides merely interfacing to new kinds of I/O devices. It's the most popular way to kludge UNIX to do something its designers never intended it to do. For example, file and record locking could be (and have been) implemented with a pseudo-device driver.

1.3 PROGRAMS AND PROCESSES

A *program* is a collection of *instructions* and *data* that is kept in an ordinary file on disk. In its i-node the file is marked executable, and the file's contents are arranged according to rules established by the kernel. (Another case of the kernel caring about the contents of a file.)

Users can create executable files any way they choose. As long as the contents obey the rules and the file is marked executable, the program can be run. In practice, most users choose to do things this way: First, the source program, in some programming language (normally C), is typed into an ordinary file (often referred to as a *text file*, because it's arranged into text lines). Next, another ordinary file, called an *object file*, is created that contains the machine-language translation of the source program. This job is done by a compiler or assembler (which are themselves programs). If this object file is complete (no missing subroutines), it is marked executable and may be run as is. If not, the *linker* (called a ''loader'' in UNIX jargon) is used to bind this object file with others previously created, possibly taken from collections of object files called *libraries*. Unless the linker couldn't find something it was looking for, its output is complete and executable.

In order to run a program, the kernel is first asked to create a new *process*, which is an environment in which a *program* executes. A process consists of three segments: *instruction segment*,[3] *user data segment*, and *system data segment*. The program is used to initialize the instructions and user data. After this initialization, there is no longer any fixed connection between a process and the program it is running. Although modern programmers don't normally modify instructions, the data does get modified. In addition, the process may acquire resources (more memory, open files, etc.) not present in the program.

Several concurrently running processes can be initialized from the same program. There is no functional relationship, however, between these processes. The kernel might be able to save memory by arranging for such processes to share instruction segments, but, since these segments are read-only, the processes involved can't detect such sharing.

A process's *system data* includes attributes such as current directory, open file descriptors, accumulated CPU time, and so on. These will be treated in subsequent sections of this chapter. A process cannot access or modify its system data directly, since it is outside of its address space. Instead, there are various system calls to access or modify attributes.

A process is created by the kernel on behalf of a currently executing process, which becomes the *parent* of the new *child* process. The child inherits most of the parent's system-data attributes. For example, if the parent has any files open, the child will have them open too. Heredity of this sort is absolutely fundamental to the operation of UNIX, as we shall see throughout this book.

1.4 SIGNALS

The kernel can send a *signal* to a process. A signal can be originated by the kernel itself, sent from a process to itself, sent from another process, or sent on behalf of the user.

An example of a kernel-originated signal is a segmentation-violation signal, sent when a process attempts to access memory outside of its address space. An example of a signal sent by a process to itself is an alarm clock signal: A process sets the clock; when the alarm goes off, the signal is sent. An example of a signal sent from one process to another is a termination signal, sent when one of several related processes decides to terminate the whole family. Finally, an example of a user-originated signal is an interrupt signal, sent to all processes created by the user when he or she presses the interrupt key (usually DEL).

There are about 19 types of signals (some versions of UNIX have a few more or a few less). For all but one (the kill signal, which is always fatal), a process can control what happens when it receives the signal. It can accept the default action,

[3]In UNIX jargon the instruction segment is called the "text segment," but we'll avoid that confusing term.

which results in termination of the process; it can ignore the signal; or it can catch the signal and execute a subroutine when the signal arrives. The signal type (an integer from 1 through 19) is passed as an argument to this subroutine. There isn't any direct way for the subroutine to determine who sent the signal, however. When the signal-handling subroutine returns, the process resumes executing at the point of interruption.

Two signals are undefined by the kernel. These may be used by an application for its own purposes.

1.5 PROCESS-IDS AND PROCESS GROUPS

Every process has a *process-ID*, which is a positive integer. At any instant these are guaranteed to be unique. Every process but one has a parent. The exception is process 0, which is created and used by the kernel itself, for swapping.

A process's system data also records its *parent-process-ID*, the process-ID of its parent. If a process is orphaned because its parent terminated, its parent-process-ID is changed to 1. This is the process-ID of the initialization process (init), which is the ancestor of all other processes. In other words, the initialization process adopts all orphans.

Sometimes programmers choose to implement a subsystem as a group of related processes instead of as a single process. For example, a complex database management system might be broken down into several processes to gain additional concurrency of disk I/O. The UNIX kernel allows these related processes to be organized into a *process group*.

One of the group members is the *group leader*. Each member of the group has the group leader's process-ID as its *process-group-ID*.[4] The kernel provides a system call to send a signal to each member of a designated process group. Typically, this would be used to terminate the entire group as a whole, but any signal can be broadcast in this way.

Any process can resign from its process group, become a leader of its own group (of one) by making its process-group-ID the same as its own process-ID, and then spawn child processes to round out the new group. Hence, a single user could be running, say, 10 processes formed into, say, three process groups.

A process group can have a *control terminal*, which is the first terminal device opened by the group leader.[5] Normally, the control terminal for a user's processes is the terminal from which the user logged in. When a new process group is formed, the processes in the new group no longer have a control terminal.

The terminal device driver sends interrupt, quit, and hangup signals coming from a terminal to every process for which that terminal is the control terminal.

---

[4]Not to be confused with a process's group-ID; see Sec. 1.6.

[5]The System III and System V manuals sometimes refer to a *tty-group ID* (the process-ID of the group leader) instead of to a control terminal.

Unless precautions are taken, hanging up a terminal, for example, will terminate all of the user's processes. To prevent this, a process can arrange to ignore hangups (this is what the `nohup` command does).

When a process group leader terminates for any reason, all processes with the same control terminal are sent a hangup signal, which, unless caught or ignored, terminates them too. This feature makes hard-wired terminals, which can't be physically hung up, behave like those that can. Thus, when a user logs off (terminating the shell, which is normally the process group leader), everything is cleaned up for the next user, just as it would be if the user actually hung up.

In summary, there are three process-IDs associated with each process:

process-ID   Positive integer that uniquely identifies this process.

parent-process-ID   Process-ID of this process's parent.

process-group-ID   Process-ID of the process-group leader. If equal to the process-ID, this process is the group leader.

1.6 PERMISSIONS

A *user-ID* is a positive integer that is associated with a user's *login name* in the *password file* (`/etc/passwd`). When a user logs in, the `login` command makes this ID the user-ID of the first process created, the login shell. Processes descended from the shell inherit this user-ID.

Users are also organized into *groups* (not to be confused with process groups), which have IDs too, called *group-IDs*. A user's login group-ID is taken from the password file and made the group-ID of his or her login shell.

Groups are defined in the *group file* (`/etc/group`). While logged in, a user can change to another group of which he or she is a member; this changes the group-ID of the process that handles the request (normally the shell, via the `newgrp` command), which then is inherited by all descendent processes.

These two IDs are called the *real user-ID* and the *real group-ID* because they are representative of the real user, the person who is logged in. Two other IDs are also associated with each process: the *effective user-ID* and the *effective group-ID*. These IDs are normally the same as the corresponding real IDs, but they can be different, as we shall see shortly. For now, we'll assume the real and effective IDs are the same.

The effective ID is always used to determine permissions; the real ID is used for accounting and user-to-user communication. One indicates the user's permissions; the other indicates the user's identity.

Each file (ordinary, directory, or special) has, in its i-node, an *owner user-ID* and an *owner group-ID*. The i-node also contains three sets of three permission bits (nine bits in all). Each set has one bit for *read permission*, one bit for *write permission*, and one bit for *execute permission*. A bit is 1 if the permission is granted and 0 if not. There is a set for the owner, for the owner group, and for others (the public). Here are the bit assignments (bit 0 is the rightmost bit):

Bit	Meaning
8	owner read
7	owner write
6	owner execute
5	group read
4	group write
3	group execute
2	others read
1	others write
0	others execute

Permission bits are frequently specified using an octal number. For example, octal 775 would mean read, write, and execute permission for the owner and the group, and only read and execute permission for others. The `ls` command would show this combination of permissions as `rwxrwxr-x`; in binary it would be 111111101; in octal it would be 775.

The permission system determines whether a given process can perform a desired action (read, write, or execute) on a given file. For ordinary files the meaning of the actions is obvious. For directories the meaning of read is obvious, since directories are stored in ordinary files (the `ls` command reads a directory, for example). "Write" permission on a directory means the ability to issue a system call that would modify the directory (add or remove a link). "Execute" permission means the ability to use the directory in a path (sometimes called "search" permission). For special files, read and write permissions mean the ability to execute the `read` and `write` system calls. What, if anything, that implies is up to the designer of the device driver. Execute permission on a special file is meaningless.

The permission system determines whether permission will be granted using this algorithm:

1. If the effective user-ID is zero, permission is instantly granted (the effective user is the *superuser*).
2. If the process's effective user-ID and the file's user-ID match, then the owner set of bits is used to see if the action will be allowed.
3. If the process's effective group-ID and the file's group-ID match, then the group set of bits is used.
4. If neither the user-IDs nor group-IDs match, then the process is an "other" and the third set of bits is used.

There are other actions, which might be called "change i-node," that only the owner or the superuser can do. These include changing the user-ID or group-ID of a file, changing a file's permissions, and changing a file's access or modification times. As a special case, write permission on a file allows setting of its access and modification times to the current time.

Occasionally we want a user to temporarily take on the privileges of another user. For example, when we execute the p a s s w d command to change our password, we would like the effective user-ID to be that of r o o t (the traditional login name for the superuser), because only r o o t can write into the password file. This is done by making r o o t the owner of the p a s s w d command (i.e., the ordinary file containing the p a s s w d program), and then turning on another permission bit in the p a s s w d command's i-node, called the *set-user-ID* bit. Executing a program with this bit on changes the effective user-ID to the owner of the file containing the program. Since it's the effective, rather than the real, user-ID that determines permissions, this allows a user to temporarily take on the permissions of someone else. The *set-group-ID* bit is used in a similar way.

Since both user-IDs (real and effective) are inherited from parent process to child process, it is possible to use the set-user-ID feature to run with an effective user-ID for a very long time.

There is a potential loophole. Suppose you do the following: Copy the s h command to your own directory (you will be the owner of the copy). Then use c h m o d to turn on the set-user-ID bit and c h o w n to change the file's owner to r o o t. Now execute your copy of s h, and take on the privileges of r o o t! Fortunately, this loophole was closed a long time ago. If you're not the superuser, changing a file's owner automatically clears the set-user-ID and set-group-ID bits.

1.7 OTHER PROCESS ATTRIBUTES

Besides those already mentioned, a few other interesting attributes are recorded in a process's system data segment.

There is one open *file descriptor* (an integer from 0 through 19) for each file (ordinary file, directory, or special file) that the process has opened, and two for each pipe that the process has created. A child doesn't inherit open file descriptors from its parent, but rather it inherits copies of them. Nonetheless, they are indices into the same systemwide open file table, which among other things means that parent and child share the same file pointer.

A process's *priority* is used by the kernel scheduler. Any process can lower its priority via the system call n i c e; a superuser process can raise its priority via the same system call. Technically speaking, n i c e sets an attribute called the *nice value*, which is only one factor in computing the actual priority.

A process's *file size limit* can be (and usually is) less than the systemwide limit; this is to prevent confused or uncivilized users from writing runaway files. A superuser process can raise its limit.

If the *trace flag* is on, the child merely stops upon receipt of a signal instead of doing its normal thing (terminating, for example). Presumably, its parent will then poke around in the child's address space and possibly restart the child. The trace flag is used only by debuggers (such as a d b and s d b). This facility is horrendously complicated to use; fortunately, since the debuggers are already written, most of us don't have to worry about using it.

1.8 INTERPROCESS COMMUNICATION

In UNIX systems prior to System III, processes could communicate with one another via shared file pointers, signals, process tracing, files, and pipes. With System III, FIFOs (named pipes) were added. With System V, semaphores, messages, and shared memory were added. As we shall see, none of these nine mechanisms are entirely satisfactory. That's why there are nine.

Shared file pointers are rarely used for interprocess communication. In theory, one process could position the file pointer to some fictitious location in a file, and a second process could then find out where it points. The location (a number between, say, 0 and 100) would be the communicated data. Since the processes must be related to share a file pointer, they might as well just use pipes.

Signals are sometimes used when a process just needs to poke another. For example, a print spooler could signal the actual printing process whenever a print file is spooled. But signals don't pass enough information to be helpful in most applications. Also, a signal interrupts the receiving process, making the programming more complex than if the receiver could get the communication when it was ready. Signals are mainly used just to terminate processes.

With *process tracing*, a parent can control the execution of its child. Since the parent can read and write the child's data, the two can communicate freely. Process tracing is used only by debuggers, since it is far too complicated and unsafe for general use. Moreover, parent and child can easily communicate over a pipe instead.

Files are the most common form of interprocess communication. For example, one might write a file with a process running e d and then format it with a process running n r o f f. However, files are inconvenient if the two processes are running concurrently, for two reasons: First, the reader might outrace the writer, see an end-of-file, and think that the communication is over (this can be handled through some tricky programming). Second, the longer the two processes communicate, the bigger the file gets. Sometimes processes communicate for days or weeks, passing millions of bytes of data. This would quickly exhaust the file system.

Using an empty file for a sempahore is also a traditional UNIX technique. This takes advantage of some peculiarities in the way UNIX creates files. More details are given in Sec. 2.5.

Pipes solve the synchronization problems of files. A pipe is not a type of file; although it has an i-node, there are no links to it. Reading and writing a pipe is somewhat like reading and writing a file, but with some significant differences: If the reader gets ahead of the writer, the reader just waits for more data. If the writer gets too far ahead of the reader, it sleeps until the reader has a chance to catch up, so the kernel doesn't have too much data queued. Finally, once a byte is read, it is gone forever, so long-running processes connected via pipes do not fill up the file system.

Pipes are well known to shell users, who can enter command lines like:

```
ls | wc
```

to see how many files they have. The kernel facility, however, is far more general than what the shell provides, as we shall see in Chap. 6.

Pipes have three major disadvantages: First, the processes communicating over a pipe must be related, typically parent and child or two siblings. This is too constraining for many applications, particularly when one process is a database manager and the other is an application that needs to access the database. The second disadvantage is that reads and writes are not guaranteed to be atomic, prohibiting the use of pipes when there are multiple readers or multiple writers.[6] If several application processes are sending requests to a database manager, their data might get intermingled. The third disadvantage is that pipes might be too slow. The data has to be copied from the writing user process to the kernel and back again to the reader. No actual I/O is performed, but the copying alone can take too long for some critical applications. It's because of these disadvantages that fancier schemes have evolved.

FIFOs, or *named pipes*, were added to System III to solve the first two disadvantages of pipes. (FIFO stands for "first-in-first-out.") A FIFO exists as a special file, and any process with permission can open it for reading or writing. Atomicity is guaranteed: The bytes written or read via a single system call are always contiguous. Hence, both multiple writer and multiple reader arrangements are easily handled. FIFOs are easy to program with, too, as we shall demonstrate in Chap. 7.

What's wrong with FIFOs? They don't eliminate the third disadvantage of pipes: They are sometimes too slow. For the most critical applications, the new interprocess communication features of System V can be used, but not easily.

A *semaphore* is a flag that prevents two or more processes from accessing the same resource at the same time (the term comes from the railroads, where the "resource" was a common track and the "processes" were trains). As we've mentioned, files can be used for semaphores too, but the overhead is far too great for many applications.

A *message* is a small amount of data (500 bytes, say) that can be sent to a *message queue*. Messages can be of different types. Any process with appropriate permissions can receive messages from a queue. It has lots of choices: either the first message, or the first message of a given type, or the first message of a group of types.

Shared memory provides the fastest interprocess communication of all. The

---

[6]Newer versions of UNIX have eliminated this problem.

same memory is mapped into the address spaces of two or more processes. As soon as data is written to the shared memory, it is instantly available to the readers. A semaphore or a message is used to synchronize the reader and writer.

Xenix 3 has semaphores and shared memory, too.

1.9 USING SYSTEM CALLS

How does a C programmer actually issue a system call? There is no difference between a system call and any other function call. For example, the `read` system call might be issued like this:

```
amt = read(fd, buf, numbyte);
```

The implementation of the subroutine `read` varies with the UNIX implementation. It is usually an assembly language program that uses a machine instruction designed specifically for system calls, which isn't directly executable from C. This instruction might be "sys," "int," "svc," and so on, depending on the computer.

The UNIX manual once documented system calls in both assembly language and C, but the assembly language documentation was omitted when UNIX was ported to machines other than the PDP-11. Nowadays, it's safe to assume that system calls are simply C subroutines. Remember, though, that since a system call involves a context switch (from user to kernel and back), it takes much longer than a simple subroutine call within a process's own address space. So avoiding excessive system calls is wise. This point will be emphasized in Sec. 2.10 when we look into buffered I/O.

Most system calls return a value. In the `read` example above, the number of bytes read is returned. To indicate an error, a system call returns a value that can't be mistaken for valid data, namely -1. Therefore, our `read` example should have been coded something like this:

```
if ((amt = read(fd, buf, numbyte)) == -1) {
    printf("Read failed!\n");
    exit(1);
}
```

Note that `exit` is a system call too, but it can't return an error.

There are lots of reasons why a system call that returns -1 might have failed. The global integer `errno` contains a code that indicates the reason. These error codes are defined at the beginning of the system call chapter of the UNIX manual [the pages titled "intro(2)"]. Note that `errno` contains valid data only if a system call actually returns -1; you can't use `errno` alone to determine whether an error occurred.

Two other useful external variables are defined: s y s _ e r r l i s t is an array of messages that correspond to the error codes, and s y s _ n e r r is one more than the highest defined subscript in the array.[7] e r r n o should be tested against s y s _ n e r r before indexing s y s _ e r r l i s t. We now can code a useful subroutine that we'll be using throughout this book whenever a system call returns an error:

```
#include <stdio.h>

void syserr(msg) /* print system call error message and terminate */
char *msg;
{
    extern int errno, sys_nerr;
    extern char *sys_errlist[];

    fprintf(stderr, "ERROR: %s (%d", msg, errno);
    if (errno > 0 && errno < sys_nerr)
        fprintf(stderr, "; %s)\n", sys_errlist[errno]);
    else
        fprintf(stderr, ")\n");
    exit(1);
}
```

We might use s y s e r r like this:

```
        if ((amt = read(fd, buf, numbyte)) == -1)
            syserr("read");
```

Since we forgot to open the file descriptor f d, here's the message we got when we executed this code:

```
        ERROR: read (9; Bad file number)
```

This message isn't particularly attractive, but it will serve our purposes just fine. You can surely improve on our s y s e r r when you get ready to write your own programs. Indeed, you may not want to make a specific system-call error fatal at all. It's often better for a subroutine to pass an error code back to its caller (who might in turn pass it to *its* caller, etc.) so that corrective action can be taken.

---

[7]Most UNIX manuals erroneously define s y s _ n e r r as the *number* of messages, but this is wrong because there is no message numbered zero.

Another function we'll use from time to time handles fatal errors that don't result from failed system calls:

```
#include <stdio.h>

void fatal(msg) /* print error message and terminate */
char *msg;
{
    fprintf(stderr, "ERROR: %s\n", msg);
    exit(1);
}
```

1.10 PROGRAMMING CONVENTIONS

The C examples in this book use some language features that were added after *The C Programming Language* was published, namely the enum and void data types.

An object of type enum is like an integer, except that it can only take on a value that has been enumerated in its definition (the idea comes from Pascal). For example:

```
enum color {RED, GREEN, BLUE} balloon;
```

This defines the enumeration type color and declares the variable balloon to be of that type. RED, GREEN, and BLUE are also declared to be constants of type color; balloon can take on one of these three values.

void is a type applicable only to functions. It specifies that the function does not return a value—it is like a Pascal procedure or a Fortran subroutine.

A few other comments about our programming conventions are appropriate to mention here. No register declarations appear in any examples. (A register declaration requests the compiler to assign an automatic variable to a hardware register.) We've omitted them because they do not affect the semantics of a function and because we want the examples to be as uncluttered as possible. The careful reader will note many other ways in which our examples could be made faster or smaller. We frequently sacrifice efficiency for clarity and reliability. On the other hand, since this is a book and not a computer, the definition of efficiency probably *is* "clarity and reliability."

In a few examples, particularly in Chap. 4, we use techniques for bit testing and setting that may not be familiar to some readers, although the C operators used aren't new (you may want to review them in your C manual). In the following example, MASK defines two bits. We test the variable flags to see if they are set. If they are, we clear them; if they are not, we set them.

```
#define MASK 0201

fixflags()
{
    int flags;

    if ((flags & MASK) == MASK)      /* see if set */
        flags &= ~MASK;              /* clear them */
    else
        flags |= MASK;               /* set them */
}
```

It's important to understand that this would have been wrong:

```
if (flags & MASK)    /* wrong */
```

If only one of the two bits were set, the expression flags & MASK would still have been nonzero (i.e., true). If the mask consisted of only one bit, this simpler if statement would have been technically correct, but it would have been poor technique because you're not supposed to be cognizant of the value of MASK.

Many example functions in this book return a value of type BOOLEAN, either TRUE or FALSE. This type is defined in the header file defs.h. Two handy macros for getting the high-order (leftmost) and low-order (rightmost) bytes of a 16-bit word are also defined there:[8]

```
typedef enum {FALSE, TRUE} BOOLEAN;

#define lowbyte(w) ((w) & 0377)
#define highbyte(w) lowbyte((w) >> 8)
```

Some system calls require a header file that defines constants or structures. We'll note these as we encounter each system call. Because a few header files are so frequently used, we won't repeat the #include statements in each example. You should assume that every example in this book begins with these four lines:

```
#include <stdio.h>
#include <errno.h>
#include <fcntl.h>
#include "defs.h"
```

We'll explain errno.h and fcntl.h when we get ready to use them in Chap. 2.

---

[8]On computers with a 32-bit word, these macros operate on the rightmost 16 bits.

We'll use standard UNIX subroutines as much as possible in our examples. These are documented in Section 3 of the UNIX manual. All standard subroutines used in this book are also listed in Appendix B.

1.11 PORTABILITY

We'll end every chapter with a discussion of portability. Here we'll discuss the issue of UNIX portability in general.

"UNIX portability" means at least three things:

1. Portability of UNIX itself from one computer model to another.
2. Portability of C programs from one computer model to another, where both computers are running the same version of UNIX.
3. Portability of C programs from one version of UNIX to another.

Portability of UNIX itself is of no concern to us here, since this book is about the *externals* of the kernel, not its *internals*.[9]

Portability of C programs across computers is of little concern to us, primarily because we will use so little of the C language in this book. A thorough discussion of this kind of portability is in *The C Programming Language*.

We are interested in the portability of C programs, especially those that use many system calls, across *versions of UNIX*. This is truly the dark side of UNIX, the part you don't read about in advertisements and promotional literature. Any nonportability is a shame, because portability of applications across computers running UNIX is perhaps the greatest strength of UNIX, at least in the commercial arena.

It's easy to use the older system calls, such as `pipe` or `write`, portably, because these system calls were simple to begin with and are so fundamental to UNIX that all versions have remained compatible with respect to them. It's the newer or more advanced features, like FIFOs or terminal control, that present the problem. It isn't enough to say "Don't use these features," or "If you use these features your programs may not be portable." Serious commercial applications *must* use these features—that's why they're there! It simply won't do to tell someone programming a screen editor not to control the terminal.

So it is our goal, at the end of each chapter, to give some advice on how to use what we've presented and still be portable. Sometimes we can do little more than identify the limits of portability: which versions work the way we've said and which don't. Other times we'll do better: We'll suggest specific coding techniques that avoid the problems.

---

[9]Readers interested in this subject are referred to S. C. Johnson and D. M. Ritchie, "Portability of C Programs and the UNIX System," *The Bell System Technical Journal* 57, no. 6, pt. 2 (July-August 1978), 2021-48.

There is some good news. With the notable exception of the new interprocess communication system calls introduced in System V, there is very little difference between System III and System V in their system call interface. Even terminal control, which traditionally changes with every version, has remained the same. As of this writing, the industry is moving rapidly to System III and System V (away from Version 7), so the situation is getting steadily better, except, that is, for users of Berkeley 4.2 BSD, which has diverged alarmingly from Version 7, its original base. We'll still do our best to help you port programs from an AT&T version to 4.2 BSD, but porting the other way is out of the question if many of the Berkeley-specific system calls are used.

Interprocess communication remains a trouble spot. We'll present a method of doing interprocess communication in an efficient but portable way in Chap. 7.

BASIC FILE I/O

2.1 INTRODUCTION

In this chapter we'll explore basic I/O on ordinary files. We'll continue in Chap. 3 with more advanced system calls. I/O on special files is in Chap. 4, I/O on pipes in Chap. 6, and I/O on FIFOs in Chap. 7.

To get started we'll show a simple example that uses five system calls you may already be familiar with: open, creat, read, write, and close. This function copies one file to another (like the cp command):

```
#define BUFSIZE 512

void copy(from, to) /* copy file (has a bug) */
char *from, *to;
{
    int fromfd, tofd, nread;
    char buf[BUFSIZE];

    if ((fromfd = open(from, 0)) == -1)
        syserr(from);
    if ((tofd = creat(to, 0666)) == -1)
        syserr(to);
    while ((nread = read(fromfd, buf, sizeof(buf))) > 0)
        if (write(tofd, buf, nread) != nread)
            syserr("write");
```

```
        if (nread == -1)
            syserr("read");
        if (close(fromfd) == -1 || close(tofd) == -1)
            syserr("close");
    }
```

Try to find the bug in this function (there's a clue in Sec. 1.9). If you can't, we'll point it out in Sec. 2.7.

We'll say just a few quick words about this function now; there will be plenty of time to go into the details later. The call to **open** opens the input file for reading (as indicated by the second argument of 0) and returns a file descriptor for use in subsequent system calls. **creat** creates a new file if none exists, or truncates an existing file. In either case, the file is opened for writing and a file descriptor is returned. The second argument to **creat** is the set of permission bits to use if the file is created (octal 666 means read and write permission for the user, group, and others). **read** reads the number of bytes given by its third argument into the buffer pointed to by its second argument. It returns the number of bytes read, or zero on end-of-file. **write** writes the number of bytes given by its third argument from the buffer given by its second argument. It returns the number of bytes written, which we treat as an error if it isn't equal to the number of bytes we asked to be written. Finally, **close** closes the file descriptors. Note that for simplicity, we treated all errors (return values of −1) as fatal (**syserr** was shown in Sec. 1.9). We'll do this in most of the examples in this book.

Our function would have been much prettier without putting every system call in an **if** statement to check for an error return, but it is extremely poor practice to ignore error returns. Many programmers do ignore them on functions that "never" return an error, such as **read** or **close**, but this is false economy. The author has wasted countless hours searching for bugs that would have been easy to spot if only a system-call error had been caught as soon as it occurred.

2.2 FILE DESCRIPTORS

Each UNIX process has 20 file descriptors at its disposal, numbered 0 through 19. By convention, the first three are already open when the process begins. File descriptor 0 is the *standard input*, file descriptor 1 is the *standard output*, and file descriptor 2 is the *standard error output*. A UNIX filter would read from the standard input and write to the standard output. File descriptor 2 should be used for important messages, since anything written to file descriptor 1 might go off down a pipe or into a file and never be seen.

Any of these standard file descriptors could be open to a file, a pipe, a FIFO, or a device. It's best to program in a way that's independent of the type of source or destination, but this isn't always possible. For example, a screen editor probably won't work at all if the standard output isn't a terminal device.

The three standard file descriptors are ready to be used immediately in **read** and **write** calls. The other 17 file descriptors are available for files, pipes, and special files that the process opens for itself. It's possible for a parent process to bequeath more than just the standard three file descriptors to a child process. This doesn't happen very often, but it might be useful in certain applications partitioned into several closely coupled processes.

There are five system calls that produce file descriptors. This chapter covers **creat** and **open**, Chap. 3 covers **fcntl**, and Chap. 6 covers **pipe** and **dup**.

2.3 creat SYSTEM CALL

We'll introduce each system call by giving a function header, as though we were going to program it in C. We use this convention (as does the UNIX manual) because it provides a compact and syntactically legal way to indicate mnemonic names and types of arguments and the type of the return value.

Here is the function header for **creat**:

```
int creat(path, perms)          /* create file */
char *path;                     /* path name */
int perms;                      /* permission bits */
/* returns file descriptor or -1 on error */
```

creat behaves differently depending on whether the file to be created already exists or not. If it doesn't exist, then a new i-node is allocated, and a link to it is placed in the directory where the file is to be created (the current directory if **path** contains no / characters). The effective user-ID or the effective group-ID of the process making the call must have write permission in this directory. The new file is assigned permissions as given by the **perms** argument; the low-order nine bits are considered (read, write, and execution permission for the owner, the group, and others).[1] Bits set in the file mode creation mask are cleared, as discussed more fully in Sec. 9.4. The effective user-ID and the effective group-ID become the owners of the file. The file is initially of length 0, and it is opened for writing. The access, modification, and status-change (creation) times of the file are set to the current time.

If the file already exists, there need not be write permission on the directory that links to it, only execute (search) permission. However, the effective user-ID or the effective group-ID must have write permission on the file itself. Neither the file's

---

[1]Actually, 12 bits are considered, including the set-user-ID and set-group-ID bits, but it is almost unheard of to set these when a file is created; the **chmod** system call (Sec. 3.9) is almost always used instead.

ownership or permissions are changed, but its length is truncated to 0 and it is opened for writing. The modification and status-change times of the file are set to the current time. The `perms` argument is ignored.

2.4 unlink SYSTEM CALL

```
int unlink(path)            /* unlink file */
char *path;                 /* path name */
/* returns 0 on success or -1 on error */
```

The `unlink` system call removes a link from a directory, reducing the link count in the i-node by one. If the resulting link count is zero, the file system will discard the file: All disk space that it used will be made available for reuse (added to the "free list"). The i-node will become available for reuse too.

If the link count goes to zero while some process still has the file open, the file system will delay discarding the file until it is closed. This feature is frequently used to make temporary files:

```
fd = creat("temp", 0666);
unlink("temp");
```

There are two advantages to this technique: First, if the process terminates for any reason, the file will be discarded. There's no need to catch a hangup signal, for example, to make sure the file is unlinked. Second, since the link is removed from the current directory as soon as the `unlink` is processed, there's less danger of a second process accidentally using the same temporary file. "Less" danger, however, is still too much; there is a small time interval between the `creat` and the `unlink`, and another process could sneak in and do a `creat` on the same file. A safer approach would be to embed the process-ID in the name of the file (e.g., "temp21763", where the process-ID is 21763), since process-IDs are guaranteed to be unique. The `getpid` system call (Sec. 5.7) can be used to obtain the process-ID. Actually, most UNIX systems already have a function `tmpnam` in the C library that makes up temporary file names.

Only the superuser can unlink a directory (see Sec. 3.2).

2.5 IMPLEMENTING SEMAPHORES WITH FILES

When `creat` makes a *new* file, it is opened for writing even if the permission argument doesn't allow writing. When `creat` truncates an *existing* file, however, it fails if there is no write permission. This allows a file to be used as a semaphore, since such a `creat` succeeds if and only if the file doesn't exist. Two processes that want exclusive access to a resource can follow this protocol: Before accessing the resource, they try to create a file (with an agreed-upon name) without write permission. Only one of them will succeed; the other process's c r e a t will fail. It can either wait and try later or just give up. When the successful process finishes with the resource, it unlinks the semaphore file. The unsuccessful process's c r e a t will then work, and it can safely proceed.

Ironically, only *ordinary* users can implement a semaphore with c r e a t—the method won't work for the *superuser*. That's because a c r e a t issued by the superuser succeeds in truncating and opening an existing file even if the file disallows writing (nothing is disallowed the superuser). In fact, the UNIX editor e d suffered from this problem once. The editor used a semaphore mechanism like the one we've described to assign each user a unique temporary file. Occasionally a user would accidentally share an editor temporary file with the superuser, who was usually editing the password file. The symptom was a hunk of the password file stuck into the middle of the user's file! We'll show how to solve this problem in the next section; for now, assume that only ordinary users use semaphores.

The semaphore protocol is best encapsulated into two functions, l o c k and u n l o c k, to be used like this:

```
if (lock("accounts")) {
    ...manipulate accounts...
    unlock("accounts");
}
else
    ...couldn't obtain lock...
```

The lock name "accounts" is abstract; it doesn't necessarily have anything to do with an actual file. If two or more processes are concurrently executing this code, the lock will prevent them from simultaneously executing the protected section ("manipulate accounts", whatever that means). Remember that if a process doesn't call l o c k, though, then there is no protection.

Here is the code for l o c k and u n l o c k:

```
#define LOCKDIR "/tmp/"
#define MAXTRIES 3
#define NAPTIME 5

BOOLEAN lock(name)    /* acquire lock */
char *name;
{
    char *path, *lockpath();
    int fd, tries;
    extern int errno;
```

```
        path = lockpath(name);
        tries = 0;
        while ((fd = creat(path, 0)) == -1 && errno == EACCES) {
            if (++tries >= MAXTRIES)
                return(FALSE);
            sleep(NAPTIME);
        }
        if (fd == -1 || close(fd) == -1)
            syserr("lock");
        return(TRUE);
}

void unlock(name)    /* free lock */
char *name;
{
        char *lockpath();

        if (unlink(lockpath(name)) == -1)
            syserr("unlock");
}

static char *lockpath(name) /* generate lock file path */
char *name;
{
        static char path[20];
        char *strcat();

        strcpy(path, LOCKDIR);
        return(strcat(path, name));
}
```

The function lockpath generates an actual file name to use as the lock. We put it in the directory /tmp because that directory is on every UNIX system and it's writable by everyone. To place a lock, we try to create the file with no permissions (in particular, no write permission). This will work only if the file doesn't exist. We're careful to check errno if creat fails, since the only reason that's acceptable is lack of write permission. The constant EACCES is documented in the introduction to Section 2 of the UNIX manual. Error number symbolic constants are defined in the header file /usr/include/errno.h. Recall from Sec. 1.10 that this file is assumed to be included.

We try to create the file up to **MAXTRIES** times, sleeping for **NAPTIME** seconds between tries. The function sleep is part of the C library; we'll see how to code it ourselves in Sec. 8.7. We close the file descriptor we got from creat because we aren't interested in actually writing anything to the file. As an enhancement, we could write our process number and the time on the file so other processes waiting on it could see who they're waiting for and how long it's been busy. If we did this, we'd want the permissions to be octal 444 instead of 0.

All unlock has to do is unlink the file. The next attempt to create it will succeed.

Using a file for a semaphore entails quite a bit of overhead, but it has the advantage of working on every version of UNIX. It's widely used by many commands that come with UNIX.

An assumption about creat is crucial to its use for semaphores. creat must be atomic: If two processes are simultaneously trying to create the same file with no write permission, then at most one of them will succeed. It is a well-known fact that this is true, and too many important commands rely on it for a future version of UNIX to make it untrue. The Version 7 manual page for creat says that it's atomic, but the System III and V manuals do not.

Another well-known but undocumented fact about creat is that the lowest available file descriptor is returned. Normally we don't care what the actual number is. However, when we set up a pipe we do care; see Sec. 6.4.

2.6 open SYSTEM CALL

There are two forms of the open system call. The older form, with two arguments, is used to read or write existing files. The newer form (new with System III), with three arguments, can do everything the older form can do, everything creat can do, and more. We'll start with the older form:

```
int open(path, flags)          /* open file */
char *path;                     /* path name */
int flags;                      /* read, write, or both */
/* returns file descriptor or -1 on error */
```

The file specified by path must already exist. If flags is 0, it is opened for reading; if 1, opened for writing; and if 2, opened for both reading and writing. The file descriptor returned may be used in subsequent system calls such as lseek, read, write, and close. The effective user-ID or the effective group-ID must have read and/or write permission, depending on the value of flags. The file pointer is positioned at the first byte of the file. If the file is opened for both reading and writing, there is still only one file pointer, so, in general, a call to lseek (see Sec. 2.11) will precede each call to read and write.

Since creat opens a file for writing only, a sequence like the following is often used to create a file and open it for both reading and writing:

```
if ((fd = creat(path, 0600)) == -1)
    syserr("creat");
if (close(fd) == -1 || (fd = open(path, 2)) == -1)
    syserr("reopen");
```

Note that this will fail if the file exists before the `creat` and doesn't have read or write permission, because in that case `creat` won't change the permissions. It might be better to place a call to `unlink` before the call to `creat`:

```
if (unlink(path) == -1)
    syserr("unlink");
```

Now for the fancier `open`:

```
#include <fcntl.h>

int open(path, flags, perms)    /* open file */
char *path;                     /* path name */
int flags;                      /* option flags */
int perms;                      /* permission bits */
/* returns file descriptor or -1 on error */
```

Here the `flags` argument takes on additional values beyond 0, 1, and 2, and there is a third argument, `perms`, that for some values of `flags` has the same significance as the second argument to `creat`. Instead of using numbers for `flags`, symbolic constants are defined in the header file `/usr/include/fcntl.h`. These may be ORed together (with the | operator) to achieve various combined effects, although not all combinations are meaningful.

Here are the symbolic constants. Note that the first three (which are mutually exclusive) have values of 0, 1, and 2, and are therefore compatible with the old form of `open`.

O_RDONLY	Open for reading.
O_WRONLY	Open for writing.
O_RDWR	Open for both.
O_NDELAY	When opening pipes, FIFOs, and communication-line special files, this flag determines whether **open** waits or returns immediately. Subsequent reads and writes are also affected. More details are given in Chaps. 4, 6, and 7. **O_NDELAY** has no effect on ordinary files and directories.
O_CREAT	If the file does not exist, create the file (in the manner of `creat`). This is the only case in which the third argument (`perms`) is used.
O_TRUNC	If the file exists, truncate its length to zero (even if it isn't to be opened for writing).
O_EXCL	If **O_CREAT** is also set, fail if the file already exists.
O_APPEND	Ensure that all subsequent writes occur at the end of the file.

O_WSYNC   This flag is available in Xenix 3, but not in any AT&T version of UNIX. It makes all writes wait until the physical output is complete. This matter will be discussed further in Sec. 2.7.

The flags O_CREAT and O_TRUNC represent an unbundling of the features of creat; one may now choose from the à la carte menu instead of taking the complete dinner. In turn, the creat system call is equivalent to the combination:

```
O_WRONLY | O_CREAT | O_TRUNC
```

A major advantage of the new form of open is that it simplifies many common tasks. For example, suppose a program is to open a file for writing if it exists, and create it if it doesn't. Conventionally, one first tries to open it; if open fails because of nonexistence, then creat is called:

```
if ((fd = open(path, 1)) == -1)
    if (errno == ENOENT) {
        if ((fd = creat(path, 0666)) == -1)
            syserr("creat");
    }
    else
        syserr("open");
```

(Note the use of curly braces to prevent the else from being paired with the wrong if.)

Programmers often make mistakes here (failing to check errno correctly is the most common one) and destroy a few files before the bugs get fixed. The new open makes this common task simpler and, therefore, easier to get right:

```
if ((fd = open(path, O_WRONLY | O_CREAT, 0666)) == -1)
    syserr("open");
```

O_TRUNC is the really dangerous flag. As long as you leave it out, you can't destroy an existing file with open.

The coding to create a file to be opened for reading and writing, shown earlier in this section with the old form of open, is now more straightforward, too:

```
if ((fd = open(path, O_RDWR | O_CREAT, 0600)) == -1)
    syserr("open");
```

One may well ask why creat is still in UNIX as a system call. After all, other old system calls such as sleep were demoted to subroutines when more general facilities were introduced (alarm and pause). The answer is probably emotional; c r e a t has been a system call since the very beginning, and has evidently been granted tenure.

The O _ E X C L flag provides an official way to use a file as a semaphore; it is no longer necessary to use the trick of creating a file without write permission as we did in the previous section. Most importantly, a semaphore implemented with O _ E X C L works for the superuser too. So, in l o c k, instead of the line:

```
while ((fd = creat(path, 0)) == -1 && errno == EACCES) {
```

we could code:

```
while ((fd = open(path, O_WRONLY | O_CREAT | O_EXCL, 0666)) == -1
&& errno == EEXIST) {
```

It's frustrating that the UNIX manual doesn't state explicitly that two processes simultaneously executing an open on the same file with O _ E X C L and O _ C R E A T set cannot both succeed (i.e., that open is atomic). The manual only implies this, but it is known to be a fact.

Why does O _ E X C L have to be paired with O _ C R E A T? That is, why can't we open existing files for exclusive access? The answer is that just because a version of UNIX has the O _ E X C L flag, that doesn't mean it has semaphores as independent entities. The existence of the file itself is still the semaphore. If an existing file could be opened exclusively, then something else would have to serve as the semaphore (another file, say). So it is rare that a file used as a semaphore actually contains any of the user's data. A file is either a semaphore or a data repository, but not both.

The flag O _ A P P E N D is designed for programs that keep an audit trail or write accounting records. Several concurrent processes may all want to write onto the end of the same file, to accumulate data in chronological sequence. But they each have their own file pointer, and hence, their own concept of where the end is. One might think that seeking to the end before each write solves the problem, but since l s e e k and w r i t e are two separate system calls, there is the possibility that during the interval between them, another process could sneak in and write. Then the first process would overwrite the second process's data. We could use our semaphore mechanism to prevent this:

```
if (!lock("accts"))
    syserr("lock");
if (lseek(fd, 0L, 2) == -1) /* seek to end; see Section 2.11 */
    syserr ("lseek");
if (write(fd, acctrec, sizeof(acctrec)) == -1)
    syserr("write");
unlock("accts");
```

This works, but with enormous overhead because of the way lock is implemented. If we open the file with the flag combination

```
O_WRONLY | O_CREAT | O_APPEND
```

then a seek to the end precedes each write automatically, and the calls to lock, lseek, and unlock aren't needed.

Again, the UNIX manual fails to state that writes to files opened with O_APPEND are atomic. For noncritical data, the assumption that they are is good enough (it might even be true); for critical data, a semaphore should be used to be safe. However, remember that our implementation of lock was based on undocumented assumptions, too.

The danger with these assumptions isn't that a specific implementation will behave erratically—we can always run experiments or speak to the vendor to get the facts. The problem is that our programs may not be portable to other versions of UNIX, since implementors are bound only by what's in the manual.[2] What's worse, even a system that doesn't force open or write to be atomic will still act that way 99 percent of the time, making the bug maddeningly elusive.

2.7 write SYSTEM CALL

```
int write(fd, buf, nbytes)      /* write on file */
int fd;                         /* file descriptor */
char *buf;                      /* buffer address */
unsigned nbytes;                /* number of bytes to write */
/* returns number of bytes written or -1 on error */
```

write writes the nbytes bytes pointed to by buf to the open file represented by fd. The write starts at the current position of the file pointer, and after the write the file pointer is incremented by the number of bytes written. The number of bytes written, or −1 if there was an error, is returned.

write is used to write to pipes and special files too, but its semantics are somewhat different in these cases. We'll postpone the discussion of writes to other than ordinary files until Chaps. 4, 6, and 7.

write is deceptively simple. One is encouraged to think that it writes the data and then returns, but a little experimentation will convince one that this is impossible. For example, on my own UNIX system I ran a program that wrote 20 blocks of 512 bytes each, seeking to a different position in the file before each write.

---

[2]It is presumably a goal of the /usr/group standards effort to document important properties like the atomicity of creat, open, and write. But their Proposed Standard doesn't do so. If this omission is deliberate—that is, a conforming implementation does *not* have to ensure that these system calls are atomic—then the standard is seriously defective.

This took a total of .3 second of real time. My disk has an average access time of about .075 second, so the elapsed real time wasn't enough for even 20 seeks, let alone the data transfer and the other kernel processing that took place. Clearly, somebody cheated.

In fact, the file system cheats. When you issue a write system call, it does not perform the write and then return. It just transfers the data to the buffer cache and returns, claiming nothing more than this:

> *I've taken note of your request, and rest assured that your file descriptor is OK, I've copied your data successfully, and there's enough disk space. Later, when it's convenient for me, and if I'm still alive, I'll try to put your data on the disk where it belongs. If I discover an error then I'll try to print something on the console, but I won't tell you about it (indeed, you may have terminated by then). If you, or any other process, tries to read this data before I've written it out, I'll give it to you from the buffer cache, so, if all goes well, you'll never be able to find out when and if I've completed your request. You may ask no further questions. Trust me. And thank me for the speedy reply.*

If all does go well, delayed writing is fantastic. The semantics are the same as if the writing actually took place, but it's much faster. However, if there is a disk error, or if the kernel stops for any reason, then the game is up. We discover that the data we "wrote" isn't on the disk at all.

In addition to the uncertainty about when the physical write occurs, there are two other problems with delayed writes. First, a process initiating a write cannot be informed of write errors. Indeed, file system buffers aren't owned by any single process; if several processes write to the same block of the same file at the same time, their data will be transferred to the same buffer. Of course, one could conceive of a scheme in which a "write error" signal would be sent to every process that wrote a particular buffer, but what is a process supposed to do about it at that late date? And how does the kernel notify processes that have already terminated?

The second problem is that the *order* of physical writes can't be controlled. Order often matters. For example, in updating a linked-list structure on a file, it is better to write a new record and then update the pointer to it, rather than the reverse. This is because a record not pointed to is usually less of a problem than a pointer that points nowhere. But even if the write system calls are issued in a particular order, that doesn't mean that the buffers will be physically written to disk in that order. So *careful replacement* techniques, of which this is but one example, are not as advantageous as they might be. They guard against the process itself terminating at an inopportune time, but not against disk errors or kernel crashes.[3]

As was mentioned in the previous section, Xenix 3 has an open flag (O_WSYNC) that forces the write system call to complete before returning. It slows down the entire system markedly, but it's worthwhile in critical cases. Non-

---

[3]Newer versions of UNIX do use careful replacement internally when flushing buffers that contain directory or free-list data. But no such control is available for user data structures.

Xenix users must resort to writing on raw files, as described in Sec. 3.3, and that is a high price to pay.

These problems with write should not be overemphasized. Considering how reliable computers are today, and how reliable UNIX implementations usually are, kernel crashes are quite rare. Most users are pleased to benefit from the quick response provided by the buffer cache and never find out that the kernel is cheating.

Now let's look once again at the file copy example at the beginning of this chapter. The bug is in the check for a write error:

```
if (write(tofd, buf, nread) != nread)
    syserr("write");
```

The UNIX manual states that it is not an error if the count returned by write is less than the requested count. Specifically, if the file has reached its limit, the next call to write will produce the error.[4] So the bug is that the call to syserr will print a meaningless value for errno. We could recode the function to absorb partial writes and to keep trying until a real error occurs:

```
#define BUFSIZE 512

void copy2(from, to)  /* copy file (second try) */
char *from, *to;
{
    int fromfd, tofd, nread, nwrite, n;
    char buf[BUFSIZE];

    if ((fromfd = open(from, 0)) == -1)
        syserr(from);
    if ((tofd = creat(to, 0666)) == -1)
        syserr(to);
    while ((nread = read(fromfd, buf, sizeof(buf))) != 0) {
        if (nread == -1)
            syserr("read");
        nwrite = 0;
        do {
            if ((n = write(tofd, &buf[nwrite], nread - nwrite))
              == -1)
                syserr ("write");
            nwrite += n;
        } while (nwrite < nread);
    }
    if (close(fromfd) == -1 || close(tofd) == -1)
        syserr("close");
}
```

---

[4]In some versions of System III, and perhaps in other versions too, the manual is wrong. When a partial write occurs, −1 is returned instead of a partial count. So our program may not have had a bug after all.

Realistically, this seems like too much trouble. Perhaps this simple solution makes more sense:

```
if ((n = write(tofd, buf, nread)) != nread) {
    if (n != -1)
        errno = EFBIG;
    syserr("write");
}
```

The constant EFBIG is defined in /usr/include/errno.h, but it isn't used by write. So it's OK to steal it.

2.8 read SYSTEM CALL

```
int read(fd, buf, nbytes)      /* read from file */
int fd;                        /* file descriptor */
char *buf;                     /* buffer address */
unsigned nbytes;               /* number of bytes to read */
/* returns number of bytes read, 0 on EOF, or -1 on error */
```

The read system call is the opposite of write. It reads the nbytes bytes pointed to by buf from the open file represented by fd. The read starts at the current position of the file pointer, and after the read the file pointer is incremented by the number of bytes read. read returns the number of bytes read, or 0 on an end-of-file, or −1 on an error.

Unlike write, the read system call can't very well cheat by passing along the data and then reading it later. If the data isn't already in a kernel buffer (due to a previous write or read), the process just has to wait for the kernel to get it from disk. Usually, the kernel tries to speed things up by noticing access patterns suggesting sequential reading of consecutive disk blocks and then reading ahead to anticipate the process's needs. If the system is lightly loaded enough for data to remain in buffers a while, and if reads are sequential, read-ahead is quite effective.

2.9 close SYSTEM CALL

```
int close(fd)                  /* close file */
int fd;                        /* file descriptor */
/* returns 0 on success or -1 on error */
```

The most important thing to know about the close system call is that it does practically nothing. It does not flush any kernel buffers; it just makes the file descriptor available for reuse. In fact, if the file descriptor isn't needed again, there's no need to call close at all (although it's better technique to do so, because someone might change your program someday). The file will be closed when the process terminates.

2.10 BUFFERED I/O

The kernel buffering we've described so far anticipates reads, postpones writes, and keeps frequently accessed data in fast internal memory. This section is concerned with a completely different kind of buffering, performed by user processes themselves without the knowledge of the kernel at all. We'll call this *user buffering*, as opposed to *kernel buffering*.

Recall from Chap. 1 that the UNIX file system is built on top of a block special file, and therefore all kernel I/O operations and all kernel buffering are in units of the block size. For most versions of UNIX this is 512 bytes, but more recently System V and 4.2 BSD have allowed larger sizes, such as 1024 and 2048. We'll assume in our examples that the block size is 512, but we'll be careful to use a symbolic constant (BUFSIZE) instead of the actual number to make it easy to change.

Reads and writes in chunks of 512 bytes that occur on a a 512-byte boundary are much, much faster than any smaller unit. To demonstrate this we recompiled copy2 from the previous section with a user buffer size of 1 by making this change:

```
#define BUFSIZE 1
```

Then we timed the two versions of copy on a 4000-byte file with these results (times are in seconds):

Method	Real Time	User Time	System Time
512-byte buffer	1.10	.02	.23
1-byte buffer	44.00	1.38	41.37

Real time is the total elapsed time (sometimes called *wall-clock* time). User time is the time spent executing instructions in the user process. System time is the time spent executing instructions in the kernel on behalf of the process.

The performance penalty for I/O with ordinary files in units smaller than 512 bytes is so drastic that one simply never does it, unless the program is just for occasional and casual use, or the situation is quite unusual (reading a file backward, for example; see the next section). If the algorithm is most easily programmed with smaller chunks, the data is moved between kernel space and user space in 512-byte blocks and then smaller pieces are dealt with in user space, using normal data move-

ment instructions, not system calls. That is, one does user buffering instead of kernel buffering.

It's convenient to use a set of subroutines that do reads, writes, seeks, and so
on, in whatever units the caller wishes. These subroutines handle the buffering automatically and never stray from the block model. An exceptionally fine example
of such a package is the so-called "Standard I/O Library," described in most books
on C and in Section 3 of the UNIX manual.[5]

To show the principles behind a user-buffering package, we'll present a simplified one here that we call STREAM. It supports reads and writes, but not seeks,
in units of a single character. First, the header file s t r e a m . h that users of the
package must include:

```
#define SENOMEM 1001
#define SEINVAL 1002
#define BUFSIZE 512

typedef struct {
    int fd;                         /* file descriptor */
    char dir;                       /* direction: r or w */
    int total;                      /* total chars in buf */
    int next;                       /* next char in buf */
    char buf[BUFSIZE];              /* buffer */
} STREAM;

STREAM *Sopen();
int Sgetc();
BOOLEAN Sputc();
BOOLEAN Sclose();
```

Now for the implementation of the package (s t r e a m . c). Don't forget that this
file starts with the four #i n c l u d e statements shown in Sec. 1.10.

```
#include "stream.h"

extern int errno;

STREAM *Sopen(path, dir) /* open stream */
char *path, *dir;
{
    STREAM *z;
    int fd, flags;
    char *malloc();
```

---

[5]Chapter 7 of *The C Programming Language*.

```
    switch (dir[0]) {
    case 'r':
        flags = O_RDONLY;
        break;
    case 'w':
        flags = O_WRONLY | O_CREAT | O_TRUNC;
        break;
    default:
        errno = SEINVAL;
        return(NULL);
    }
    if ((fd = open(path, flags, 0666)) == -1)
        return(NULL);
    if ((z = (STREAM *)malloc(sizeof(STREAM))) == NULL) {
        errno = SENOMEM;
        return(NULL);
    }
    z->fd = fd;
    z->dir = dir[0];
    z->total = z->next = 0;
    return(z);
}

static BOOLEAN readbuf(z)   /* fill buffer */
STREAM *z;
{
    switch (z->total = read(z->fd, z->buf, sizeof(z->buf))) {
    case -1:
        return(FALSE);
    case 0:
        errno = 0;
        return(FALSE);
    default:
        z->next = 0;
        return(TRUE);
    }
}
static BOOLEAN writebuf(z)   /* flush buffer */
STREAM *z;
{
    int n, total;

    total = 0;
    while (total < z->next) {
        if ((n = write(z->fd, &z->buf[total], z->next - total)) == -1)
            return(FALSE);
        total += n;
    }
```

```
    z->next = 0;
    return(TRUE);
}


int Sgetc(z)   /* get character */
STREAM *z;
{
    int c;

    if (z->next >= z->total && !readbuf(z))
        return(-1);
    return(z->buf[z->next++] & 0377);
}


BOOLEAN Sputc(z, c)   /* put character */
STREAM *z;
char c;
{
    z->buf[z->next++] = c;
    if (z->next >= sizeof(z->buf))
        return(writebuf(z));
    return(TRUE);
}


BOOLEAN Sclose(z)   /* close stream */
STREAM *z;
{
    int fd;

    if (z->dir == 'w' && !writebuf(z))
        return(FALSE);
    fd = z->fd;
    free(z);
    return(close(fd) != -1);
}
```

Finally, we recode our file-copy function to use the new package:

```
#include "stream.h"

void copy3(from, to) /* copy file (uses STREAM package) */
char *from, *to;
{
    STREAM *stfrom, *stto;
    int c;
    extern int errno;
```

```
    if ((stfrom = Sopen(from, "r")) == NULL)
        syserr(from);
    if ((stto = Sopen(to, "w")) == NULL)
        syserr(to);
    while ((c = Sgetc(stfrom)) != -1)
        if (!Sputc(stto, c))
            syserr("Sputc");
    if (errno != 0)
        syserr("Sgetc");
    if (!Sclose(stfrom) || !Sclose(stto))
        syserr("Sclose");
}
```

Note the careful attention to error checking and error reporting in this package. It uses errno to specify the error type, just as system calls do. Two new error types are defined: SENOMEM (not enough space; similar to the kernel's ENOMEM), and SEINVAL (invalid argument; similar to EINVAL). Thus the user of STREAM can just check errno when a call returns an error. Sometimes it will contain a kernel error code, and sometimes a STREAM error code. Sgetc sets errno to 0 on end-of-file, to distinguish that reason for a −1 return from an error return (something that the Standard I/O Library doesn't do).

It is unfortunate that there are three different error return values: NULL, FALSE, and −1. However, this is symptomatic of UNIX subroutines in general, and C programmers quickly get used to it.[6]

You will notice a strong resemblance between STREAM and a subset of the Standard I/O Library. Here's a version of copy using that package:

```
void copy4(from, to)  /* copy file (uses Standard I/O) */
char *from, *to;
{
    FILE *stfrom, *stto;
    int c;

    if ((stfrom = fopen(from, "r")) == NULL)
        syserr(from);
    if ((stto = fopen(to, "w")) == NULL)
        syserr(to);
    while ((c = getc(stfrom)) != EOF)
        putc(c, stto);
    if (fclose(stfrom) == EOF || fclose(stto) == EOF)
        syserr("Sclose");
}
```

---

[6]Even though NULL and FALSE have the same definition (0), they are distinct symbols because they serve different purposes. NULL is an invalid pointer, whereas FALSE is a Boolean value.

To see the great benefits of user buffering, the following table shows the times in seconds for the file copy using STREAM and the Standard I/O Library (for convenience we've reproduced the times we got with straight system calls):

Method	Real Time	User Time	System Time
512-byte buffer	1.10	.02	.23
1-byte buffer	44.00	1.38	41.37
STREAM package	1.63	1.33	.18
Standard I/O	1.43	1.08	.20

With user buffering we've almost got the best of both worlds: We process the data as we like, even 1 byte at a time, yet we achieve a system time about the same as the 512-byte buffer method, with user times no worse than with the 1-byte buffer method. So user buffering is definitely the right approach.

The almost universal acceptance of the Standard I/O Library is ironic. The ability to do I/O in arbitrary units on ordinary files has always been one of the really notable features of the UNIX kernel. Yet in practice, the feature is almost never used, because it's too inefficient.

2.11 lseek SYSTEM CALL

```
long lseek(fd, offset, interp)          /* move file pointer */
int fd;                                 /* file descriptor */
long offset;                            /* offset in file */
int interp;                             /* interpretation of offset */
/* returns file pointer value or -1 on error */
```

The lseek system call just sets the file pointer for use by the next read or write. No actual I/O is performed, and no commands are sent to the disk controller. If interp is zero, then offset is an actual file offset (the first byte of the file is at offset 0). If interp is 1, the file pointer is incremented by offset (which might be negative). If interp is 2, the file pointer is set to the size of the file plus offset. This last option is normally used to seek backward from the end of the file, so offset is usually negative or zero when interp is 2.

The second argument may be any value at all, as long as the resulting file pointer would not be negative. The file pointer may point beyond the end of the file. If so, the next write stretches the file to the necessary length, filling the interval with garbage bytes. On the other hand, a **read** with the file pointer set at or past the end generates a 0 (end-of-file) return. A **read** of the stretched interval caused by a **write** past the end succeeds, but the data is meaningless.

When a **write** beyond the end of a file occurs, most UNIX systems don't actually store the intervening blocks of garbage. Thus it is possible for a disk with, say, 30,000 available blocks to contain files whose combined lengths are greater than 30,000 blocks. This can create a serious problem if files are backed up to tape and then restored, since because the files have to be read to transfer them to tape, more than 30,000 blocks will be on the tape! Programmers who create many files with holes in them usually hear about it from their system administrator.

Of all the possible ways to use **lseek**, three are the most popular. First, **lseek** may be used to seek to an absolute position in the file:

```
if (lseek(fd, offset, 0) == -1)
    syserr("lseek");
```

Second, **lseek** may be used to seek to the end of the file:

```
if (lseek(fd, 0L, 2) == -1)
    syserr("lseek");
```

Third, **lseek** may be used to find out where the file pointer currently is:

```
if ((where = lseek(fd, 0L, 1)) == -1)
    syserr("lseek");
```

Other ways of using **lseek** are much less common.

A few words of warning about using **lseek**: Don't forget to declare **lseek** in your program, or else the return value will be misinterpreted. This is sufficient:

```
long lseek();
```

And don't forget that the second argument must be a long integer. Note the use of the long constant **0L** rather than a plain **0**. Remember that the C compiler neither checks nor converts arguments to functions. It converts returned values, but only if you declare the function properly.

Most seeks done by the kernel are implicit rather than as a result of explicit calls to **lseek**. When **open** or **creat** is called, the kernel seeks to the first byte. When **read** or **write** is called, the kernel increments the file pointer by the number of bytes read or written. When a file is opened with the **O_APPEND** flag set, a seek to the end of the file precedes each write.

The name "lseek" is strange. What does the "l" stand for? In the old days of UNIX the system call was **seek**. This was before the C language had long integers. With **seek**, the second argument was an integer (16 bits only; UNIX wasn't portable then), and there were *six* values for the third argument. For three of them the offset was interpreted as a block number (multiple of 512 bytes), and for the other three the offset was in terms of bytes. So, to seek to location 1726, say, one did this:

```
if (seek(fd, 3, 3) == -1 || seek (fd, 190, 1) == -1)
    syserr("seek");
```

The first s e e k seeks to the fourth block (location 1536); the second seeks 190 bytes further. Once long integers were added to C, this awkward approach wasn't needed because file pointers could be expressed directly. The new function was called "lseek" to avoid confusion.[7] In fact, a subroutine named "seek," written in terms of l s e e k, stayed around for a while.

To illustrate the use of l s e e k, here is a function b a c k w a r d that prints a file backward, a line at a time. For example, if the file contains:

```
                          dog
                          bites
                          man
```

then b a c k w a r d will print:

```
                          man
                          bites
                          dog
```

Here is the code:

```
void backward(path) /* print file backward */
char *path;
{
    char s[101], c;
    int i, fd, nread;
    long where, lseek();

    if ((fd = open(path, 0)) == -1)
        syserr(path);
    if ((where = lseek(fd, -1L, 2)) == -1)
        syserr("lseek");
    i = sizeof(s) - 1;
    s[i] = '\0';
```

---

[7]The extra letter was available, since c r e a t was one letter short.

```
while ((nread = read(fd, &c, 1)) == 1) {
    if (c == '\n') {
        printf("%s", &s[i]);
        i = sizeof(s)-1;
    }
    if (i == 0)
        fatal("line too long");
    s[--i] = c;
    if (where == 0)
        break;
    if ((where = lseek(fd, -2L, 1)) == -1)
        syserr("lseek");
}
switch (nread) {
case 0:
    fatal("end-of-file");
case -1:
    syserr("read");
}
printf("%s", &s[i]);
if (close(fd) == -1)
    syserr("close");
}
```

There are two tricky things to observe in this function: First, since read implicitly seeks the file forward, we have to seek backward by *two* bytes to read the previous byte. Second, there's no such thing as a "beginning-of file" return from read, as there is an end-of-file return. So we have to watch the file pointer (the variable where) and stop after we've read the first byte. Alternatively, we could wait until lseek tries to make the file pointer negative. However, this is unwise because the error code in this case (EINVAL) is also used to indicate other kinds of invalid arguments.

2.12 PORTABILITY

The system calls introduced in this chapter are basic enough so that portability among UNIX versions shouldn't be much of a problem. Of course, if one relies too heavily on peculiarities of a particular implementation (values of bytes inserted by a write past the end of a file, for instance), then trouble is bound to arise.

If you anticipate porting to systems based on Version 7, the new form of open (three arguments) should be avoided if possible. The new form is supported in 4.2 BSD, however.

The toughest decision is what to do about writing portable software when writes are required to be physically complete before write returns. Xenix 3 offers the most attractive method, the O_WSYNC flag, but realistically, it is probably essential for commercial software to be portable to AT&T System III and System V. AT&T has not adopted this Xenix feature, and it is not in the /usr/group Proposed Standard either. That leaves raw files as the only portable approach, even though that requires a much more extensive development effort. We'll look at how one uses raw files in Sec. 3.3.

EXERCISES

2.1. Change l o c k in Sec. 2.5 to store the login name in the lock file (use the standard function g e t l o g i n). Add an argument to be used when l o c k returns **FALSE** that provides the login name of the user who has acquired the lock.

2.2. Write a program that opens a file for writing with the **O_APPEND** flag and then writes a line of text on the file. Run several concurrent processes executing this program to convince yourself that the text lines won't get intermixed. Then recode the program without **O_APPEND**, and use l s e e k to seek to the end before each **w r i t e**. Rerun the concurrent processes to see if the text gets intermixed now.

2.3. Rerun the buffered I/O timing tests in Sec. 2.10 with buffer sizes of 2, 57, 128, 256, 511, 513, and 1024. Try some other interesting numbers if you wish. If you have access to several versions of UNIX, run the experiment on each version and assemble the results into a table.

2.4. Enhance the STREAM package to open a file for both reading and writing.

2.5. Add an **Sseek** function to the STREAM package.

2.6. Write a B-tree package for UNIX. You'll need functions to create a B-tree file, to open an existing file, to close a file, and to store, fetch, and delete records. Since a major advantage of a B-tree is that it keeps the records in order, you should also have functions to scan the entire tree. For further information about B-trees, see Douglas Comer, "The Ubiquitous B-Tree," *Computing Surveys* 11, no. 2 (June 1979), 121-37, or D. E. Knuth, *The Art of Computer Programming, Vol. 3: Sorting and Searching* (Reading, Mass.: Addison-Wesley Publishing Company, Inc.), 1973.

2.7. Same as Exercise 2.6, but design your disk-update algorithms to use careful replacement (see Sec. 2.7).

3

ADVANCED
FILE I/O

3.1 INTRODUCTION

This chapter picks up where Chap. 2 left off. First we'll extend the use of the I/O system calls already introduced to work on directories and disk special files. Then we'll introduce additional system calls that allow us to create new directories (and other things), link to existing files, and obtain or modify file status information.

You're much less likely to use the advanced features covered in this chapter than those in Chap. 2. You'll still benefit from knowing how to use them, however, because that will give you a more complete understanding of how file I/O works.

The program examples in this chapter are more extensive than those that have appeared so far. Careful study of these will be well worth your time, since they illustrate details not covered explicitly in the text.

3.2 I/O ON DIRECTORIES

Recall that directories are identical to ordinary files except that they have a special bit set in their i-node and the kernel does not permit writing on them. Any I/O system call may be freely used on a directory, provided the contents of the directory are not modified. Forbidden are `creat`, `open` with flags `O_WRONLY`, `O_RDWR`, or `O_TRUNC`, and `write`. This is not to say that other system calls are useful, only that they are legal. For example, lseek makes little sense on a directory, since the links are kept in no particular order.

Typically, you open a directory for reading and then you read through the links. This is in fact what the ls command does. To assist in interpreting the contents of a directory, there is a standard header file /usr/include/sys/dir.h that defines the structure of one link (struct direct): a two-byte word containing an i-number followed by a 14-byte file name. The file name is padded with null bytes if it is less than 14 bytes, so it may in that case be treated as a null-terminated C string. Unfortunately, the file name is not null-terminated if it is exactly 14 bytes. Hence, the supplied structure in dir.h is less convenient to use than one that has room after the file name to hold a null byte. This is illustrated by the following function that reads and prints a directory:

```
#include <sys/dir.h>

directory(path) /* list directory */
char *path;
{
    struct directx {
        ino_t d_ino;
        char d_name[DIRSIZ + 1];
    } dlink;
    int fd, nread;
    char *dname;

    if ((fd = open(path, 0)) == -1)
        syserr(path);
    dlink.d_name[DIRSIZ] = '\0';
    while ((nread = read(fd, &dlink, sizeof(struct direct))) ==
        sizeof(struct direct)) {
        if (dlink.d_ino == 0)
            dname = "--- UNUSED ---";
        else
            dname = dlink.d_name;
        printf("%-14s %4d\n", dname, dlink.d_ino);
    }
    switch (nread) {
    case 0:
        return;
    case -1:
        syserr("read");
    default:
        fatal("partial read");
    }
}
```

The structure directx is exactly like the official one (direct) except the array d_name is one byte longer. We are careful to read sizeof(struct `direct`) bytes for each link instead of `sizeof(struct directx)`, since the latter would read too much. Note that an i-number of zero indicates an unused link.

This is the output from a test run:

.	678
..	578
`memos`	676
`data`	681
`--- UNUSED ---`	0
`AugustAccounts`	682

Note the entries for `.` and `..`, which are installed automatically when the kernel creates a new directory. Since `.` is a link from this directory to itself, this directory must be i-node 678. Its parent is i-node 578. We don't know the name of the parent directory; that information is only in the parent's parent.

The `unlink` system call works on directories exactly as it does for ordinary files, except that only a process with an effective user-ID of zero (the superuser) may issue it. This is to avoid removing a nonempty directory and thereby creating orphan files, which exist but are not linked to by any directory.[1] The superuser is assumed to know better.

Normal users are expected to partake of the `rmdir` command instead of using `unlink` directly. This command is programmed to make sure that only empty directories are unlinked. The superuser owns the file containing `rmdir`, and the set-user-ID bit is on. Hence, when a normal user executes this command, the effective user-ID is set to that of the superuser.

To create a directory the system call `mknod` is used; it is analogous to `creat` for ordinary files. The contents of a directory are modified by `link`, which installs a new link, and `unlink`, which removes one. `link` and `mknod` are discussed in Sec. 3.6 and Sec. 3.8.

Since directories are in essence ordinary files, and since ordinary files can't shrink to any size other than zero, it isn't possible to directly reclaim the disk space once occupied by a large directory that has many unused links. This fact is not always apparent to UNIX users. Sometimes a user guesses (correctly) that a very large directory is slowing down his or her file accesses, and guesses (incorrectly) that moving most of the files to subdirectories will help. In fact, to effectively shrink a directory, one must make a new sibling directory, move all the links to the new directory, unlink the old directory, and then rename the new directory to have the old name. There isn't any system call to "move" links, although of course there are commands (`mv` and `mvdir`). At the system call level a move is done using `link` and `unlink`, as we shall see in Sec. 3.6.

---

[1]The `fsck` program that repairs file systems acts as an adoption agency. It links orphan files to the `/lost+found` directory, using the i-number as the file name.

3.3 I/O ON DISK SPECIAL FILES

Until now we have done I/O exclusively through the kernel file system, using relatively high level abstractions like file, directory, and i-node. As discussed in Sec. 2.7, the file system is implemented on top of the block I/O system, which uses the buffer cache. The block I/O system is accessed via a block special file, or block device, that interfaces directly to the disk. The disk is treated as a sequence of fixed-size blocks (typically 512 bytes), numbered sequentially starting with 0.

There may be several physical disks, and each physical disk may be divided into pieces, each of which is called a *volume* or *file system*. The term *file system* is confusing because it also describes part of the kernel. The context in which we use the term will make our intended meaning clear.

Each volume corresponds to a special file whose name is formed from a device name, such as rp or hd, followed by a number or letter. These special files are always linked into the /dev directory, although they don't have to be. The disk special files might be named /dev/hd0, /dev/hd1, and so on, up to /dev/hd7.

In principle, a disk special file may be operated on with I/O system calls just as if it were an ordinary file. It may be opened for reading and/or writing, read or written (in arbitrary units), seeked (to any byte boundary), and closed. The buffer cache is used (since it is a block special file), but within the volume, there are no directories, files, i-nodes, permissions, owners, sizes, times, and so on. One just deals with a giant array of numbered blocks.

In practice, most people can't perform any of these operations because permission is denied to them. Reading a disk that contains other users' files compromises their privacy, even though the disk appears haphazard when viewed as a special file (blocks are assigned to UNIX files and directories in no particular order). And writing to a disk without going through the kernel file system would create even worse havoc.

On the other hand, if a volume is reserved for a user, and not used for other users' files and directories, then there is no conflict. Users implementing database managers or data acquisition systems may indeed want to have a volume set aside so they can access it as a block special file. This allows much faster I/O. A limitation, of course, is that there are only so many disk special files to go around. Usually when a disk special file is used by an application, that application is the only one, or certainly the main one, on the computer.

Much, much faster than disk special files are *raw* disk special files. These device drivers deal with the same areas of disk, and their names are even similar; usually an r is prepended (/dev/rhd0, /dev/rhd1, etc.). However, these raw special files are *character* devices, not block devices. That means they do not follow the block model, and they do not use the buffer cache. They do something even better.

When a read or write is initiated on a raw special file, the process is locked into memory (prevented from swapping) so no physical data addresses can change. Then the disk is ordered to transfer data using DMA (direct memory access). Data flows directly between the process's data segment and the disk controller, without going through the kernel at all. The size of the transfer may be more than a block at a time.

Usually, I/O on raw devices is less flexible than it is with ordinary files and block special files. I/O in multiples of a disk sector may be required. The DMA hardware may require the process's buffer address to be on a word boundary. Seeks may be required to be to a block boundary only. These restrictions probably mean little to designers of database-oriented file systems, since they find it convenient to view a disk as being made of fixed-size pages anyhow.

So far, we have seen that UNIX features vary somewhat from version to version. Here, however, we have a variation that depends also on the *port*. Since computers vary enormously in their I/O hardware, device drivers vary accordingly. Also, the goals of the porting effort affect the importance of making raw I/O fast. On a general-purpose desktop system, for example, it may be of very little importance.

Raw I/O has one tremendous advantage and one tremendous disadvantage. The tremendous advantage is that, since the process waits for a `write` to complete, and since there is no question of which process owns the data, the process can be informed about physical write errors via a −1 return value and an `errno` code. There is a code defined (`EIO`), but whether it is ever passed on is up to the device driver implementor. Most implementors do support this code, but since most UNIX manuals are little more than reproductions of the AT&T-issued manual, they seldom give sufficient detail about raw I/O on a specific hardware configuration. It is best either to look at the source code for the device driver itself, if it's available (which it usually isn't), or ask the vendor. Experimentation is a poor way to find out how the error reporting works, because I/O errors are just too difficult to generate, let alone reproduce consistently.

The tremendous disadvantage of raw I/O is that, since the process waits for a `read` or `write` to complete, and since the design of UNIX allows a process to issue only a single system call at a time, the process does I/O very fast but not very often. For example, in a multi-user database application with one centralized database manager process (a common arrangement), there will be a colossal I/O traffic jam if raw I/O is used, since only one process does the I/O for everyone. But I/O on ordinary files isn't very desirable either, so the situation appears hopeless at first glance. This is one reason why UNIX has a reputation for being unsuited for database applications.

The only way to alleviate the traffic jam (short of changing the kernel) is for the central database manager process to create several *drone* processes to do the actual I/O. Rather than the central process doing a read or a write for itself, it passes the request, via an interprocess communication mechanism, to a drone, which issues the read or write and waits. The central process can later interrogate the drone to find out if the I/O is complete. In other words, after centralizing the database management function, we then decentralize the actual I/O. The problem with this scheme is that it greatly increases the amount of interprocess communication. On older versions of UNIX that creates a bottleneck of its own, but with System V or Xenix 3 it is workable (see Chap. 7). The programming of such a high-performance database manager, however, is far from easy.

A minor disadvantage of raw I/O that we can dispose of immediately is that while the process is locked in memory, other processes may not be able to run because there is no room to swap them in. This would be a shame, because DMA does not use the CPU, and these processes could otherwise actually execute. The solution is just to add some more memory. At today's prices (about a tenth of a penny per byte) there is no excuse for not having enough memory to avoid most, if not all, swapping, especially on a computer that runs an application important enough to be doing raw I/O.

The following table summarizes the functional differences between I/O on ordinary files, on disk devices, and on raw disk devices:

Feature	Ordinary File	Disk Device	Raw Disk Device
directories, files, i-nodes, permissions, etc.	Yes	No	No
buffer cache	Yes	Yes	No
I/O error returns, DMA	No	No	Yes

To show the speed differences, we timed a loop that read 204,800 bytes in 100 reads of 2048 bytes each. We read an ordinary file, a disk device (/dev/hd0), and a raw disk device (/dev/rhd0). As we did in Sec. 2.10, we report real time, user time, and system time, in seconds:

File Type	Real Time	User Time	System Time
Ordinary File	10.77	.00	4.60
Disk Device	6.40	.02	2.63
Raw Disk Device	4.13	.02	.58

As you can see, the speed advantages of raw I/O are enormous. We didn't bother running a comparison for writes, since we know that the two file types that use the buffer cache would have won hands down, and because we didn't have a spare volume to scribble on. Of course, it wouldn't have been a fair comparison, since the times with the buffer cache wouldn't have included the physical I/O, and the raw I/O time would have included little else.

It's illuminating to look at the internal structure of a volume by reading it as a disk device (assuming you have read permission). Block 0 (the first block) of a file system is unused. Block 1 is called the *super block*; it contains assorted structural information such as the number of i-nodes, the number of blocks in the volume, the head of a linked list of free blocks, and so on. A C structure describing the super block is available in the header /usr/include/sys/filsys.h.

The i-list, consisting of a sequence of 64-byte i-nodes, starts with block 2. I-nodes are numbered starting with 1, but i-node 1 itself isn't used for an actual file. Instead, it may be used for a pseudo-file consisting of defective disk blocks, to prevent them from being assigned to the free list or to a file. I-node 2 is reserved for the root directory (/), so that when the kernel is given an absolute path it can start from a known place. No other i-numbers have any particular significance; they are assigned to files as needed. All remaining blocks after the i-list are available for data blocks. Initially, they are linked into a free list. As a file grows, blocks are taken off the free list and assigned to it. When a file is truncated or discarded, its blocks are put back on the free list.

The header /usr/include/sys/ino.h contains the C structure for an i-node (struct dinode). The following function prints information from the first five i-nodes:

```
#include <sys/types.h>
#include <sys/ino.h>

inodes() /* print i-node info */
{
    struct dinode di;
    int fd, inumber, nread;
    long lseek();

    if ((fd = open("/dev/hd0", 0)) == -1)
        syserr("open");
    if (lseek(fd, 1024L + sizeof(di), 0) == -1) /* seek to i-node 2 */
        syserr("lseek");
    for (inumber = 2; inumber <= 6; inumber++) {
        if ((nread = read(fd, &di, sizeof(di))) != sizeof(di))
            switch (nread) {
            case 0:
                fatal("EOF");
            case -1:
                syserr("read");
            default:
                fatal("partial read");
            }
        printf("i-node %d; owner = %3o; size = %7ld\n", inumber,
          di.di_uid, di.di_size);
    }
}
```

Here's what this program printed:

```
i-node 2; owner =      2; size =         256
i-node 3; owner =      0; size =          27
i-node 4; owner =      2; size =        1280
i-node 5; owner =      2; size =         744
i-node 6; owner =      2; size =       11182
```

To get information out of an i-node you don't have to read the disk device directly, as we did. You can use the **s t a t** system call, which we'll explain in Sec. 3.12.

3.4 DATES AND TIMES

Two kinds of time are commonly used in UNIX: *execution time* and *calendar time*. Execution time is used to measure timing intervals (as we have done in the previous section) and for accounting records. The kernel automatically records each process's execution time; the system-call **t i m e s** (Sec. 9.10) may be used to obtain it. Execution times are in units of "ticks," which vary from computer to computer (60 or 100 ticks per second).

Calendar time is kept as a count of the number of seconds since midnight, January 1, 1970 GMT (Greenwich Mean Time). It is used for the access, modification, and status-change times of files, for recording when a user logged in, and so on. GMT is also a good way for application programs to store times in data files, but sometimes local time is used instead. Since the system-call **t i m e** (Sec. 9.11) returns a long integer, the count must fit into 31 bits, but that's enough seconds to take us to January 19, 2038, by which time someone surely will have moved the epoch.

The UNIX kernel isn't concerned with time zones other than GMT, but users are. It's convenient to use local time when times are entered or printed out, and this complicates things. There must be some way for the computer to know what time zone the user is in and whether it is currently standard or daylight time. Worse, when printing past times, the computer must know whether it was standard or daylight time back then. There is a collection of subroutines called **c t i m e** that attempts to deal with the problem.[2] Time zones are handled well; the standard/daylight offset is handled imperfectly but well enough.

The user's time zone is recorded in the environment variable **T Z**, which must be set correctly (just once, unless the computer is moved) by the system administrator. The first three characters of the value of **T Z** are the name of the time zone; the last three are the name during daylight saving time (if it is observed); the middle characters are the offset in hours from GMT, positive for zones west of Greenwich and negative for zones east. An example is **M S T 7 M D T** for Colorado.

---

[2]The **c t i m e** package, including the functions **l o c a l t i m e** and **a s c t i m e**, is documented in Section 3 of the UNIX manual.

A trickier question is whether a particular time is daylight or standard. As of this writing, daylight time begins at 2 A.M. on the last Sunday of April and ends on the last Sunday of October. But that's only true of the United States, and not for Arizona and Hawaii. To complicate matters further, in 1974 and 1975 daylight time was observed during the winter and early spring (to save energy). A table inside the ctime subroutines records this historical information. If a time zone observes daylight time, as indicated by the TZ variable, then ctime assumes that it always did, and the internal table is used. This doesn't allow for states or countries that change their policy of observance. Fortunately, if we know past times to within an hour we're usually satisfied. *Comparisons* between times are more critical, but there is no problem here because these take place within the computer, where only GMT is used.

The ctime subroutines help only in displaying time. They don't help in entering it, and there are no standard UNIX subroutines that do. To translate from a convenient notation, such as year-month-day-hour-minute-second (YYMMDDhhmmss) to the offset in seconds since 1970 is surprisingly complex. You must take into account the varying number of days per month, leap years, time zones, and the observance of daylight saving time. To show how this conversion is done, we present a program that converts a 12-digit number of the form YYMMDDhhmmss to internal form:

```
#include <time.h>

static long timecvt(atime)  /* convert YYMMDDhhmmss to internal */
char *atime;
{
    long tm;
    int i, n, days, tzone;
    char s[3], *getenv(), *tz;
    BOOLEAN isleapyear;
    extern struct tm *localtime();

    if (strlen(atime) != 12) {
        printf("Time must be 12 digits (YYMMDDhhmmss)\n");
        return(0);
    }
    for (i = 0; i < 12; i++)
        if (atime[i] < '0' || atime[i] > '9') {
            printf("Time contains non-numeric character\n");
            return(0);
        }
    if ((tz = getenv("TZ")) == NULL)
        tzone = 5;  /* Eastern Time Zone */
    else
        tzone = atoi(&tz[3]);
    s[2] = '\0';
```

```
for (i = 0; i < 12; i += 2) {
    s[0] = atime[i];
    s[1] = atime[i + 1];
    n = atoi(s);
    switch (i) {
    case 0: /* YY: year */
        isleapyear = n != 0 && n % 4 == 0;  /* 2000 isn't */
        if (n < 70)
            n += 100; /* years after 2000 */
        days = (n - 70L) * 365L;
        days += ((n - 69L) / 4); /* previous years' leap days */
        continue;
    case 2: /* MM: month */
        switch (n) {
        case 12:
            days += 30;  /* Nov */
        case 11:
            days += 31;  /* Oct */
        case 10:
            days += 30;  /* Sep */
        case 9:
            days += 31;  /* Aug */
        case 8:
            days += 31;  /* Jul */
        case 7:
            days += 30;  /* Jun */
        case 6:
            days += 31;  /* May */
        case 5:
            days += 30;  /* Apr */
        case 4:
            days += 31;  /* Mar */
        case 3:
            days += (isleapyear ? 29 : 28); /* Feb */
        case 2:
            days += 31;  /* Jan */
        case 1:
            break;
        default:
            printf("Invalid month\n");
            return(0);
        }
        continue;
```

```
case 4: /* DD: day */
    if (n > 31) {
        printf("Invalid day\n");
        return(0);
    }
    tm = (days + n - 1) * 24L * 60L * 60L;
    continue;
case 6: /* hh: hour */
    if (n > 23) {
        printf("Invalid hour\n");
        return(0);
    }
    n += tzone; /* correct for time zone */
    tm += n * 60L * 60L;
    continue;
case 8: /* mm: minute */
    if (n > 59) {
        printf("Invalid minute\n");
        return(0);
    }
    tm += n * 60L;
    continue;
case 10: /* ss: second */
    if (n > 59) {
        printf("Invalid second\n");
        return(0);
    }
    tm += n;
}
if (localtime(&tm)->tm_isdst)
    tm -= 60L * 60L; /* adjust for daylight savings time */
return(tm);
    }
}
```

The standard function getenv gets the value of an environment variable (TZ, in this case).

We cheated in determining whether the entered time was standard or daylight: We calculated the internal time as though it were standard, and then asked localtime (part of the ctime package) to figure out for us whether daylight saving time was in effect then. This isn't completely accurate around 2 A.M. on the switch-over days. We leave the minor correction as an exercise for those readers who care.

3.5 **FILE MODES**

In Chaps. 1 and 2 we explained that the rightmost nine bits of a file's mode are its permissions, to be interpreted as read, write, and execute permission for the owner, for the group, and for others. Here we look at the leftmost seven bits.

The following table indicates the meaning of each bit. The bits are numbered from 15 at the left to 0 at the right.

Bits	Symbol	Value	Meaning
15—12	S_IFMT	0170000	Type of file:
	S_IFREG	0100000	Ordinary
	S_IFDIR	040000	Directory
	S_IFCHR	020000	Character special
	S_IFBLK	060000	Block special
	S_IFIFO	010000	FIFO
11	S_ISUID	04000	Set-user-ID
10	S_ISGID	02000	Set-group-ID
9	S_ISVTX	01000	Save swapped text
8—0			Permission bits

The symbols are defined in the header /usr/include/sys/stat.h to have the indicated values. Given a 16-bit mode, these symbols can be used to mask off and test specific bits. For example, the expression:

```
(mode & S_IFMT) == S_IFDIR
```

is true for directories. You must not use the symbols S_IFDIR and S_IFCHR as masks, because block special files are marked with both of those bits on. That is, if we had erroneously written the above expression as:

```
(mode & S_IFDIR) == S_IFDIR  /* wrong */
```

then it would falsely report a block special file to be a directory. The symbols that aren't part of the four-bit file-type field may be used as masks, since they define only a single bit.

There are some symbols defined for the nine-bit permission field too, but it's easier and just as readable to use the familiar octal numbers. For example, a mode for a FIFO might be

```
S_IFIFO | 0664
```

The rightmost 12 bits of a mode may be used in all system calls that use a file mode: creat, open, chmod, stat, fstat, and mknod. The leftmost four bits (the file type) are used only with s t a t, f s t a t, and m k n o d. The ordinary-file bit (S _ I F R E G) is also set by c r e a t and o p e n.

The meaning of the "save swapped text" bit (S _ I S V T X) hasn't been explained yet, so we'll do so now. A program may be marked as having *sharable text*, or, a better term, *sharable instructions*. (The term *pure-procedure* is also sometimes used.) The requirements for this are that the instructions and data be in separate segments (that is, data starts on a segment boundary) and that the instructions be read-only. The benefit is that if two or more processes are concurrently executing that program, they may share the physical memory holding the instruction segment. This is easily done by the kernel by simply making their instruction segment registers all point to the same memory locations. A further economy occurs when a process running a sharable-instruction program is swapped out: There is no need to swap the instruction segment out. Instead, when the process is swapped back in, the instructions will be reloaded from the program file.

Now, the effect of the S _ I S V T X bit, sometimes called the *sticky bit*, is to swap the instruction segment out once only, and then to leave it on the swap device, even after the process terminates. Then when a future process executes the same program, the text may be loaded from the swap device instead of from the program file. This slightly improves performance if the program is frequently used and if the swap device is appreciably faster than the device holding the program. Usually only two programs qualify: the shell and the most popular text editor (normally, e d or v i).

This is as good a place as any to explain one other concept related to programs with sharable instructions: *text busy*. While such a program is in execution, its instructions must not be modified. If they were, then the next time the process got swapped in, it would load the *new* instructions (from the program file) along with the *old* data (from the swap device), with indescribable results. To prevent such a thing, the kernel refuses to load a program from a file that is currently open for writing or to open for writing a file containing a sharable-instruction program that is currently executing. In either case the offending system call returns − 1 with an e r r n o value of E T X T B S Y.

3.6 link SYSTEM CALL

```
int link(oldpath, newpath)    /* link to file */
char *oldpath;                 /* existing file */
char *newpath;                 /* new directory entry */
/* returns 0 on success or -1 on error */
```

The l i n k system call adds a new link to a directory. The first argument, *oldpath*, must be an existing link; it provides the i-number to be used. The second argument, *newpath*, indicates the name of the new link. The links are equal in every way, since UNIX has no notion of primary and secondary links. The effective user-ID or the effective group-ID must have write permission on the directory that is to contain the new link. The link specified by the second argument must not already exist; link can't be used to change an existing link. In this case the old link must first be removed with unlink.

If the . and .. links present in every directory are ignored, the directory structure is a strict tree. That is, there are no loops. Programs that recursively descend the hierarchy (such as the command find) can then be programmed without fear of passing through the same directory twice, or, even worse, actually getting stuck in an endless loop. To ensure that this rule is obeyed, only the superuser is allowed to establish a second link (other than . and ..) to a directory.

Why does even the superuser need to link twice to a directory? This is to allow a directory to be moved to another part of the tree, or to allow a directory to be renamed. As long as the second link is quickly removed, little harm is done.

The overall strategy for the mv command, then, is to unlink the new name, in case it already exists; make a link from the old name to the new; and then unlink the old name. If we're the superuser this works for directories too, except that we don't want to risk unlinking the new name, since that directory may not be empty. This is embodied in the following function:

```
mv(from, to) /* move file or directory; must be superuser */
char *from, *to;
{
    BOOLEAN isdir();
    extern int errno;

    if (!isdir(to))
        if(unlink(to) == -1 && errno != ENOENT)
            syserr("unlink1");
    if (link(from, to) == -1)
        syserr("link");
    if (unlink(from) == -1)
        syserr("unlink2");
}

BOOLEAN isdir(path) /* is path a directory? */
char *path;
{
    BOOLEAN ans;
    int fd;
    extern int errno;

    ans = (fd = open(path, 1)) == -1 && errno == EISDIR;
    if (fd != -1 && close(fd) == -1)
        syserr("close");
    return(ans);
}
```

The trick we used to determine if a file was a directory was to try to open it for writing, and see if we fail because it's a directory. A much cleaner way would be to rewrite `isdir` to use `stat`, as we shall see in Sec. 3.12. If the new file is not a directory, we go ahead and try to unlink it. It's perfectly OK if this fails because the file doesn't exist (`ENOENT`), but not for any other reason.

This function always works on files, but it works on directories only if the effective user-ID is zero (superuser). If we wanted to make this function generally available as a command, we would make the superuser the owner of the file and turn on the set-user-ID bit (`S_ISUID`, as explained in the previous section). But we dare not do that, for if this command runs as superuser then anyone could move or rename anyone else's files and directories!

There was a time when the real UNIX `mv` command actually worked pretty much like our example. You really did run as superuser when moving or renaming a directory. This could be exploited by a clever user to break in and become superuser, like this:[3]

1. Make a copy of the password file (`/etc/passwd`) in `/tmp`. You will be the owner of the copy, and you will have write permission on it.
2. Edit `/tmp/passwd` to remove the superuser password. (The superuser's login name is `root`.)
3. Rename `/tmp` to be `/etc`:

```
mv /etc /etc2
mv /tmp /etc
```

4. Log in as `root`. No password will be needed.
5. As quickly as you can, restore everything to the way it was.
6. Send your system administrator some mail, which will be coming from `root`!
7. *Log out*. After all, you don't want to damage anything but the system administrator's pride.

The fix for this bug was to enhance `mv` so that it checks that the *real* user-ID has permission to do what it is about to do. We want to make sure that the effect of running as superuser is to allow us to execute `link` and `unlink` on directories and nothing else. The `access` system call, detailed in the next section, makes this check quite straightforward.

One more bug in using `mv` on directories is still there to this day. There is a small window of time between the call to `link` and the call to `unlink`. During this time, the directory has two links to it. If a program that assumes the directory

---

[3]Alan L. Glasser and I used this scheme to break into Dennis Ritchie and Ken Thompson's system back in 1973 or 1974.

hierarchy is a strict tree is concurrently running, it may visit the same directory twice. The chances of this are slim, and the chances of any real harm is slimmer. But to be safe, you should run programs that traverse the directory structure on an otherwise idle system.

link can only build a link from a directory to a file or directory on the same volume. This is because a mounted volume is restricted to a single mount point. Rather than go into this here, we'll defer the discussion of mountable volumes until Sec. 9.14.

3.7 access SYSTEM CALL

```
int access(path, pattern)    /* check permissions */
char *path;                  /* file to be checked */
int pattern;                 /* permission bits */
/* returns 0 if requested access is allowed or -1 on error */
```

Unlike any other system call that deals with permissions, access checks the *real* user-ID or group-ID, not the *effective* ones. The argument pattern is taken as three permission bits: read, write, and execute. If the real user-ID and the owner user-ID of path match, then the pattern is compared to the file's owner permission bits (bits 8, 7, and 6 of the mode). If the real user-ID has each permission specified by the pattern, then access returns 0; it returns -1 otherwise. If the user-IDs don't match, but the group-IDs do, then the group permission bits of the mode (5, 4, and 3) are tested. If the group-ID doesn't match either, then the other bits (2, 1, and 0) are tested.

If pattern is zero, access just checks to see if path exists. Each directory in path must have execute (search) permission.

We can use access to fix the security breach in the mv example of the previous section. We want to ensure that the real user-ID has write permission on the parent directory of the file or directory to be moved and on the new parent. To help, we need a function parent that takes a path specifying a file or directory and gives us the directory containing it. Given /usr/marc/book, for example, parent would return /usr/marc. The task is easy: We just remove the rightmost / and everything to its right. The only slight complication is that paths without / characters and paths that have only a leading / must be handled correctly too. Here is our version of parent:

```
char *parent(path, dir)  /* get parent directory */
char *path, *dir;
{
    char *lastslash, *strrchr();
```

```
        strcpy(dir, path);
        lastslash = strrchr(dir, '/');
        if (lastslash == NULL) /* current directory */
            strcpy(dir, ".");
        else if (lastslash == dir) /* root */
            strcpy(dir, "/");
        else
            *lastslash = '\0';
        return(dir);
    }
```

The standard function `strrchr` returns a pointer to the last occurrence of a character in a string, or **NULL** if it doesn't occur.

Now we can fix **mv** by adding these lines at the start of the function:

```
        char dir[50], *parent();

        if (access(parent(from, dir), 2) == -1 ||
            access(parent(to, dir), 2) == -1)
                syserr(dir);
```

Let's reflect on what we've had to do. Because we needed to use `link` and `unlink` on directories, we had to run as superuser. But that meant the kernel's permission system was completely bypassed, so it wasn't available to prevent users from doing unauthorized things. We had to implement our own permission system, using `access`. This points out the central security problem with UNIX: not that it can't be made secure, but that responsibility is so widely distributed. There is no programming methodology for UNIX that prevents security breaches, and no practical way to audit a UNIX system to determine whether it's secure. The loopholes have been discovered piecemeal over a period of years. Today, if the system administrator is on the ball, a UNIX system is probably quite safe. *But no one knows for sure*!

3.8 mknod SYSTEM CALL

```
        #include <sys/types.h>
        #include <sys/stat.h>

        int mknod(path, mode, device)   /* make file */
        char *path;                      /* file to be created */
        int mode;                        /* mode of new file */
        int device;                      /* device number */
        /* returns 0 on success or -1 on error */
```

mknod makes a file of any type. All 16 bits of the second argument mode are used, as explained in Sec. 3.5. It is the only way to make directories, special files, and FIFOs. Ordinary files are almost always made with creat or open instead.

When making a special file you must supply the device number, which, as we mentioned in Sec. 1.2.3, is an index into a table inside the kernel that specifies the appropriate device driver. The actual interpretation of a device number is configuration dependent, but the rightmost byte is usually the *minor* device number and the next byte is the *major* device number. The major device number indicates which device driver is to be used, whereas the minor device number indicates the specific physical device. A single device driver for a disk, say, could handle several actual disks. By convention, all special files are put in the directory /dev.

mknod is only used to make a device when a new device driver is installed or a new minor device number becomes active. Once a UNIX system is set up, mknod for special files ceases to be of much interest.

Except when making a FIFO, only the superuser can execute mknod. For special files this restriction is understandable, but for directories (and ordinary files, for that matter) it seems to be a mistake. UNIX has always been that way, however, so programmers have had a long time to get used to it.

System programmers new to UNIX often look in vain for the mkdir system call. You know, the one the mkdir command uses? There is no such system call, but it's easy enough to program a function to do the same job:

```
int mkdir(path) /* make directory; must be superuser */
char *path;
{
    return(mknod(path, S_IFDIR | 0775, 0));
}
```

Since only the superuser can execute mknod, the mkdir command simply runs with the set-user-ID bit on. But normal users often write programs that have to make directories too. They can just execute the mkdir command as a subprocess. Here's a version of the function that anybody can run:

```
int mkdir2(path) /* make directory */
char *path;
{
    char cmd[50];

    sprintf(cmd, "mkdir %s", path);
    if (system(cmd) == 0)
        return(0);
    else
        return(-1);
}
```

This is a time-consuming way to make a directory, but directories aren't made often enough for it to matter much.

When FIFOs were first introduced, how to make one was a real mystery. The term doesn't even appear in the UNIX manual's permuted index! Programmers eventually discovered that mknod was assigned the job, as illustrated by this handy function:

```
int mkfifo(path)  /* make FIFO */
char *path;
{
     return(mknod(path, S_IFIFO | 0666, 0));
}
```

We'll have much more to say about FIFOs in Chap. 7.

3.9 chmod SYSTEM CALL

```
int chmod(path, mode)      /* change mode of file */
char *path;                /* file to be changed */
int mode;                  /* new mode */
/* returns 0 on success or -1 on error */
```

The chmod system call changes the mode of an existing file of any type. It can't be used to change the type itself, however, so only the rightmost 12 bits of the mode argument are used. The caller's effective user-ID must match the owner user-ID of the file, or the caller must be the superuser. It's not enough for the caller's effective group-ID to match that of the file. Only the superuser can turn on the save-swapped-text bit.

Incidentally, don't ever use a mode like 4777. This turns on the set-user-ID bit and allows others to write on the file. Someone else could then copy the shell onto your file, execute it, and become (effectively) you! A good system administrator will run a program from time to time that looks for files with such a mode and clears the gratuitous write bits.

An example using chmod is in Sec. 3.12.

3.10 chown SYSTEM CALL

```
int chown(path, owner, group)      /* change owner of file */
char *path;                        /* file to be changed */
int owner;                         /* new owner ID */
int group;                         /* new group ID */
/* returns 0 on success or -1 on error */
```

chown changes the owner user-ID and group-ID of a file. Only the owner or the superuser may execute it.

Unless the caller is the superuser, chown clears the set-user-ID and set-group-ID bits. This is to prevent a rather obvious form of break-in:

```
$ cp /bin/sh mysh          [get a personal copy of the shell]
$ chmod 4700 mysh          [turn on the set-user-ID bit]
$ chown root mysh          [make the superuser the owner]
$ mysh                     [become superuser]
```

If you want your own superuser shell, you must reverse the order of chmod and chown. But, unless you are already the superuser, you won't be allowed to execute the chmod. So another loophole is plugged.

Section 3.12 has an example of chown.

3.11 utime SYSTEM CALL

```
#include <sys/types.h>

int utime(path, timep)      /* change file times */
char *path;                 /* file to be changed */
struct utimbuf {
    time_t atime;           /* new access time */
    time_t mtime;           /* new modification time */
} *timep;
/* returns 0 on success or -1 on error */
```

utime changes the access and modification times of a file of any type. time_t is actually a long, and the times are in standard calendar-time form as defined in Sec. 3.4 (number of seconds since 1970). If the second argument timep is NULL, the access and modification times are set to the current time. This is done to force a file to appear up-to-date without rewriting it, and is primarily for the benefit of the touch command.

If timep is not NULL, only the owner or the superuser can change the times. If it is NULL, then anyone with write permission on the file can also change the times. This concession was introduced to make the touch command more reasonable. After all, if you can rewrite a file, surely you should be able to update its times!

Aside from touch, utime is most often used when restoring files from a dump tape or when receiving files across a communication line. The times are reset to the values they had originally. The status-change time can't be reset, but that's appropriate since the i-node didn't move anywhere—a new one got created.

Although the System III and System V manuals describe the timep argument in terms of a structure, those UNIX versions don't include a header file containing its definition. This is no doubt because Version 7 defined **t i me p** somewhat differently:

```
time_t timep[2];
```

Apparently the System III manual writers decided to be a little classier.

The next section shows an example using **ut i me**.

3.12 stat AND fstat SYSTEM CALLS

```
#include <sys/types.h>
#include <sys/stat.h>

int stat(path, sbuf)                    /* get file status */
char *path;                             /* path name */
struct stat *sbuf;                      /* status information */
/* returns 0 on success or -1 on error */

int fstat(fd, sbuf)                     /* get file status */
int fd;                                 /* file descriptor */
struct stat *sbuf;
/* returns 0 on success or -1 on error */
```

stat and **fstat** are used to get status information from an i-node. **stat** takes a path and finds the i-node by following it; **fstat** takes an open file descriptor and finds the i-node from the active i-node table inside the kernel. Data from the i-node is rearranged and placed into the user supplied **stat** structure, which is defined in the header **/usr/include/sys/stat.h**.

fstat can be used on a file descriptor open to a pipe, which isn't normally thought of as being associated with an i-node. In fact, the kernel does dedicate an i-node for each pipe, and **fstat** interrogates this hidden i-node. The file type is that of a FIFO. Since pipes, unlike FIFOs, don't have names, the link count is zero, and this fact may be used to distinguish pipes from FIFOs should it ever be necessary to do so. The permission bits are zero. The size reflects the number of bytes in the pipe waiting to be read. The owner, group, and times fields have the same interpretation as for files.

The following table lists the members of the **stat** structure. The type name as it appears in the structure definition and the actual C type as defined in **/usr/include/sys/types.h** are given in parentheses. You need to know this to use the member in a program (**localtime**, for example, takes a **long**, not a **time_t**). The type **ushort** means **unsigned short**.

st_dev	The device number of the device containing the i-node. In the usual interpretation, the leftmost byte is the major num-

	ber and the rightmost byte is the minor number. (d e v _ t; s h o r t)
st_ino	The i-number. (i n o _ t; u s h o r t)
st_mode	The 16-bit mode (see Sec. 3.5). (u s h o r t)
st_nlink	The link count; 0 for pipes. (s h o r t)
st_uid	The owner user-ID. (u s h o r t)
st_gid	The group-ID. (u s h o r t)
st_rdev	For a special file, the device number of the device it refers to. For other file types this field is meaningless. (d e v _ t; s h o r t)
st_size	The current size of the file; zero for special files. (o f f _ t; l o n g)
st_atime	The access time as the number of seconds since 1970 (see Sec. 3.4). Updated whenever the file is read, but not when a directory is searched. (t i m e _ t; l o n g)
st_mtime	The modification time, updated when the file is written. Updated when a link is added to or removed from a directory. (t i m e _ t; l o n g)
st_ctime	The status-change time, updated when the file is written or when the mode, owner, group, link count, or modification time is changed. Updated when the access time is changed explicitly via u t i m e, but not when the file is read. (t i m e _ t; l o n g)

To show how s t a t is used, and also to give the examples for c h m o d, c h o w n, and u t i m e that we promised earlier, we present an interactive utility program, s t a t u t i l, that can print status information; change the owner, mode, and times; and even execute arbitrary shell commands. You may find it useful to run this program for yourself to see how the status changes when various operations are performed.

Here is a sample s t a t u t i l session. Characters typed by the user are underlined.

```
$ statutil
a    change access time
f    new file name
m    change modification time
o    change owner
p    change permissions
q    quit
s    display status
!    execute UNIX command
?    display command summary
```

```
Command? f

File? /dev/hd0

File "/dev/hd0"
Block special file
Device number: 0, 0
Resides on device: 0, 0
I-node: 93; Links: 1; Size: 0
Owner ID: 2; Name: bin
Group ID: 2; Name: bin
Permissions: 644
Last access:                    Thu Aug 23 10:02:22 1984
Last modification:              Wed Dec 31 22:00:00 1969
Last status change:             Mon Aug 20 11:03:05 1984

Command? f

File? statutil

File "statutil"
Ordinary file
Resides on device: 0, 0
I-node: 698; Links: 1; Size: 22604
Owner ID: 200; Name: marc
Group ID: 1; Name: staff
Permissions: 755
Last access:                    Thu Aug 23 11:49:44 1984
Last modification:              Thu Aug 23 11:49:39 1984
Last status change:             Thu Aug 23 11:49:40 1984

Command? p

Mode (up to 4 octal digits)? 6755

Command? s

File "statutil"
Ordinary file
Resides on device: 0, 0
I-node: 698; Links: 1; Size: 22604
Owner ID: 200; Name: marc
Group ID: 1; Name: staff
Set-user-ID
Set-group-ID
Permissions: 755
Last access:                    Thu Aug 23 11:49:44 1984
Last modification:              Thu Aug 23 11:49:39 1984
Last status change:             Thu Aug 23 11:51:53 1984
```

```
Command? m

Time (YYMMDDhhmmss)? 781107085236

Command? s

File "statutil"
Ordinary file
Resides on device: 0, 0
I-node: 698; Links: 1; Size: 22604
Owner ID: 200; Name: marc
Group ID: 1; Name: staff
Set-user-ID
Set-group-ID
Permissions: 755
Last access:              Thu Aug 23 11:49:44 1984
Last modification:        Tue Nov  7 08:52:36 1978
Last status change:       Thu Aug 23 11:53:40 1984

Command? q
$
```

In programming s t a t u t i l we used several standard functions: To access the password and group files (/ e t c / p a s s w d and / e t c / g r o u p) to convert between numerical IDs and names, we used g e t p w u i d, g e t p w n a m, g e t g r g i d, and g e t g r n a m. We used a s c t i m e and l o c a l t i m e, which were also used back in Sec. 3.4, as well as t i m e c v t, which appeared in that section as well.

Here is s t a t u t i l. You'll want to read through it carefully, since it's capable of lots more than we showed in the sample session.

```
#include <sys/types.h>
#include <sys/stat.h>
#include <pwd.h>
#include <grp.h>
#include <time.h>

main() /* statutil */
{
    setbuf(stdout, NULL);
    help();
    mainloop();
}

static void mainloop() /* process commands */
{
    char path[50], cmd[10], shcmd[100];
```

```
    while (1) {
        prompt("Command", cmd);
        if (strlen(cmd) > 1)
            cmd[0] = '\1';  /* force unknown command message */
        switch (cmd[0]) {
        case '\0':
        case 'q':
            exit(0);
        case 'a':
        case 'm':
            chtime(path, cmd[0]);
            continue;
        case 'f':
            prompt("File", path);
            if (access(path, 0) == -1) {
                printf("%s nonexistent\n", path);
                continue;
            }
            status(path);
            continue;
        case 'o':
            chowner(path);
            continue;
        case 'p':
            chperms(path);
            continue;
        case 's':
            status(path);
            continue;
        case '!':
            prompt("Shell command", shcmd);
            system(shcmd);
            continue;
        case '?':
            help();
            continue;
        default:
            printf("Unknown command; use ? for help");
            continue;
        }
    }
}

static void help()  /* display menu */
{
```

```
    printf("a    change access time\n");
    printf("f    new file name\n");
    printf("m    change modification time\n");
    printf("o    change owner\n");
    printf("p    change permissions\n");
    printf("q    quit\n");
    printf("s    display status\n");
    printf("!    execute UNIX command\n");
    printf("?    display command summary\n");
}

static void prompt(msg, result) /* prompt user */
char *msg, *result;
{
    printf("\n%s? ", msg);
    if (gets(result) == NULL)
        exit(0);
}

static void status(path) /* "s" command */
char *path;
{
    struct stat sb;

    if (stat(path, &sb) == -1) {
        syserrmsg("stat");
        return;
    }
    printf("\nFile \"%s\"\n", path);
    dspstatus(&sb);
}

static void dspstatus(sbp) /* display status */
struct stat *sbp;
{
    BOOLEAN isdevice = FALSE;
    struct passwd *pw, *getpwuid();
    struct group *gr, *getgrgid();
    char *name, *asctime();
    struct tm *localtime();

    if ((sbp->st_mode & S_IFMT) == S_IFDIR)
        printf("Directory\n");
    else if ((sbp->st_mode & S_IFMT) == S_IFBLK) {
        printf("Block special file\n");
        isdevice = TRUE;
    } else if ((sbp->st_mode & S_IFMT) == S_IFCHR) {
        printf("Character special file\n");
        isdevice = TRUE;
```

```
    } else if ((sbp->st_mode & S_IFMT) == S_IFREG)
        printf("Ordinary file\n");
    else if ((sbp->st_mode & S_IFMT) == S_IFIFO)
        printf("FIFO\n");
    if (isdevice)
        printf("Device number: %d, %d\n", (sbp->st_rdev >> 8) & 0377,
            sbp->st_rdev & 0377);
    printf("Resides on device: %d, %d\n", (sbp->st_dev >> 8) & 0377,
        sbp->st_dev & 0377);
    printf("I-node: %d; Links: %d; Size: %ld\n", sbp->st_ino,
        sbp->st_nlink, sbp->st_size);
    if ((pw = getpwuid(sbp->st_uid)) == NULL)
        name = "???";
    else
        name = pw->pw_name;
    printf("Owner ID: %d; Name: %s\n", sbp->st_uid, name);
    if ((gr = getgrgid(sbp->st_gid)) == NULL)
        name = "???";
    else
        name = gr->gr_name;
    printf("Group ID: %d; Name: %s\n", sbp->st_gid, name);
    if ((sbp->st_mode & S_ISUID) == S_ISUID)
        printf("Set-user-ID\n");
    if ((sbp->st_mode & S_ISGID) == S_ISGID)
        printf("Set-group-ID\n");
    if ((sbp->st_mode & S_ISVTX) == S_ISVTX)
        printf("Save swapped text after use\n");
    printf("Permissions: %o\n", sbp->st_mode & 0777);
    printf("Last access:          %s",
        asctime(localtime(&sbp->st_atime)));
    printf("Last modification:    %s",
        asctime(localtime(&sbp->st_mtime)));
    printf("Last status change: %s",
        asctime(localtime(&sbp->st_ctime)));
}


static void chtime(path, which)   /* "a" and "m" commands */
char *path, which;
{
    char atime[20];
    long seconds, timecvt();
    struct stat sb;
    struct utimbuf {
        time_t actime;
        time_t modtime;
    } tb;
```

```
    if (stat(path, &sb) == -1) {
        syserrmsg("stat");
        return;
    }
    prompt("Time (YYMMDDhhmmss)", atime);
    if ((seconds = timecvt(atime)) <= 0)
        return;
    switch (which) {
    case 'a':
        tb.actime = seconds;
        tb.modtime = sb.st_mtime;
        break;
    case 'm':
        tb.actime = sb.st_atime;
        tb.modtime = seconds;
    }
    if (utime(path, &tb) == -1)
        syserrmsg("utime");
}

static void chowner(path)  /* "o" command */
char *path;
{
    char oname[20], gname[20];
    int owner, group;
    struct passwd *pw, *getpwnam();
    struct group *gr, *getgrnam();

    prompt("Owner name", oname));
    if ((pw = getpwnam(oname)) == NULL) {
        printf("Unknown name\n");
        return;
    }
    owner = pw->pw_uid;
    prompt("Group name", gname);
    if ((gr = getgrnam(gname)) == NULL) {
        printf("Unknown name\n");
        return;
    }
    group = gr->gr_gid;
    if (chown(path, owner, group) == -1)
        syserrmsg("chown");
}
```

```
static void chperms(path)  /* "p" command */
char *path;
{
    char smode[20];
    int mode;

    prompt("Mode (up to 4 octal digits)", smode);
    if (sscanf(smode, "%o", &mode) != 1) {
        printf("Invalid mode\n");
        return;
    }
    if (chmod(path, mode) == -1)
        syserrmsg("chown");
}

static void syserrmsg(msg)  /* display error message */
char *msg;
{
    extern int errno, sys_nerr;
    extern char *sys_errlist[];

    fprintf(stderr, "ERROR: %s (%d", msg, errno);
    if (errno > 0 && errno < sys_nerr)
        fprintf(stderr, "; %s)\n", sys_errlist[errno]);
    else
        fprintf(stderr, ")\n");
}
```

The function syserrmsg is just a nonfatal form of syserr, since in an interactive program we usually want to return to command level when an error occurs rather than quitting altogether.

3.13 fcntl SYSTEM CALL

```
#include <fcntl.h>

int fcntl(fd, cmd, arg)     /* control file */
int fd;                     /* file descriptor */
int cmd;                    /* command */
int arg;                    /* argument */
/* returns value, file descriptor, or -1 on error */
```

In contrast to many of the system calls in this chapter that change properties of a file (such as chmod and utime), fcntl changes properties of an open *file descriptor*. There are five commands that can be used, symbols for which are defined in the header /usr/include/fcntl.h (the same header used with open):

F_DUPFD   Return a new file descriptor that is a duplicate of the first argument fildes. This service will be explained along with the dup system call in Sec. 6.3.

F_GETFD   Return the close-on-exec flag, which indicates whether the file descriptor will be closed when an exec system call is issued. Close-on-exec is detailed further in Sec. 5.3.

F_SETFD   Set the close-on-exec flag.

F_GETFL   Return the file status flags. Not to be confused with the file status as described in the previous section, these correspond to the second argument of open (Sec. 2.6). Given a file descriptor, one can determine whether it is opened for writing only (O_WRONLY), reading and writing (O_RDWR), and so on.

F_SETFL   Set the file status flags from the third argument. The flags O_RDONLY, O_WRONLY, and O_RDWR can't be changed; these can be set only by open or, in the case of O_WRONLY, by creat. Only O_NDELAY and O_APPEND can be set with fcntl.

At this point in this book, the only functions of fcntl that pertain to material already presented are getting the file status flags or toggling the O_APPEND flag. We'll come back to fcntl as we have more use for it, starting with the next chapter.

As an example, here is a function to turn on the O_APPEND flag. Note that we have to get the file status first, since we don't want to disturb any other flags:

```
int setappend(fd)  /* set O_APPEND flag */
int fd;
{
    int flags;

    if ((flags = fcntl(fd, F_GETFL, 0)) == -1)
        syserr("fcntl");
    return(fcntl(fd, F_SETFL, flags | O_APPEND));
}
```

If we had wanted to turn *off* the O_APPEND flag instead, the expression for setting the flags would have been:

```
flags & ~O_APPEND
```

3.14 PORTABILITY

There is no difference between System III and System V as far as the system calls introduced in this chapter are concerned. There are some differences with Version 7, however. Here is a list of the nontrivial ones:

1. fcntl is completely missing, as might be expected from the fact that the three-argument form of open is missing, too. The F_DUPFD features are pretty much handled by dup and dup2. (dup2 has been removed from System III and System V.) The F_SETFD command to turn the close-on-exec flag on or off is handled by Version 7's form of ioctl (see Sec. 4.4). Version 7 provides no way to interrogate the value of the close-on-exec flag, although this is far from a major defect since such an interrogation serves no practical purpose.

2. fstat on a pipe indicates an ordinary file rather than a FIFO, which doesn't exist in Version 7. Version 7 defines additional file types for "multiplexed" files, which don't exist in System III or System V.

3. utime doesn't accept a NULL second argument to set the access and modification times to the current time. The Version 7 touch command actually reads and rewrites a byte of the file to accomplish the same thing (sounds good enough to me).

Berkeley 4.2 BSD does implement fcntl, but for some reason, the flag status symbols used for F_SETFD and F_GETFD have different names from those used with open. stat is in general compatible, but additional structure members have been added to support 4.2 BSD-only features. There are no FIFOs, but rather "sockets" instead, which are about a thousand times fancier and more complicated to use. utime is present as a subroutine; the system call is utimes. Interestingly, a mkdir system call has been added, and you don't have to be the superuser to issue it.

As usual, the best advice for portability is to stay on common ground if at all possible. One rarely cares too much about the file type when using stat, the close-on-exec flag can normally be left alone, and fcntl doesn't do much on nonspecial files (special files are completely nonportable anyhow, as we shall see in the next chapter). So most programs can be written to avoid anything that varies from version to version.

If you must use a nonportable feature, you can resort to a single-interface, multiple-implementation approach. The C preprocessor helps, as illustrated in this function to toggle the close-on-exec flag:

```
#ifdef V7
#include <sgtty.h>
#else
#include <fcntl.h>
#endif
```

```
int clex(fd, on)  /* turn close-on-exec flag on or off */
int fd;
BOOLEAN on;
{
#ifdef V7
      return(ioctl(fd, on ? FIOCLEX : FIONCLEX, NULL));
#else
      return(fcntl(fd, F_SETFD, on ? 1 : 0));
#endif
}
```

EXERCISES

3.1. Implement the pwd command (it displays the full path name of the current directory). You may assume that only the root file system is mounted (see Sec. 9.14).

3.2. Write a program to copy an entire tree of directories and files. It should have two arguments: the root of the tree (e.g., /usr/marc/book), and the root of the copy (e.g., /usr/marc/backup/book).

3.3. Write a program to print out all the information in the super block of a file system. Your system administrator will have to give you read permission on the special file in order to test your program.

3.4. Write a program to calculate the number of days between two dates.

3.5. Rewrite isdir in Sec. 3.6 to use stat instead of open.

3.6. Write access as a function. You may use any system call except access.

3.7. Implement the ls command.

4

TERMINAL I/O

4.1 INTRODUCTION

Terminal I/O is so complex that it needs most of a chapter all to itself. The problem isn't with normal terminal I/O, which we'll start with—that's even simpler than file I/O. The numerous variations possible with the i o c t l system call are what complicate matters.

Standard terminal I/O on UNIX treats a terminal like an old-fashioned hard-copy Teletype, the model with the massive type box that makes a terrible racket as it bounces around. There is no support for CRT screens, function keys, mice and other pointing devices, or bit-mapped displays. Some of these modern devices, such as CRT screens and function keys, can be handled by subroutines that call on the standard device driver (c u r s e s is the best-known such package); others, like bit-mapped displays, require custom-designed device drivers that haven't yet found their way into the standard AT&T UNIX product.

Because this chapter's subject is a device driver rather than an inherent part of the kernel like the file system, specific features vary even more than usual from one UNIX version to another. Sometimes even individual UNIX sites make modifications to the terminal device driver. Remember also that not all attributes of terminal I/O are caused by UNIX itself. With the increasing use of smart terminals, local-area networks, and front-end processors, the character stream is subject to much processing before UNIX sees it and after UNIX has sent it on its way. Details of this pre- and post-processing vary much too widely to be given here. As usual, we'll concentrate on the standard device driver supplied with System III and System V. With this as background you should be able to figure out your own system from its manual.

Also in this chapter is a brief discussion of I/O on devices other than disks and terminals.

4.2 NORMAL TERMINAL I/O

We'll start by explaining how normal terminal input and output work; that is, how they work when you first log in and before you've used the s t t y command to customize them to your taste. Then, in subsequent sections, we'll show how the f c n t l and i o c t l system calls can be used to vary the normal behavior.

There are three ways to access a terminal for input or output:

1. You can open the character special file / d e v / t t y for reading, writing, or, most commonly, both reading and writing. This special file is a synonym for the process's control terminal (see Sec. 1.5).

2. If you know the actual name of the special file (e.g., / d e v / t t y 0 4), you can open it instead. If you just want the control terminal, this has no advantages over using the generic name / d e v / t t y. It is mainly used to access terminals other than the control terminal.

3. Conventionally, each process inherits three file descriptors already open: the standard input, the standard output, and the standard error output. These may or may not be open to the control terminal, but normally, they should be used anyhow, since if they are open to a file or a pipe instead, it is because the user decided to redirect input or output.

If the terminal itself must be accessed, then a special file should be opened just to make sure; this would be done for a screen editor or for an emergency error message. Otherwise, it's best to just use the already-open file descriptors. Just be careful that your I/O programming is device-independent, because you won't know in advance whether you are dealing with a terminal, a file, or a pipe.

The basic I/O system calls for terminals are o p e n, r e a d, w r i t e, and c l o s e. To open a terminal for writing c r e a t can be used also, but since the terminal special file must already exist, and since you usually want it opened for reading too, o p e n is almost always better. l s e e k has no effect on terminals.

The r e a d system call acts on terminals differently from the way it acts on files: It never returns more than one line of input, and no characters are returned until the entire line is ready, even if the r e a d requests only a single character. This is because until the user has ended the line we can't assume it's in final form—the erase (**#**) and kill (**@**) characters can be used to revise it or to cancel it entirely. The count returned by r e a d is used to determine how many characters were actually read.

The user can end a line in one of two ways. Most often, a newline character is the terminator. The return key is actually pressed, but the device driver translates the return (octal 15) to a newline (octal 12). Alternatively, the user can generate an EOT (end-of-transmission) character by pressing Control-D. In this case the line is made available to read as is, without a newline terminator. One special case is important: If the user generates an EOT at the *start* of the line, read will return with a zero count, since the line that the EOT terminated is empty. This looks like an end-of-file, and that's why Control-D can be thought of as an end-of-file "character."

The following function can be used to read a terminal using file descriptor 0. It removes a terminating newline character if one is present, and adds a terminating null character to make the line into a C string.

```
BOOLEAN getln(s, max)  /* read line from terminal */
char *s;
int max;
{
    int nread;

    switch (nread = read(0, s, max-1)) {
    case -1:
        syserr("read");
    case 0:
        return(FALSE);
    default:
        if (s[nread-1] == '\n')
            nread--;
        s[nread] = '\0';
        return(TRUE);
    }
}
```

This function is efficient for terminals because it reads the entire line with a single system call. Furthermore, it doesn't have to search for the end—it just goes by the count returned by read. But it doesn't work on files or pipes at all, because since the one-line limit doesn't apply, read will in general read too much. Instead of getln reading a line, it will read the next max −1 characters.

A more universal version of getln would ignore that unique property of terminals: reading one line at most. It would simply examine each character, looking for a newline:

```
BOOLEAN getln2(s, max)  /* read line from anywhere */
char *s;
int max;
{
    int i;
    char c;
```

```
    i = 0;
    while (TRUE)
        switch (read(0, &c, 1)) {
        case -1:
            syserr("read");
        case 0:
            return(FALSE);
        default:
            if (i >= max)
                fatal("getln2 overflow");
            if (c == '\n') {
                s[i] = '\0';
                return(TRUE);
            }
            s[i++] = c;
        }
}
```

This version treats an EOT typed anywhere but the beginning of the line differently than does the earlier version. Since the string s isn't properly terminated with a null byte until a newline is read, and since its value isn't intended to be used when getln2 returns FALSE, a line ended with an EOT will be skipped entirely. In some applications this may even be an advantage. If it's a disadvantage, it can be fixed easily by adding some code to the end-of-file case (case 0) to check if any characters have been added to s. If so, s is terminated and TRUE is returned. A flag is set so that FALSE is immediately returned the next time getln2 is called.

Although getln2 reads terminals, files, and pipes properly, it reads the latter two sources more slowly than it might because it doesn't buffer the input as described in Sec. 2.10. This is easily fixed by changing getln2 to call Sgetc, which is part of the STREAM package introduced in that section. Sopen is already suitable for opening terminal special files (e.g., /dev/tty). However, to allow us to use Sgetc on the standard input we need to add a function called Sfdopen that initializes a STREAM pointer from an already open file descriptor instead of from a path. Then we could read a character from the standard input, whether it's a terminal, file, or pipe, like this:

```
STREAM *stin;
char c;

if ((stin = Sfdopen(0, "r")) == NULL)
    syserr("Sfdopen");
c = Sgetc(stin);
```

We're now reading as fast as we can in each case: a block at a time on files and pipes, and a line at a time on terminals. The "lost line" bug that we mentioned earlier isn't inherent in the STREAM package itself. Whether we lose a line ended with an EOT depends on how we code the function that calls `Sgetc`, and the solution that we suggested for `getln2` would work here as well.

Our implementation of the STREAM package doesn't allow the same STREAM pointer to be used for both input and output, so if output is to be sent to the terminal, a second STREAM must be opened using file descriptor 1.

The UNIX Standard I/O Library provides three predefined FILE pointers to access the terminal: `stdin`, `stdout`, and `stderr`, so the function `fdopen`, which is like our `Sfdopen`, usually need not be called.

Output to a terminal is more straightforward than input, since nothing like erase and kill processing is done. As many characters as we output with `write` are sent to the terminal immediately, whether a newline is present or not. Indeed, this is essential or we wouldn't be able to do things like prompt the user without returning the carriage, as we did in the `statutil` program of Sec. 3.12.

`close` on a file descriptor open to a terminal doesn't do any more than it does for a file. It just makes the file descriptor available for reuse. But since the file descriptor is most often 0, 1, or 2, no obvious reuse comes readily to mind. So no one bothers to close these file descriptors at the end of a program.[1]

4.3 NONBLOCKING TERMINAL I/O

If a line of data isn't available when `read` is issued on a terminal, `read` waits for the data. Since the process can do nothing in the meantime, this is called *blocking*. No analogous situation occurs with files; either the data is available or the end-of-file has been reached.

The O_NDELAY (no delay) flag, set with `open` or `fcntl`, makes `read` nonblocking. If a line of data isn't available, `read` returns immediately with a count of zero. This is indistinguishable from an end-of-file indication, which is generated when the user types an EOT character. This ambiguity must be taken into account whenever nonblocking terminal I/O is used. The simplest solution is to dispense with EOT (Control-D) and instead use an alternative such as q (for "quit") or Control-X.

The /usr/group Proposed Standard has fixed this problem by defining `read` to return −1 with an `errno` code of EAGAIN when no data is ready. But none of the major UNIX versions has yet adopted their proposal. And even if a future version does, we can assume that other versions that work the old way will be around for many years.

Frequently we want to turn blocking on and off at will, so we'll code a function `setblock` to call `fcntl` appropriately. We can't just call `fcntl` with O_NDELAY as an argument, since we must be careful to preserve the other flags.

---

[1] We will be closing them in Chap. 6 when we connect two processes with a pipe.

While it's true that there are no other flags that apply to terminals today, since the only other flag settable by `fcntl` is `O_APPEND`, it's a good idea to make our programs immune to future disruptions, if possible.

```
void setblock(fd, on) /* turn blocking on or off */
int fd;
BOOLEAN on;
{
    static int blockf, nonblockf;
    static BOOLEAN first = TRUE;
    int flags;

    if (first) {
        first = FALSE;
        if ((flags = fcntl(fd, F_GETFL, 0)) == -1)
            syserr("fcntl");
        blockf = flags & ~O_NDELAY; /* make sure O_NDELAY is off */
        nonblockf = flags | O_NDELAY; /* make sure O_NDELAY is on */
    }
    if (fcntl(fd, F_SETFL, on ? blockf : nonblockf) == -1)
        syserr("fcntl2");
}
```

You can also set the `O_NDELAY` flag when you open a terminal special file with `open`. In this case `O_NDELAY` affects `open` as well as `read`: If there is no connection (carrier is absent), `open` returns without waiting for one.

One application for nonblocking input is to monitor several terminals. The terminals might be laboratory instruments that are attached to a UNIX computer through terminal ports. Characters are sent in sporadically, and we want to accumulate them as they arrive, in whatever order they show up. Since there's no way to predict when a given terminal might transmit a character, we can't use blocking I/O, for we might wait for one terminal that has nothing to say while other talkative terminals are being ignored. With nonblocking I/O, however, we can poll each terminal in turn; if a terminal is not ready, `read` will return zero and we can just go on. If we make a complete loop without finding any data ready, we sleep for a second before looping again so as not to hog the CPU.

This algorithm is illustrated by the function `readany`. Its arguments are an array `fds` of `nfds` file descriptors. It doesn't return until a `read` of one of those file descriptors returns a character. Then it returns the subscript in `fds` of the file descriptor from which the character was read. The character itself is the value of the function. The caller of `readany` is presumably accumulating the incoming data in some useful way for later processing. To be fair, we keep track of where we left off so that we start the next round of polling from there.[2]

---

[2]Assume the laboratory instruments are inputting newline-terminated lines, as silly as it may seem. In Sec. 4.4.8 we'll see how to read data without waiting for a complete line to be ready.

```
int readany(fds, nfds, whichp)  /* poll for input */
int fds[], nfds, *whichp;
{
    static int lasti;
    int i;
    char c;

    i = lasti + 1;
    while (1) {
        if (i >= nfds)
            i = 0;
        setblock(fds[i], FALSE);
        switch (read(fds[i], &c, 1)) {
        case -1:
            syserr("read");
        case 0:
            if (i == lasti)
                sleep(1);
            i++;
            continue;
        default:
            *whichp = lasti = i;
            return(c & 0377); /* prevent sign extension */
        }
    }
}
```

Calling s l e e p to pass the time has two disadvantages: First, there could be a delay of as long as a second before an incoming character is processed, which might be a problem in a time-critical application. Second, we might wake up and make another futile loop, perhaps many times, before a character is ready. Best would be a system call that said, ''Put me to sleep until an input character is ready on any file descriptor.'' Alas, UNIX offers no such feature, although a custom-designed device driver very well might.

Since this function handles several concurrent events (terminals transmitting data), it is a primitive form of multitasking. While this example is quite reasonable, we don't want to get carried away with do-it-yourself multitasking—after all, UNIX itself is already a multitasking system. It is usually easier to use multiple processes to handle concurrent events than to program a single multitasking process using techniques like nonblocking input. In the case of our laboratory instruments, for example, we could have programmed a process to handle just one instrument, and then let the UNIX kernel run the processes concurrently for us. In fact, this is exactly the way UNIX normally works, where the ''instruments'' are the time-sharing users.

Sometimes we just want to know if a character is ready, without reading it. Then, when we're ready, we'll take the character. Unfortunately, **r e a d** can't do this; if a character is ready, it is returned. We can do what we want by keeping the prematurely read character in a buffer. Then the function we call to get a character can look in the buffer first. If the character is there, we just return it; if not, we turn on blocking and call read. This scheme is used in the following pair of functions: cready just tells us whether a character is ready, and cget gets a character, waiting if necessary.

```
#define EMPTY '\0'
static char cbuf = EMPTY;

BOOLEAN cready()  /* is a character ready? */
{
    if (cbuf != EMPTY)
        return(TRUE);
    setblock(0, FALSE);
    switch (read(0, &cbuf, 1)) {
    case -1:
        syserr("read");
    case 0:
        return(FALSE); /* could be EOF too */
    default:
        return(TRUE);
    }
}

int cget()  /* get a character */
{
    char c;

    if (cbuf != EMPTY) {
        c = cbuf;
        cbuf = EMPTY;
        return(c & 0377); /* prevent sign extension */
    }
    setblock(0, TRUE);
    switch (read(0, &c, 1)) {
    case -1:
        syserr("read");
    case 0:
        return(-1); /* must be EOF */
    default:
        return(c & 0377);
    }
}
```

We've preempted the null byte as our empty-buffer indicator (EMPTY), which means that null bytes read by cready will be ignored. If this isn't acceptable, a separate BOOLEAN variable can be used as an empty-buffer flag.

Notice the way c r e a d y and c g e t shift back and forth between blocking and nonblocking input. Since we're reading only one input stream, there's no need to stay in the nonblocking state while we test for an available character, as we had to do in r e a d a n y. We just revert to blocking and issue a r e a d. After all, waiting for a character is what blocking means.

c r e a d y and c g e t are most useful when a program has some discretionary work to do, work that can wait if a character is ready. A good example is a program that uses c u r s e s, the screen-output package from Berkeley.[3] To update the screen, a variety of subroutines are called that modify a screen-size buffer. Then, whenever the programmer is ready, r e f r e s h is called to update the physical screen. This is time-consuming, because r e f r e s h compares what is currently on the screen with the new image so as to minimize the number of characters transmitted. A fast typist can easily get ahead of the updates, especially if the screen must be updated on each keystroke, as it must with a screen editor. A neat solution is to call r e f r e s h from within the input routine, but only if input is not waiting. If input is waiting, then the user has obviously typed ahead without waiting for the screen to catch up, so the screen update is skipped. The screen will be updated next time the input routine is executed, unless a character is waiting then too. When the user stops typing, the screen will become current. On the other hand, if the program can process characters faster than the typist types them, then the screen will get updated with each keystroke.

This may sound complex, but by using functions we've already developed it takes only three lines of code:

```
if (!cready())
    refresh();
c = cget();
```

4.4 ioctl SYSTEM CALL

```
#include <termio.h>

int ioctl(fd, cmd, tbuf)    /* control terminal device */
int fd;                     /* file descriptor */
int cmd;                    /* command */
struct termio *tbuf;        /* terminal information */
/* returns 0 on success or −1 on error */
```

---

[3] c u r s e s is part of 4.1 BSD and 4.2 BSD, but many vendors license it from Berkeley and include it in their non-Berkeley versions (it's in Xenix 3 and PC/IX). It's almost always available whenever the screen editor v i is.

```
int ioctl(fd, cmd, arg)
int fd;
int cmd;
int arg;                        /* command argument */
/* returns 0 on success or -1 on error */
```

For terminals there are two calling sequences for ioctl.[4] In the first form the third argument is a pointer to a terminal-information structure that is either input to the call or is filled in by the call. In the second form the third argument is just an integer flag. Other nonterminal device drivers may define the third argument differently—it's up to the device-driver designer.

4.4.1 Basic ioctl Usage

The terminal-information structure (struct termio) contains about 50 flag bits that tell the driver how to process characters coming in and going out, how to set communication-line parameters, such as the baud rate, and so on. The structure also defines several control characters, such as erase (normally #), kill (normally @), and EOT (normally Control-D). Here's the definition of the structure from /usr/include/termio.h:

```
#define NCC 8
struct termio {
    unsigned short      c_iflag;        /* input flags */
    unsigned short      c_oflag;        /* output flags */
    unsigned short      c_cflag;        /* control flags */
    unsigned short      c_lflag;        /* line discipline flags */
    char                c_line;         /* line discipline */
    unsigned char       c_cc[NCC];      /* control characters */
};
```

Before getting into the depths of this structure, let's examine the available commands:

TCGETA	Fill in the termio structure with information on the terminal referenced by fd.
TCSETA	Set the terminal according to the information in the structure.
TCSETAW	Similar to the previous command, but wait for all pending output characters to be sent first. This should be used when output-affecting changes are made, to ensure characters previously output are processed under the rules in effect when they were written.

---

[4]The name is inconsistent with fcntl —is "control" abbreviated "ctl" or "cntl"?

TCSETAF   Similar to the previous command, but the input queue is flushed (characters are discarded). When beginning a new interactive mode, as when starting a screen editor, this is the safest command to use because it prevents characters that may have been typed ahead from causing an unintended action.

The next three commands use the second form of ioctl:

TCSBRK   Wait for the output queue to be sent. If arg is 0, then send a break (a quarter second of 0 bits).

TCXONC   If arg is 0, immediately suspend output; if 1, restart it.

TCFLSH   If arg is 0, flush the input queue; if 1, flush the output queue; if 2, flush both.

The termio structure is described in considerable detail in the UNIX manual in the section on device drivers, usually under "tty" or "termio." We won't repeat all the details here, just the more important ones. We'll refer to specific flags only by their symbolic names. Consult the manual for the actual bit pattern.

4.4.2 Speed, Character Size, and Parity

Flags in c_cflag set the baud rate (from 50 to 9600), the character size (5 to 8 bits), the number of stop bits (1 or 2), and the parity (even, odd, or none). There's no creativity here; one is usually quite satisfied to find a combination that works.

You can also get more information about characters that fail the parity check. If the PARMRK flag is on, bad characters are preceded with the two characters 0377 and 0. Otherwise, characters with incorrect parity are input as null bytes. Alternatively, flag IGNPAR can be set to ignore characters with bad parity entirely.

4.4.3 Character Mapping

The mapping of newlines to returns and returns to newlines on input is controlled by flags INLCR and ICRNL in c_iflag. For terminals that input both a return and a newline when the return key is pressed, the return can be ignored (IGNCR).

On output we usually want to map a newline to a return-newline pair; flag ONLCR in c_oflag does this job. Other flags cause a return to be changed to a newline, and a return at column 0 to be suppressed. If a newline also causes a return, there's a flag to tell the terminal driver this so it can keep track of the column (for tabs and backspaces).

The driver can also handle uppercase-only terminals, which are much less common than they once were. If **XCASE** in c_lflag is set, **IUCLC** in c_iflag is set, and **OLCUC** in c_oflag is set, then uppercase letters are mapped to lowercase on input, and lowercase letters are mapped to uppercase on output. Since UNIX uses lowercase more than upper, this is desirable. To input or output uppercase, the letter is preceded with a backslash (\).

If the **ISTRIP** flag in c_iflag is set, input characters are stripped to seven bits (after parity is checked). Otherwise, all eight bits are input. Most terminals use ASCII, which is a seven-bit code, so stripping is normally desirable. Specialized devices may, however, transmit a full eight bits. On output, all bits written by the process are sent. If eight data bits are to be sent to the terminal, then parity generation must be turned off by clearing the **PARENB** flag in c_cflag.

4.4.4 Delays and Tabs

Some terminals, particularly mechanical ones, require time to perform various motions, such as to return the carriage. Flags in c_oflag can be set to adjust delays for newlines, returns, backspaces, horizontal and vertical tabs, and form-feeds.

Another flag, **TAB3**, causes output tabs to be replaced by an appropriate number of spaces. This is useful when the terminal has no tabs of its own, when it's too much trouble to set them, or when the terminal is really another computer that is downloading the output, and only spaces are wanted.

4.4.5 Flow Control

Output to the terminal can be stopped momentarily either by the user pressing Control-S or by a process calling ioctl with the **TCXONC** command (see Sec. 4.4.1). Flow is restarted by the user typing Control-Q or by ioctl.

If the **IXANY** flag in c_iflag is set, the user can type any character to restart the flow, not just Control-Q. If the **IXON** flag is off, no output flow control is available to the user at all; Control-S and Control-Q have no special meaning.

The terminal driver also supports input flow control. If the **IXOFF** flag is set, then, when the input queue gets full, the driver will send a Control-S to the terminal to suspend input. When the queue length drops because a process read some queued-up characters, a Control-Q will be sent to tell the terminal to resume input. Of course, this feature can be used only with those terminals that support it.

4.4.6 Control Characters

Several control characters can be changed from their defaults by setting elements of the c_cc array in the termio structure. The following chart gives, for each settable control character, the subscript in c_cc and the default value:

Character	Subscript	Default
Interrupt	0	DEL
Quit	1	Control-\ (FS)
Erase	2	#
Kill	3	@
EOT	4	Control-D (EOT)
EOL	5	NUL

On many systems the defaults for erase and kill are different from what we've shown; for example, erase may be backspace and kill may be Control-U. EOL is a line delimiter (like newline), but it's rarely used.

To suppress a control character, you can set it to octal 377. Alternatively, you can suppress interrupt and quit by clearing the ISIG flag in c_lflag.

4.4.7 Echo

Terminals normally run in full duplex, which means that data can flow across the communication line in both directions simultaneously. Consequently, the computer, not the terminal, echoes typed characters, to provide verification that they were correctly received. The usual output character mapping applies, so, for example, a return is mapped to a newline and then, when echoed, the newline is mapped to a return and a newline.

To turn echo off, the ECHO flag in c_lflag is cleared. This is done either to preserve secrecy, as when typing a password, or because the process itself must decide if, what, and where to echo, as when running a screen editor.

Two special kinds of echo are available for the erase and kill characters. If the erase character is backspace, the flag ECHOE can be set so that backspace echoes as backspace-space-backspace. This has the pleasing effect of clearing the erased character from a CRT screen (it has no effect at all on hard-copy terminals, except to wiggle the type element). The flag ECHOK can be set to echo a newline (possibly mapped to return and newline) after a kill character; this gives the user a fresh line to work on.

4.4.8 Punctual Input

Normally, input characters are queued until a line is complete, as indicated by a newline or an EOT. Only then are any characters made available to a read, which might only ask for and get one character. In many applications, such as screen editors and form-entry systems, the reading process wants the characters as they are typed, without waiting for a line to be assembled. Indeed, the notion of "lines" may have no meaning.

If the flag I CANON ("canonical") is clear, input characters are not assembled into lines before they are read; therefore, erase and kill editing are unavailable. The erase and kill characters lose their special meaning. Two parameters, MIN and TIME, determine when a read is satisfied. When the queue becomes MIN characters long, or when TIME tenths of a second have elapsed, the characters in the queue become available.

The EOT and EOL positions (subscripts 4 and 5) of the c _ c c array are used to hold MIN and TIME, since those positions aren't needed for their usual purpose when I CANON is clear. Make sure you set these or you'll get the current EOT and EOL characters for MIN and TIME, which will cause very strange results. If you ever find a process getting input on every fourth character typed, this is probably what's happened. (Control-D, the usual EOT character, is 4).

The idea behind MIN and TIME is to allow a process to get characters as, or soon after, they are typed without losing the benefits of reading several characters with a single read system call. Unless you code your input routine to buffer input, however, you might as well set MIN to 1 (TIME is then irrelevant), since your read system calls will be reading only a single character anyhow.

Here's a buffering, but punctual, input routine called keystroke. Since it will change the terminal flags, we've also provided the companion routine restore to restore the terminal to the way it was before the first call to keystroke. The calling program must call restore before terminating.

```
#include <termio.h>

static struct termio tbufsave;

char keystroke()  /* get character from terminal */
{
    static char buf[10];
    static int total, next;
    static BOOLEAN first = TRUE;
    struct termio tbuf;

    if (first) {
        first = FALSE;
        if (ioctl(0, TCGETA, &tbuf) == -1)
            syserr("ioctl");
        tbufsave = tbuf;
        tbuf.c_lflag &= ~ICANON;
        tbuf.c_cc[4] = sizeof(buf); /* MIN */
        tbuf.c_cc[5] = 2; /* TIME */
        if (ioctl(0, TCSETAF, &tbuf) == -1)
            syserr("ioctl2");
    }
```

```
        if (next >= total)
            switch (total = read(0, buf, sizeof(buf))) {
            case -1:
                syserr("read");
            case 0:
                fatal("Mysterious EOF");
            default:
                next = 0;
            }
        return(buf[next++]);
}

void restore()  /* restore terminal flags */
{
        if (ioctl(0, TCSETAF, &tbufsave) == -1)
            syserr("ioctl3");
}
```

Note that we've cleared only **ICANON** (and set MIN and TIME, of course). Typically, we would want to clear more flags, to turn off echo, output character mapping, and so on. This is addressed in the next section.

In a specific application, you will want to experiment with values for MIN and TIME. We've used 10 characters and .2 seconds, which seems to work well.

4.5 RAW TERMINAL I/O

In Version 7 and earlier versions, a single flag could be cleared to put the terminal into *raw* mode, which means that no special input or output processing is done and that characters are readable immediately, without waiting for a line to be assembled. Things have since gotten much more complicated. The **stty** command still has a **raw** option, but to achieve the equivalent with **ioctl** requires several flags to be adjusted.

We want raw terminal I/O to have the following attributes:

1. *Punctual input*. Clear **ICANON** and set MIN and TIME.
2. *No character mapping*. Clear **OPOST** in **c_oflag** to turn off output processing. For input, clear **INLCR**, **ICRNL**, and **IUCLC**. Clear **ISTRIP** to get all eight bits.
3. *No flow control*. Clear **IXON**.
4. *No control characters*. Clear **BRKINT** and **ISIG**.
5. *No echo*. Clear **ECHO**.

These operations are encapsulated in the function **setraw**. Note that it saves the old **termio** structure for use by **restore**.

```
void setraw() /* put terminal into raw mode */
{
    struct termio tbuf;

    if (ioctl(0, TCGETA, &tbuf) == -1)
        syserr("ioctl");
    tbufsave = tbuf;
    tbuf.c_iflag &= ~(INLCR | ICRNL | IUCLC | ISTRIP | IXON | BRKINT);
    tbuf.c_oflag &= ~OPOST;
    tbuf.c_lflag &= ~(ICANON | ISIG | ECHO);
    tbuf.c_cc[4] = 5; /* MIN */
    tbuf.c_cc[5] = 2; /* TIME */
    if (ioctl(0, TCSETAF, &tbuf) == -1)
        syserr("ioctl2");
}
```

Now that we have **setraw** we can rework **keystroke** to call it instead of clearing **ICANON** for itself. Usually, programs that want punctual input also want the other attributes of raw I/O.

Sometimes during (or after!) debugging, a program that's put the terminal in raw mode aborts before it can restore the original settings. Programmers often think the computer has crashed or that their terminal has "locked up"—they can't even use EOT to log off. But it's possible to recover from raw mode. First, recall that **ICRNL** is clear; this means you'll have to end your input lines with the line feed (newline) key or with Control-J instead of using the return key.[5] Second, you won't see what you type because **ECHO** is off, too. Start by typing a few line feeds; you should see a series of shell prompts, but not at the left margin because output processing (**OPOST**) is turned off. Then type this, followed by a line feed:

```
stty echo icanon icrnl opost
```

Interaction should now be much improved, even though you still don't have erase, kill, flow control, and a few other features. You can either turn them on with another **stty** or just log off.

Some UNIX systems have a **sane** option on **stty** that sets the flags to reasonable values all at once, so on these systems you can make an even speedier recovery.

4.6 OTHER SPECIAL FILES

Besides those for disks and terminals, UNIX systems normally come with several other special files for devices such as floppy disks, magnetic tapes, line printers, a

---

[5]A nice enhancement to the shell would be for it to accept a return as a line terminator, as well as a newline.

console, and internal memory. These vary from system to system, so you will have to consult your specific UNIX manual to determine how to use them.

Section 4 or 7 of your system's UNIX manual should have a write-up on each special file. The use of `open`, `close`, `read`, and `write` is usually straight-forward. The complexity, as we've seen in the case of terminals, is with `ioctl`. A device-driver designer can use this system call in any way he or she wishes, and these wishes are sometimes rather strange. But you have a right to expect header files to be documented (and included with your system) and for each of the pertinent `ioctl` commands to be completely documented.

4.7 PORTABILITY

We've described terminals as they work on System III, System V, and on systems based on those versions, such as Xenix 3. Even on these systems, however, you may find that extensions have been made. For example, if your computer has an integrated console, additional `ioctl` options may have been added to control the keyboard and the screen (to pause every so many lines of CRT output, for example).

The other major UNIX versions act similarly insofar as `open`, `close`, `read`, and `write` are concerned (Version 7 lacks `O_NDELAY`). The main deviations are in `ioctl` and its associated structure.

In Version 7 `ioctl` uses different commands, and the structure is defined in the header `sgtty.h`.[6] The structure defined there is entirely different from `termio`, but the principles are the same. If you've followed the presentation in this chapter you'll have little trouble with Version 7, since its terminal device driver is much simpler than the ones in Systems III and V.

As we've come to expect, Berkeley 4.2 BSD has diverged even more (their header is called `ioctl.h`). But again, the principles are similar, and you should be able to figure things out from the `tty` write-up in Section 4 of the 4.2 BSD manual.

Unless you confine yourself to System III, System V, and the versions based on them, you can't write portable programs that use `ioctl` directly. Instead, figure out what features you really need, such as putting the terminal in raw mode, and code single-interface multiple-implementation functions, as we did in Sec. 3.14. It's a shame that UNIX never came with a set of subroutines (similar to `setraw` and `restore`) to perform the common operations in a portable way.

Another idea is to use the technique from the `mkdir2` function of Sec. 3.8 and execute the `stty` *command,* since it's more portable than `ioctl`:

```
system("stty raw");
```

------

[6]Older versions had system calls named `stty` and `gtty`. Version 7 includes these for compatibility, but they were dropped in System III.

Although this seemed elegant with `mkdir2`, here it seems to be a kludge. This is probably because we have alternatives here. We had no choice with `mkdir2` — we had to create a child process in order to set the effective user-ID to superuser.

The /usr/group Proposed Standard doesn't help with terminals at all. Apparently there were too many variations for the committee to come to agreement. `ioctl` is in the standard as a place holder, but its arguments are not defined. Instead of trying to agree on the individual bits, it would be more practical to define a set of high-level functions along the lines of `setraw` and `restore`. Then each conforming implementor could define these appropriately, and programs could use the high-level functions instead of `ioctl` itself. It's doubtful that /usr/group will take this approach. In the past they have selected features from existing UNIX implementations (primarily System III) rather than inventing new system calls or subroutines.

If your program interfaces with a CRT terminal, by all means try to use `curses` (it handles the keyboard, too). It's not only reasonably portable across those UNIX versions that include it, but it's portable across more than 100 terminal types, too.

Rather than treating the CRT screen as a terminal, many personal computers provide a faster way to access it by mapping screen memory used by the display controller directly into the CPU's address space. This is called *memory-mapped video*. On a simple computer it's possible for a UNIX process to access this memory directly, but on computers with memory-management hardware such access is disallowed.[7] The implementor may instead provide a device driver that gives rapid access to the screen—more rapid access than if traditional escape sequences were used. Such a feature permits a more responsive human interface to be programmed, and it makes applications like spreadsheets feasible. But it makes the portability problems even worse, since memory-mapped video is much less standardized than escape sequences. And even if the computer has memory-mapped video, it can be used only to access the built-in screen, not the screens of remote terminals.

In most cases it's probably best to treat all screens like terminals, even if one screen is memory-mapped. Unfortunately, this puts UNIX-based systems at a disadvantage relative to simpler personal computers (outweighed by other factors, to be sure). A good solution to the screen-access problem is one of the most critical design challenges facing the UNIX community. The answer probably involves three areas: a redefinition of what a terminal should be able to do (scroll sideways, for example), a redesign (again!) of the UNIX terminal driver, and a rethinking of how memory management should work on a computer with an integrated screen (the shared memory system calls described in Sec. 7.7 may be of use).

---

[7]I use the screen editor EDIX this way under PC/IX. To update the screen, EDIX simply turns off interrupts and grabs hold of the segmentation registers to access display memory, which is way outside its address space. The IBM PC is powerless to stop it.

EXERCISES

4.1. Change get ln2 to return lines ended with an EOT, as discussed in Sec. 4.2.

4.2. Implement Sfdopen, as discussed in Sec. 4.2.

4.3. Implement a simplified version of the stty command that just prints out the current terminal status.

4.4. Implement a version of the stty command that allows the user to change only the 10 most commonly used flags. You have to decide which 10 these are.

4.5. Implement a simple screen editor. Decide on a small selection of functions that allow reasonable editing, but without too many bells and whistles. Keep the text being edited in internal memory. Pick a terminal model that you have access to, and update the screen using appropriate escape sequences.

4.6. If you have access to it, use the curses package (see Sec. 4.3) to do Exercise 4.5.

5
PROCESSES

5.1 INTRODUCTION

We now leave the subject of input and output to begin investigating the multitasking features of UNIX. This chapter deals with techniques for invoking programs and processes, using `exec`, `fork`, `wait`, and related system calls. The next chapter explains simple interprocess communication using pipes. Chapter 7 continues with more advanced interprocess communication mechanisms.

Our presentation is organized with the goal of implementing a fairly complete command interpreter, or shell. We'll start with a limited shell that's barely usable. Then we'll keep adding features until we end up, in the next chapter, with a shell that can handle I/O redirection, pipelines, background processes, quoted arguments, and environment variables.

5.2 ENVIRONMENT

We'll begin with a discussion of the environment, which most UNIX users are already familiar with at the shell level. The UNIX manual fails to document methods for updating the environment, however, so our first order of business is to fill in this gap.

When a UNIX program is executed, it receives two collections of data from the process that invoked it: the *arguments* and the *environment*. To C programs both are in the form of an array of character pointers, all but the last of which point to a null-terminated character string. The last pointer is zero (**NULL**). A count of the number of arguments is also passed on. Other UNIX languages, such as Fortran or Pascal, use a different interface, but we're concerned here only with C.

A C program begins like this:

```
extern char **environ;

main(argc, argv, envp)
int argc;
char *argv[], *envp[];
```

Both envp and environ contain the same value, so envp is normally omitted. Each argument string can be anything at all, as long as it is null-terminated. Environment strings are more constrained. By convention, each is in the form *variable = value*, with the null byte after the value. Environment variables are normally set by a shell assignment command, like this:

```
$ PATH=/bin:/usr/bin:/usr/marc/bin::
```

A process can get the value of an environment variable with the standard function getenv, which we used earlier in Sec. 3.4 to get the value of TZ. Alternatively, a process can access the environment directly through the pointer environ, as illustrated by this simple program that prints the entire environment:

```
extern char **environ;

main(argc, argv)
int argc;
char *argv[];
{
    int i;

    for (i = 0; environ[i] != NULL; i++)
        printf("%s\n", environ[i]);
    exit(0);
}
```

Here is the output we got:

```
HOME=/usr/marc
LOGNAME=marc
MAIL=/usr/mail/marc
PATH=/bin:/usr/bin:/usr/marc/bin::
PS1=$
PS2=>
TZ=MST7MDT
```

Updating the environment, however, is not so easy. Although the internal storage it occupies is the exclusive property of the process, and may be modified freely, there is no extra room for any new variables or for longer values. So unless the update is trivial, a completely new environment must be created. If the pointer environ is then made to point to this new environment, it will be passed on to any programs subsequently invoked, as we shall see in Sec. 5.3.

If lots of updating is to be done, it's convenient to recast the environment from its packed format into a data structure that provides enough flexibility to add variables and to assign longer values. Such a data structure is called a *symbol table*. Then, before a new program is invoked, we can construct a version in the packed format and set environ appropriately. This is in fact what sh (the standard shell) does, since it needs this flexibility to process assignment commands.

We'll be implementing our own shell in this and the next chapter, so we need an environment symbol table too. We'll present an example symbol-table structure and its associated accessing routines. We'll use linear searching to access variables, which is adequate for small symbol tables; in other situations hashing or binary trees might be used to gain speed at the expense of complexity and code size.[1]

Since sh is a programming language as well as a command interpreter, it stores many variables in its symbol table that are of interest only in the specific shell program under execution; examples are loop counters and variables that hold file names. Passing these *local* variables on to other programs would be wasteful and possibly misleading. So, to distinguish between local variables and *global* variables, which should be entered into the environment, sh allows a variable to be designated as *export*, using a command like this:

export PATH

When an environment is constructed from the symbol table, it includes the original environment plus new values of exported variables. Changes to unexported variables are ignored.

Exporting works in one direction only: from a process to any programs it invokes. Because each program inherits a copy of the environment (in its own address space), it isn't possible for a process to pass data back to its parent via the environment.

We'll use the following array as the symbol table:

```
#define MAXVAR 25

static struct varslot {
    char *name;            /* variable name */
    char *val;             /* variable value */
    BOOLEAN exported;      /* is it to be exported? */
} sym[MAXVAR];
```

[1]For further information on symbol-table techniques, see any good data structures or compiler construction textbook, such as Ellis Horowitz and Sartaj Sahni, *Fundamentals of Data Structures* (Potomac, Md.: Computer Science Press, Inc., 1976).

This is similar in concept to the environ array, except that we've separated the variable name and value strings to permit easier access and modification, and we've included an exported flag to tell us what to include when we construct the environment in packed form. There are slots for only 25 variables, which is enough for our example programs, although perhaps not for a real shell. A vacant slot will be denoted by a name pointer of NULL. Since external variables are initialized to zero, all slots are initially vacant.

To assign a value to a variable we just scan the sym array looking for a var structure with a matching name member. If we find it, we update the corresponding val member. If we don't find it, we take the first vacant slot and put the name and value there. If there are no vacant slots, the symbol table is full. The work of finding either a matching or a vacant slot is performed by the function find:

```
static struct varslot *find(name) /* find symbol table entry */
char *name;
{
    int i;
    struct varslot *v;

    v = NULL;
    for (i = 0; i < MAXVAR; i++)
        if (sym[i].name == NULL) {
            if (v == NULL)
                v = &sym[i];
        }
        else if (strcmp(sym[i].name, name) == 0) {
            v = &sym[i];
            break;
        }
    return(v);
}
```

find returns a pointer to a slot, or NULL if the symbol table is full. The caller has to check the pointed-to name member; if it's NULL, no matching name was found and the caller is free to install a new variable and value in the slot.

The equivalent of sh's assignment command is done by EVset, whose arguments are two strings: a variable name and its assigned value. EVset calls find to locate the slot (existing or vacant), and then uses assign to do the actual work of copying in the name and value strings:

```
BOOLEAN EVset(name, val)  /* add name & value to environment */
char *name, *val;
{
    struct varslot *v;
```

```
    if ((v = find(name)) == NULL)
        return(FALSE);
    return(assign(&v->name, name) && assign(&v->val, val));
}
```

Recall that when f i nd returns NULL the name is not currently in the symbol table, and there is no vacant slot in which to add it. So EVset fails.

Next comes assign. Its first argument is a pointer to a name or val member, and its second argument is the new name or value string. If the member is currently NULL, then malloc allocates sufficient space to hold the string. Otherwise, some space already exists to hold the old value, so realloc ensures that it is large enough. Then the string is copied into the allocated space. Since realloc might have to move the space, the pointer (name or val) given to assign might be changed. This is why a pointer to the member is passed to assign, which is the usual C method of returning a value through an argument. Here is the code for assign:

```
char *malloc(), *realloc();

static BOOLEAN assign(p, s)  /* initialize name or value */
char **p, *s;
{
    int size;

    size = strlen(s) + 1;
    if (*p == NULL) {
        if ((*p = malloc(size)) == NULL)
            return(FALSE);
    }
    else if ((*p = realloc(*p, size)) == NULL)
            return(FALSE);
    strcpy(*p, s);
    return(TRUE);
}
```

To set the exported flag we call EVexport. The only complication is that the variable we're marking for export may not exist yet, in which case we assign it a null value to reserve its slot:

```
BOOLEAN EVexport(name)  /* set variable to be exported */
char *name;
{
    struct varslot *v;
```

```
        if ((v = find(name)) == NULL)
            return(FALSE);
        if (v->name == NULL)
            if (!assign(&v->name, name) || !assign(&v->val, ""))
                return(FALSE);
        v->exported = TRUE;
        return(TRUE);
}
```

Getting a value from the symbol table is easy. The function **EVget** is similar to the standard function **getenv**, except that it accesses the symbol table, not the packed environment pointed to by **environ**:

```
        char *EVget(name) /* get value of variable */
        char *name;
        {
            struct varslot *v;

            if ((v = find(name)) == NULL || v->name == NULL)
                return(NULL);
            return(v->val);
        }
```

A program will normally want to initialize the symbol table from the environment it inherited. Since by definition it only received exported variables, all inherited variables should be so marked in the symbol table.[2] **EVinit**, which should be called before any of the other symbol-table functions, performs this initialization:

```
BOOLEAN EVinit() /* initialize symbol table from environment */
{
    int i, namelen;
    char name[20];

    for (i = 0; environ[i] != NULL; i++) {
        namelen = strcspn(environ[i], "=");
        strncpy(name, environ[i], namelen);
        name[namelen] = '\0';
        if (!EVset(name, &environ[i][namelen + 1]) || !EVexport(name))
            return(FALSE);
    }
    return(TRUE);
}
```

---

[2]This treatment of exported variables is somewhat different from that of **sh**.

The standard function s t r c s p n returns the number of characters preceding the first = in an environment string.

Now we take all exported variables out of the symbol table and build a new environment in a packed format that can be passed on to other programs. We won't use the storage occupied by the environment we inherited, even though it belongs to us, because it's probably not large enough (we may have exported additional variables or lengthened some values). So, the first time we construct a new environment, we allocate storage for the array of pointers and for the strings pointed to. We set the flag updated so that we won't allocate everything next time we have an environment to construct. We only have to use realloc next time to ensure that the string spaces are large enough; the array itself will be OK. The construction job is done by EVupdate:

```
BOOLEAN EVupdate()  /* build environment from symbol table */
{
    int i, envi, nvlen;
    struct varslot *v;
    static BOOLEAN updated = FALSE;

    if (!updated)
        if ((environ = (char **)malloc((MAXVAR + 1) * sizeof(char *)))
            == NULL)
            return(FALSE);
    envi = 0;
    for (i = 0; i < MAXVAR; i++) {
        v = &sym[i];
        if (v->name == NULL || !v->exported)
            continue;
        nvlen = strlen(v->name) + strlen(v->val) + 2;
        if (!updated) {
            if ((environ[envi] = malloc(nvlen)) == NULL)
                return(FALSE);
        }
        else if ((environ[envi] = realloc(environ[envi], nvlen)) == NULL)
                return(FALSE);
        sprintf(environ[envi], "%s=%s", v->name, v->val);
        envi++;
    }
    environ[envi] = NULL;
    updated = TRUE;
    return(TRUE);
}
```

Finally, since we may want to print the symbol table, we'll add one more function:

```
void EVprint()  /* print environment */
{
    int i;

    for (i = 0; i < MAXVAR; i++)
        if (sym[i].name != NULL)
            printf("%3s %s=%s\n", sym[i].exported ? "[E]" : "",
                sym[i].name, sym[i].val);
}
```

Printed variables are preceded with an **E** in brackets if they are exported. This is a different approach from that of s h, which provides the s e t command (without arguments) to print all variables and values, and the e x p o r t command (without arguments) to print the names of the exported variables.

To show how these symbol-table functions are used, here is a small program that adds two variables to the symbol table and prints it:

```
main()
{
    if (!EVinit())
        fatal("can't initialize environment");
    printf("Before update:\n");
    EVprint();
    if (!EVset("count", "0"))
        fatal("EVset");
    if (!EVset("BOOK", "/usr/marc/book") || !EVexport("BOOK"))
        fatal("EVset or EVexport");
    printf("\nAfter update:\n");
    EVprint();
    exit(0);
}
```

Here is the output:

```
        Before update:
        [E] TZ=MST7MDT
        [E] PS2=>
        [E] PS1=$
        [E] PATH=/bin:/usr/bin:/usr/marc/bin::
        [E] MAIL=/usr/mail/marc
        [E] LOGNAME=marc
        [E] HOME=/usr/marc

        After update:
        [E] TZ=MST7MDT
        [E] PS2=>
```

```
[E] PS1=$
[E] PATH=/bin:/usr/bin:/usr/marc/bin::
[E] MAIL=/usr/mail/marc
[E] LOGNAME=marc
[E] HOME=/usr/marc
    count=0
[E] BOOK=/usr/marc/book
```

In our example we didn't call EVupdate and we didn't invoke any programs to inherit our updated environment. We'll do that in the next section, once we learn how to invoke a program.

5.3 exec SYSTEM CALLS

It's impossible to understand the exec or fork system calls without fully understanding the distinction between a *process* and a *program*. If these terms are new to you, you may want to go back and review Sec. 1.3. If you're ready to proceed now, we'll just summarize the distinction in one sentence: A process is an execution environment that consists of instruction, user-data, and system-data segments, whereas a program is a file containing instructions and data that are used to initialize the instruction and user-data segments of a process.

The exec system calls reinitialize a process from a designated program; the program changes while the process remains. On the other hand, the fork system call (the subject of Sec. 5.4) creates a new process that is a clone of an existing one, by just copying over the instruction, user-data and system-data segments; the new process is not initialized from a program.[3]

Without fork, exec is of limited use; without exec, fork is of no practical use at all. Keep this in mind as we present them separately, and don't be alarmed if you think they're useless—just try to understand what they do. In Sec. 5.4, when we use them together, you'll see that they are a powerful pair. Why two system calls that are useful only when used together haven't been combined into a single system call is a good question for which we will give an excellent answer, but we won't have the necessary background to understand the answer until Chap. 6.

Aside from booting the UNIX kernel itself, exec is the only way programs get executed on UNIX. Not only does the shell use exec to execute our programs, but the shell and its ancestors were invoked by exec, too. And fork is the only way new processes get created.

There are six exec system calls, but we'll first describe just one of them in detail. Then we'll introduce the others and explain how they differ.

---

[3]The AT&T System III and V manuals confuse the reader by stating that exec "transforms the calling process into a new process." This is wrong; there is no new process.

```
int execl(path, arg0, arg1, ..., argn,      /* execute program */
  null)
char *path;                                  /* path of program file */
char *arg0;                                  /* first arg (file name) */
char *arg1;                                  /* second arg */
  ...
char *argn;                                  /* last arg */
char *null;                                  /* NULL */
/* returns on error (value is -1) */
```

The argument **path** must name a program file that is executable by the effective user-ID (mode 755, say) and has the correct contents for executable programs. The process's instruction segment is overwritten by the instructions from the program, and the process's user-data segment is overwritten by the data from the program. Then the process executes the new program from the top (that is, its **main** function is called).

There can be no return from a successful **execl** because the return location is gone. An unsuccessful **execl** does return, with a value of −1, but there's no need to test for that value, for no other value is possible. The most common reasons for an unsuccessful **execl** is that the **path** doesn't exist or it isn't executable, both usually because the user mistyped a command.

The arguments to **execl** that follow **path** are collected into an array of character pointers; the last argument, which must be **NULL**, stops the collection and terminates the array. The first argument, by convention, is the name of the program file (not the entire path). The new program may access these arguments through the familiar **argc** and **argv** arguments of **main**. The environment pointed to by **environ** is passed on too, and is accessible through the new program's **environ** pointer.

Since the process continues to live, and since its system-data segment is mostly undisturbed, almost all of the process's attributes are unchanged, including its process-ID, parent-process-ID, process-group-ID, real user-ID and group-ID, current and root directories, priority, accumulated execution times, and usually, open file descriptors. It's simpler to list the attributes that *do* change, all for good reasons:[4]

- If the process had arranged to catch any signals, they are reset to the default action, since the instructions designated to catch them are gone. Ignored or defaulted signals stay that way. (More about signals in Chapter 8.)
- If the set-user-ID or set-group-ID bit of the new program file is on, the effective user-ID or group-ID is changed to the owner-ID or group-ID of the file.[5] There's no way to get the former effective IDs back, if they were themselves different from the real IDs.

[4]See also Appendix A.

[5]Congratulations! You're only in Chapter 5 and you already understand the quotation at the start of the Preface!

- If the process was profiling (see Sec. 9.8), profiling is turned off. Since profile data makes sense only with respect to a particular program, a mess would otherwise result.

To show how exec l is used, here's a rather contrived example:

```
exectest()
{
    printf("The quick brown fox jumped over ");
    execl("/bin/echo", "echo", "the", "lazy", "dogs.", NULL);
    syserr("execl");
}
```

This function worked just fine when we first tried it, printing this:

```
The quick brown fox jumped over the lazy dogs.
```

But then we redirected the standard output to a file, so we could insert it into the text of this chapter, and all we got was this:

```
the lazy dogs.
```

What went wrong? Well, it turns out that the Standard I/O Library, of which printf is a part, buffers its output into blocks of 512 bytes (just as we did in Sec. 2.10) when writing to a file or a pipe, but not when writing to a terminal. We don't normally notice any problem because the last buffer is automatically flushed when the process exits. But the process didn't exit before exec l was called, and the buffer, being in the user-data segment, got overlaid before it could be flushed.
    The problem can be fixed by either forcing unbuffered output, like this:

```
setbuf(stdout, NULL);
```

or by flushing the buffer just before calling exec l, like this:

```
fflush(stdout);
```

As we've mentioned, open file descriptors normally stay open across an exec l. If we don't want a file descriptor to stay open, we just close it first, with close. But sometimes we can't. Suppose we are invoking a program that requires all file descriptors to be closed (an extremely unconventional requirement). We might therefore try this:

```
for (i = 0; i < 20; i++)
    close(i); /* ignore errors */
execl(path, arg0, arg1, arg2, NULL);
syserr("execl");
```

Note that we want so badly to close all file descriptors here that we don't even care if they're all open—we close them anyhow. It's one of the rare instances where ignoring system-call error returns is appropriate.

All is fine if the execl succeeds, but if it fails we'll never see the error message because file descriptor 2 has been closed. Here's where the close-on-exec flag that we encountered in Sec. 3.13 can be used. When set, with fcntl, the file descriptor is closed upon a successful execl, but left alone otherwise. We can either set this flag for only the important file descriptors, or just set it for all of them, like this:

```
for (i = 0; i < 20; i++)
    fcntl(i, F_SETFD, 1); /* ignore errors */
execl(path, arg0, arg1, arg2, NULL);
syserr("execl");
```

Close-on-exec is practically never used since conventionally the first three file descriptors are to be left open across an execl and the other 17 are to be closed. In certain multiple-process application systems, however, it may be necessary to stray from this convention.

The other five exec system calls provide three features not available with execl:

- Putting the arguments into an array, instead of listing them explicitly. This is necessary when the number of arguments is unknown at compile time, as in programming a shell, for example.
- Searching for the program file using the value of the PATH variable, just as sh does.
- Manually passing an explicit environment pointer, instead of automatically using environ. Since a successful exec overwrites the existing environment anyhow, there's no advantage to this feature.

The distribution of these features amongst the six exec variants is shown in this table:

System Call	Argument Format	Environment Passing	PATH Search?
execl	list	auto	no
execv	array	auto	no
execle	list	manual	no
execve	array	manual	no
execlp	list	auto	yes
execvp	array	auto	yes

Since **PATH** searching and automatic environment passing are almost always wanted, the choice is usually between **execlp** and **execvp**.

Here are the function headers for the **exec** variants we haven't yet shown:

```
int execv(path, argv)
char *path;
char *argv[];              /* ptrs to args */

int execle(path, arg0, arg1, ..., argn, null, envp)
char *path;
char *arg0;
char *arg1;
  ...
char *argn;
char *null;
char *envp[];              /* ptrs to environment vars */

int execve(path, argv, envp)
char *path;
char *argv[];
char *envp[];

int execlp(file, arg0, arg1, ..., argn, null)
char *file;                /* program file name */
char *arg0;
char *arg1;
  ...
char *argn;
char *null;

int execvp(file, argv)
char *file;
char *argv[];
```

Note that the **argv** argument as used here is identical in layout to the **argv** argument of a **main** function. A minor difference is that when using the **execv** variants, the last pointer must be **NULL**, whereas C programmers are taught to go by the argument count (**argc**).[6]

If a **file** argument to **execlp** or **execlv** has no slashes, the strings listed in the value of the **PATH** variable are prepended to it one by one until an ordinary file with the resulting path name that has execute permission is located. If

---

[6]*The C Programming Language* does not state anywhere that **argv[argc]** is **NULL**. Neither do most UNIX manuals. So it's unwise to assume that **argv** is terminated with **NULL**, because in non-UNIX systems or in UNIX clones it may not be true.

this file contains a program (as indicated by a code number in its first word), it is executed. If not, it is assumed to be a shell command file; to run it /bin/sh is executed with the path as its first argument.[7]

If the PATH search turns up nothing executable, the exec fails. If the file argument has slashes in it, no search is done—the path is assumed to be complete. It still may be a command file, however.

It's possible to program execvp and execlp as subroutines that call on execv or execl. Here is a version of execvp:

```
#define MAXPATH 50
#define MAXARGS 20

int execvp2(file, argv)
char *file, *argv[];
{
    char *colon, *pathseq, path[MAXPATH], *newargv[MAXARGS];
    char *getenv(), *strchr();
    int i, len;
    extern int errno;

    if (strchr(file, '/') != NULL ||
      (pathseq = getenv("PATH")) == NULL)
        pathseq = ":";
    for (; (colon = strchr(pathseq, ':')) != NULL;
      pathseq = colon + 1) {
        len = colon - pathseq;
        strncpy(path, pathseq, len);
        path[len] = '\0';
        if (len > 0)
            strcat(path, "/");
        strcat(path, file);
        execv(path, argv);
        if (errno == ENOEXEC) {
            i = 0;
            do {
                if (i >= MAXARGS-1) {
                    errno = E2BIG;
                    return(-1);
                }
                newargv[i + 1] = argv[i];
            } while (argv[i++] != NULL);
```

[7]Amazingly, no UNIX manual in this writer's library, for any version, mentions that execlp and execvp can handle command files, although it is rather well known among UNIX system programmers. Actually, this feature is implemented by the C interface to these system calls, not by the kernel itself.

```
            newargv[0] = "sh";
            execv("/bin/sh", newargv);
            syserr("execv");
        }
    }
    return(-1);
}
```

The standard function s t r c h r returns a pointer to the first occurrence of a character in a string, or NULL if there is none. We use it to scan quickly for a slash and to find the first colon. Rather than treating a file name with a slash as a special case, we just use a null path sequence. Then we pick off the path prefixes one by one, build the full path, and try to execute it. If we fail because the file wasn't in the form of a program, we assume it's a shell command file; we have to copy the arguments to a new array to make room for the new command name, s h. If we fail for any other reason, we try another path. Only when no more candidate paths remain do we give up.

We now know enough system calls to write a shell, although not a very good one. Its chief deficiency is that it has to commit suicide in order to execute a command, since there is no return from e x e c. Perversely, if you type in bad commands, you can keep running. While we're at it, we'll implement some built-in commands to modify and access the environment: assignment (e.g., BOOK=/usr /marc/book); s e t, which prints the environment; and e x p o r t, which exports the variables given as its arguments. If e x p o r t has no arguments, it behaves just like s e t.

The first task is to break up a command line into arguments. For simplicity, we'll do without quoted arguments. Moreover, since this shell can't handle background processes, sequential execution, or piping, we don't have to worry about the special characters &, ;, and |. We'll leave out redirection (>, >>, and <) also. Therefore, a command line is just a series of words separated by blanks or tabs. We just have to gather them up and put them into an a r g v array:

```
static BOOLEAN getargs(argcp, argv, max)  /* read and parse args */
int *argcp;
char *argv[];
int max;
{
    static char cmd[100];
    char *cmdp, *strtok();
    int i;

    if (gets(cmd) == NULL)
        exit(0);
```

```
    cmdp = cmd;
    for (i = 0; i <= max; i++) {
        if ((argv[i] = strtok(cmdp, " \t")) == NULL)
            break;
        cmdp = NULL; /* tell strtok to keep going */
    }
    if (i > max) {
        printf("Too many args\n");
        return(FALSE);
    }
    *argcp = i;
    return(TRUE);
}
```

Since this function reads the standard input, we've arranged for it to just exit when it reads an end-of-file; there's no cleanup work to be done before terminating. The standard function strtok grabs the next token from a string. A pointer to the string is supplied with the first call; subsequent calls are distinguished by a NULL first argument. The second argument lists the characters that delimit tokens—blank and tab in this case. In addition to filling the argv array, we return an argument count through the pointer argcp to save the caller the trouble of figuring it out.

Next, we need functions to handle the three built-in commands, assignment, set, and export. These are easy, since we can use the environment manipulation routines from the previous section.

```
void asg(argc, argv)  /* assignment command */
int argc;
char *argv[];
{
    char *name, *val, *strtok();

    if (argc != 1)
        printf("Extra args\n");
    else {
        name = strtok(argv[0], "=");
        val = strtok(NULL, "\1"); /* get all that's left */
        if (!EVset(name, val))
            printf("Can't assign\n");
    }
}

void export(argc, argv)  /* export command */
int argc;
char *argv[];
{
    int i;
```

```
        if (argc == 1) {
            set(argc, argv);
            return;
        }
        for (i = 1; i < argc; i++)
            if (!EVexport(argv[i])) {
                printf("Can't export %s\n", argv[i]);
                return;
            }
    }
    void set(argc, argv)  /* set command */
    int argc;
    char *argv[];
    {
        if (argc != 1)
            printf("Extra args\n");
        else
            EVprint();
    }
```

Next, we complete the program with a `main` function that prints the prompt character (we use "prompt string 2", kept in the environment variable `PS2`), gets the arguments, checks to see if the command is built in, and if it's not, tries to execute it.

```
    #define MAXARG 20

    main()  /* one-shot shell */
    {
        char *argv[MAXARG + 1], *prompt, *EVget();
        int argc;

        if (!EVinit())
            fatal("can't initialize environment");
        if ((prompt = EVget("PS2")) == NULL)
            prompt = "> ";
        while (1) {
            printf("%s", prompt);
            if (!getargs(&argc, argv, MAXARG) || argc == 0)
                continue;
            if (strchr(argv[0], '=') != NULL)
                asg(argc, argv);
            else if (strcmp(argv[0], "export") == 0)
                export(argc, argv);
            else if (strcmp(argv[0], "set") == 0)
                set(argc, argv);
            else
                execute(argc, argv);
        }
    }
```

```
static void execute(argc, argv)  /* execute command */
int argc;
char *argv[];
{
    if (!EVupdate())
        fatal("can't update environment");
    execvp(argv[0], argv);
    printf("Can't execute\n");
}
```

Note that we loop back to print another prompt only if **e x e c v p** fails. That's why we're unlikely to find this shell useful. Here's a sample session anyhow:

```
$ sh0
> Book=/usr/marc/book
> export BOOK
> envprint
HOME=/usr/marc
LOGNAME=marc
MAIL=/usr/mail/marc
PATH=/bin:/usr/bin:/usr/marc/bin::
PS1=$
PS2=>
TZ=MST7MDT
BOOK=/usr/marc/book
$
```

The command **e n v p r i n t** was the program we wrote to print the environment in the previous section.

As we've said, normally **e x e c** is paired with **f o r k**, but occasionally it's useful by itself. Sometimes a large program is split into phases, and **e x e c** brings in the next phase. But since *all* instructions and user-data are overlaid, the phases would have to be quite independent for this to be workable—data can only be passed through arguments, the environment, or files. So this application is rare, but not unknown. More commonly, **e x e c** is used by itself when we need to do a very small amount of preliminary work before invoking a command. An example is the **n o h u p** command, which just suppresses hangup signals before calling **e x e c v p** to invoke the user's command. Another example is the **n i c e** command, which changes a command's priority.

5.4 fork SYSTEM CALL

```
int fork()   /* create new process */
/* returns process-ID and 0 on success or -1 on error */
```

f o r k is somewhat the opposite of **e x e c**: It creates a new process, but it does not initialize it from a new program. Instead, the new process's instruction, user-data, and system-data segments are almost exact copies of the old process's. After f o r k returns, both processes (parent and child) receive the return. The return value is different, however, which is crucial, because this allows their subsequent actions to differ. Usually, the child does an e x e c and the parent either waits for the child to terminate or goes off to do something else.

The child receives a 0 return value from f o r k; the parent receives the process-ID of the child. As usual, a return of −1 indicates an error, but since f o r k has no arguments, the caller could not have done anything wrong. The only cause of an error is resource exhaustion, such as insufficient swap space or too many processes already in execution. Rather than give up, the parent may want to wait a while (with s l e e p) and try again, although this is not what the shell does—it just prints a message and reprompts.

Recall that a program invoked by an e x e c system call retained many attributes because the system-data segment was left mostly alone. Similarly, a child created by f o r k inherits most attributes from its parent because its system-data segment is copied from its parent. It is this inheritance that allows a user to set certain attributes from the shell, such as current directory, effective user-ID, and priority, that then apply to each command subsequently invoked. One can imagine these attributes to belong to the "session," even though UNIX has no such concept—inheritance makes it unnecessary.

Only a few attributes are not inherited:[8]

- Obviously, the child's process-ID and parent-process-ID are different, since it's a different process.
- The child gets copies of the parent's open file descriptors. Each is opened to the same file, and the file pointer has the same value. The file pointer is shared. If the child changes it with l s e e k, then the parent's next read or write will be at the new location. The file descriptor itself, however, is distinct: If the child closes it, the parent's copy is undisturbed.
- The child's accumulated execution times are reset to zero, because it is at the beginning of its life.

Here's a simple example to show the effect of a f o r k:

```
forktest()
{
    int pid;

    printf("Start of test\n");
    pid = fork();
    printf("Returned %d\n", pid);
}
```

---

[8]See also Appendix A.

The output:

                        Start of test
                        Returned 0
                        Returned 93

We can use fork and execvp together to make our shell from the previous section far more useful—it won't just exit after running a command, but will actually prompt for another one! We replace the function execute with execut2:

```
static void execut2(argc, argv)  /* execute command and wait */
int argc;
char *argv[];
{
    int code;

    switch (fork()) {
    case -1:
        printf("Can't create new process\n");
        return;
    case 0:
        if (!EVupdate())
            fatal("can't update environment");
        execvp(argv[0], argv);
        printf("Can't execute\n");
        exit(1);
    default:
        if (wait(NULL) == -1)
            syserr("wait");
    }
}
```

We'll present the details of wait fully in Sec. 5.6; for now, you just need to know that it waits for the child process to terminate before returning.

This function treats an error from fork differently from an error from execvp. If fork returns −1, we have not created a new process, so we just print a message and return. The caller (main from the previous section) will then prompt the user again, which is what we want. But if execvp returns, we are in the *child* process, not the parent, and we had better exit. Otherwise, the child would keep running and we would have *two* shells prompting for commands. If we actually tried to type a command, the two processes would compete for characters and each would get some of them, since a single character can only be read once. This could have serious consequences if, for example, we typed rm t * and one of the shells read rm * while the other read t.

The cost of a fork is enormous. It goes to all the trouble of cloning the parent, perhaps copying a large data segment (the instruction segment is usually read-only and can be shared) only to execute a few hundred instructions before reinitializing the code and data segments. This seems wasteful, and it is. A clever solution has been used in some virtual-memory versions of UNIX, in which copying is particularly expensive, called *copy-on-write*. It works this way: On a fork, the parent and child share the data segment, which consists of a collection of *pages*. As long as a page stays unmodified, this shortcut causes no harm. But as soon as parent or child attempts to write on a page, it is copied to give each its own version.[9] This is easy and efficient with the right kind of paging hardware (on a VAX, for example). Since the exec follows very quickly in almost all cases, very few pages will have to be copied. Even if they all have to be copied, we are no worse off—in fact, we're better off, since we were able to start running the child earlier. Remember that a copy-on-write scheme is internal to the kernel; it does not change the semantics of fork, and, apart from better performance, users are unaware of it. The approach adheres to an important guideline for system programmers: Go ahead and optimize the system, but *don't hassle the users*—it's not their problem.

5.5 exit SYSTEM CALL

```
void exit(status)      /* terminate process */
int status;            /* exit status */
/* does not return */
```

exit terminates the process that issued it, with a status code equal to the rightmost byte of status. All open file descriptors are closed. Thanks to a trick played by the C library, all Standard I/O Library streams are closed too, and their buffers are flushed, just as though fclose had been called. However, the kernel knows nothing about this.

If child processes are still alive when exit is called, they are not disturbed, but since their parent is about to die, their parent-process-ID is changed to 1, which is the ID of the init process (see Sec. 1.5).

exit is the first system call that everybody learns. In fact, most C programmers are probably unaware that it's actually a *system call* rather than a mere subroutine. It has one other distinction: It's the only system call that *never* returns.

This is not to say that exit can't be misused; in fact, it often is, when called like this:

```
exit();
```

---

[9]Berkeley 4.2 BSD has a system call named vfork, which accomplishes the same goals, but less elegantly and not transparently. It suspends the parent until the child calls exec or exits. Since it is a different system call from fork, programs ported to 4.2 BSD don't benefit. But of course, the Berkeley shell (csh) uses vfork, which helps enormously.

or when one flows off the end of a `main` function. A word of garbage is returned as the process's status code, which may or may not hurt anything. It's better to do things right, of course. By convention, a status code of zero means that the process terminated normally, and a nonzero code (usually 1) means that an error occurred. But all 256 possible codes may be used.

The exiting process's parent receives its status code via a `wait` system call.

5.6 wait SYSTEM CALL

```
int wait(statusp)       /* wait for child */
int *statusp;           /* exit status */
/* returns process-ID or -1 on error */
```

If there are any child processes, `wait` sleeps until one of them terminates. The caller can't specify which child is to be waited for. `wait` returns the child's process-ID and stores its status code into the integer pointed to by `statusp`, unless the argument is `NULL`, in which case no status is stored. `wait` also returns if a caught signal is received or if a child stops in trace mode, but we'll ignore those events for now and come back to them in Sec. 8.3 and Sec. 9.9.

Note that there can be no grandchildren if there are no children, since when a child dies its children are adopted by `init`, not by their grandparent. Therefore, a process will not receive a return from `wait` upon the termination of a grandchild; the grandchild's parent is still alive, and it has the privilege of waiting.

A process may terminate at a time when its parent is not waiting for it. Because the kernel must ensure that every process gets waited for, such an unwaited-for process becomes a *zombie* process. Its instruction, user-data, and system-data segments are discarded, but it still occupies a process-table slot in the kernel.[10] When its turn comes to be waited for it finally goes away.

If there are no children, because there never were any or because an earlier `wait` already returned their IDs, then `wait` returns −1 immediately with `errno` set to `ECHILD`.

There's no reason why every process must be waited for. It's perfectly OK for a process to create some children and just go on about its business, leaving them to run until completion.

There are three ways for a process to terminate: It can call `exit`, it can receive a fatal signal, or the computer can crash. The status code returned through `statusp` indicates which of the first two cases caused termination; in the third case the parent and the kernel are dead too, so status is moot. If the rightmost byte of the status is zero, then the byte to its left is the child's argument to `exit`. If the rightmost byte is nonzero, the rightmost seven bits are the number of the signal

---

[10]A dictionary definition of *zombie* that fits very well is ''a person of the lowest order of intelligence suggestive of the so-called walking dead.'' (*Webster's New Collegiate Dictionary*, 6th ed. [Springfield, Mass.: G. & C. Merriam Co., 1960].)

that killed the child. If the leftmost bit of the rightmost byte is 1, a core dump was produced (in a file named `core` in the current directory).

Here is a function to interpret a status code and, if it contains a signal number, to print out an appropriate phrase (the phrases are explained in Sec. 8.2):

```
#define MAXSIG 19

void statusprt(pid, status)  /* interpret status code */
int pid, status;
{
    int code;
    static char *sigmsg[] = {
        "",
        "Hangup",
        "Interrupt",
        "Quit",
        "Illegal instruction",
        "Trace trap",
        "IOT instruction",
        "EMT instruction",
        "Floating point exception",
        "Kill",
        "Bus error",
        "Segmentation violation",
        "Bad arg to system call",
        "Write on pipe",
        "Alarm clock",
        "Terminate signal",
        "User signal 1",
        "User signal 2",
        "Death of child",
        "Power fail"
    };
    if (status != 0 && pid != 0)
        printf("Process %d: ", pid);
    if (lowbyte(status) == 0) {
        if ((code = highbyte(status)) != 0)
            printf("Exit code %d\n", code);
    } else {
        if ((code = status & 0177) <= MAXSIG)
            printf("%s", sigmsg[code]);
        else
            printf("Signal #%d", code);
        if ((status & 0200) == 0200)
            printf("-core dumped");
        printf("\n");
    }
}
```

We introduced the macros lowbyte and highbyte back in Sec. 1.10.

This function is similar to one the shell uses to print messages familiar to all but the most timid programmers, such as:

```
Bus error-core dumped
```

Now that we have statusprt, we can improve on execut2 from Sec. 5.4:

```
static void execut3(argc, argv)  /* execute command and wait */
int argc;
char *argv[];
{
    int status, code;

    switch (fork()) {
    case -1:
        printf("Can't create new process\n");
        return;
    case 0:
        if (!EVupdate())
            fatal("can't update environment");
        execvp(argv[0], argv);
        fatal("can't execute");
    default:
        if (wait(&status) == -1)
            syserr("wait");
        statusprt(0, status);
    }
}
```

We didn't bother to take the process-ID returned by wait and pass it on to statusprt because this shell has only one child at a time. In Chap. 6, when we develop a more complete shell, we will be making use of the process-ID.

Our latest attempt actually works as a shell should:

```
$ sh3
> date
Thu Sep  6 17:15:39 MDT 1984
> who
marc  console Sep  6 12:00
> echo This shell is much better!
This shell is much better!
> EOT
$
```

We've shown where we typed a Control-D with the letters EOT.

5.7 SYSTEM CALLS TO GET IDS

```
int getuid()        /* get real user-ID */
/* returns ID */

int getgid()        /* get real group-ID */
/* returns ID */

int geteuid()       /* get effective user-ID */
/* returns ID */

int getegid()       /* get effective group-ID */
/* returns ID */

int getpid()        /* get process-ID */
/* returns ID */

int getpgrp()       /* get process-group-ID */
/* returns ID */

int getppid()       /* get parent-process-ID */
/* returns ID */
```

Each of these system calls returns a single ID, as indicated by the comments following their function headers. Few of them are used with any frequency.

The process-ID is often used to compose temporary file names. Since each active process has a unique ID, embedding the ID in a file name guarantees uniqueness across all processes. The following coding is typical:

```
char file[10];
int tempfd;

sprintf(file, "TMP%d", getpid());
if ((tempfd = open(file, O_RDWR | O_CREAT | O_TRUNC, 0666)) == -1)
    syserr("open");
```

You can't create more than one temporary file for the same process with this technique—the names would all be the same. If you know exactly what temporary files are needed, you can just distinguish them with successive letters (TMP23142a, TMP23142b, etc.). Or, to be completely safe, you can start with a, use the O_EXCL flag with open (see Sec. 2.6), and, if it fails because the file already exists, try b and so on until you find an unused name.

5.8 setuid AND setgid SYSTEM CALLS

```
int setuid(uid)    /* set user-IDs */
int uid;           /* user-ID */
/* returns 0 on success or -1 on error */

int setgid(gid)    /* set group-IDs */
int gid;           /* group-ID */
/* returns 0 on success or -1 on error */
```

If the caller is the superuser, these two system calls set the real and effective user-IDs or group-IDs to the argument. They allow the superuser to become any other user.

The most important UNIX command that uses these calls is login. After prompting for a login name and a password, login verifies them by consulting /etc/passwd and, if they are valid, executes setuid and setgid to set the real and effective user-IDs and group-IDs according to the numbers in the /etc/passwd entry. Then login makes the login directory the current directory, and uses exec to execute the user's designated shell.

Ordinary users can also execute setuid and setgid, but only to change the *effective* user-ID or group-ID back to the corresponding *real* ID. In this case the argument to setuid or setgid must match the real user-ID or group-ID. This feature is typically used when a program must start out with a particular effective user-ID, do some privileged work, and revert to the real ID for the rest of the process's life.

5.9 setpgrp SYSTEM CALL

```
int setpgrp()   /* set process-group-ID */
/* returns new process-group-ID */
```

This system call forms a new process group. When called, it sets the process-group-ID equal to the process-ID. This removes the process from its existing group, and since all its children will inherit the new process-group-ID, they and all their descendants will be members of the new group (unless yet another new group is formed by one of them).

The significance of process groups has to do with signaling; see Sec. 1.5 and Sec. 8.5. Usually, processes in the same group are logically connected in some way. For example, a multiple-process database manager might consist of a master process and several subsidiary processes. To make the suite of database processes a process group, the master process would simply call setpgrp before creating the subsidiaries. Recall that the process-group-ID is one of the attributes a child inherits from its parent.

5.10 chdir SYSTEM CALL

```
int chdir(path)      /* change current directory */
char *path;          /* path name */
/* returns 0 on success or -1 on error */
```

The c h d i r system call changes the current directory to the directory specified by its argument. Execute (search) permission is required on the new current directory, but not read nor write permission.

The most important use of c h d i r is, of course, for the c d command, which is built into the shell. If it were not built in, but instead performed by a child process, it would be ineffective. This is because an attribute changed by a child process (current directory, in this case) is not passed back to the parent.

5.11 chroot SYSTEM CALL

```
int chroot(path)      /* change root directory */
char *path;           /* path name */
/* returns 0 on success or -1 on error */
```

This system call changes the root directory of the process, the directory whose name is /. Only the superuser can execute it. c h r o o t is handy when a command with built-in path names (such as / e t c / p a s s w d) is to be run on other than the usual files. A new tree can be constructed wherever convenient, the root can be changed, and then the command can be executed. This is primarily useful in testing new commands before they are installed.

The restriction to a superuser prevents ordinary users from counterfeiting system files and then changing the root to fool a command. Otherwise one could become a superuser with this scheme (a few details have been omitted):

1. Make an e t c directory anywhere; / u s r / m a r c / e t c will do.
2. Copy / e t c / p a s s w d there.
3. Edit the copy to remove the password for r o o t (the superuser login name).
4. Write a program that calls c h r o o t to change the root to / u s r / m a r c and then executes l o g i n.
5. Run the program and log in as the superuser.

Fortunately, since you have to be a superuser to use c h r o o t, this scheme doesn't work.

You might think that l o g i n could be programmed to prevent this by including the call:

```
chroot("/");
```

to force the root back to where it belongs, but you would be mistaken. Such a call does absolutely nothing, because the new root applies to chroot too. In fact, once the root has been changed, there is no way to get the old one back. We know that the normal root has an i-number of 2, but it's not possible to exploit that fact. And we can't move upward from the root, because the path .. relative to the root just leads back to the root.

5.12 nice SYSTEM CALL

```
int nice(incr)        /* change nice value */
int incr;             /* increment */
/* returns new nice value or -1 on error */
```

Each process has a *nice value*, which until now we have called the *priority*.[11] The nice system call adds incr to the nice value. The resulting nice value must be between 0 and 39, inclusive; if an invalid value results, the nearest valid value is used. Higher nice values give poorer service. Processes start with a value of 20. Only the superuser can lower the nice value, getting better-than-average service.

nice actually returns the new nice value minus 20, so the returned value is in the range -20 through 19. However, the returned value is rarely of much use. This is just as well, because a new nice value of 19 is indistinguishable from an error return $(19-20 = -1)$. That this bug has remained unfixed, if not unnoticed, for so many years is indicative of how little most UNIX system programmers care about error returns from minor system calls like nice.

Most UNIX users are familiar with the nice *command,* which runs a program at a lower priority (or a higher one if run by a superuser). Here is our version of this command:

```
#define USAGE "usage: nice [-num] command\n"

main(argc, argv) /* nice command */
int argc;
char *argv[];
{
    int incr, cmdarg;

    if (argc < 2) {
        fprintf(stderr, USAGE);
        exit(1);
    }
}
```

---

[11]We introduce the awkward term *nice value* because that's what the ps command uses in its output. Technically, the *priority* is another number entirely, affected by the nice value as well as by other attributes.

```
        if (argv[1][0] == '-') {
            incr = atoi(&argv[1][1]);
            cmdarg = 2;
        }
        else {
            incr = 10;
            cmdarg = 1;
        }
        if (cmdarg >= argc) {
            fprintf(stderr, USAGE);
            exit(1);
        }
        nice(incr); /* ignore return value */
        execvp(argv[cmdarg], &argv[cmdarg]);
        syserr("execvp");
    }
```

Note how we reuse the incoming argv in the call to execvp. The variable cmdarg holds the subscript of the command name (either 1 or 2, depending on whether an increment was specified). That part of argv starting with cmdarg is the part to be passed on. You might want to contrast this with the more extensive manipulation needed for execvp2 in Sec. 5.3. There we had to *insert* an argument, which required us to recopy the entire array.

　　Note also that we used execvp without a fork. Having changed the priority, there's no need to wait around. The nohup command uses a similar method. On the other hand, the time command must wait around to print the times, so it does create a child process to run the command.

5.13 PORTABILITY

System calls execvp and execlp are absent from Version 7 and 4.2 BSD; chroot is absent from Version 7. This need not affect portability unduly, since those exec variants can be coded as subroutines (see execvp2 in Sec. 5.3), and chroot is seldom used (and almost never embedded in an application program).

　　Version 7's nice returns nothing, which is fine, because the more modern nice has a useless return value anyhow (see Sec. 5.12).

　　So much of this chapter is portable because it is such old stuff. These system calls lie at the heart of UNIX and, except in the minor ways noted, have remained unchanged for many years. It's regrettable that portability comes from old age rather than from a scrupulously implemented design philosophy, but we'll take it any way we can get it.

EXERCISES

5.1. Rewrite the environment manipulation functions in Sec. 5.2 to treat exported variables as the standard shell (s h) does. That is, an updated value for a variable is exported only if it is specifically declared in an e x p o r t command.

5.2. Change the environment manipulation functions to use hashing instead of linear searching.

5.3. Write a program that scans its arguments for assignments of the form *variable = value*, updates the environment appropriately, and then executes the program specified by the first nonassignment argument. The other nonassignment arguments become arguments to the invoked program. Don't use f o r k.

5.4. Write a function e x e c l p 2 that is analogous to e x e c v p 2 in Sec. 5.3.

5.5. Design an experiment to measure the CPU time used by f o r k. (You may want to use the timing functions in Sec. 9.10.) Try different versions of UNIX, if you can, and different computer models, if you can. If you have access to Berkeley UNIX, compare the time for f o r k with the time for v f o r k.

5.6. Investigate the equivalent system calls to e x e c and f o r k that are provided in other operating systems, such as VMS (DEC) and MVS (IBM). Compare their features and summarize their advantages and disadvantages.

6

BASIC
INTERPROCESS
COMMUNICATION

6.1 INTRODUCTION

Now that we know how to create processes, we want to connect them so they can communicate. We'll do this with pipes in this chapter, using techniques that work on all versions of UNIX. In the next chapter we'll explore interprocess communication using techniques unique to System III, System V, and Xenix 3, such as FIFOs and messages.

Pipes are familiar to most UNIX users as a shell facility. For instance, to print a sorted list of who is logged on, you can enter this command line:

```
who | sort | pr
```

There are three processes here, connected with two pipes. Data flows in one direction only, from who to sort to pr. It is also possible to set up bidirectional pipelines (from process A to B, and from B back to A) and pipelines in a ring (from A to B to C to A) using system calls. The shell, however, provides no notation for these more elaborate arrangements, so they are unknown to most UNIX users.[1]

We'll begin by showing some simple examples of processes connected by a one-directional pipeline. Then we'll improve on the primitive shell we developed in

---

[1]These arrangements can be set up with FIFOs, but the shell is an innocent bystander—it thinks they are files.

Chap. 5. Our new shell will be complete enough to be called "real"—it will handle pipelines, background processes, I/O redirection, and quoted arguments. It will lack file-name generation (`ls t*.?`) and programming constructs. We'll also show how to connect processes with bidirectional pipes and expose the deadlock problems that can arise.

6.2 pipe SYSTEM CALL

```
int pipe(pfd)                    /* create pipe */
int pfd[2];                      /* file descriptors */
/* returns 0 on success or -1 on error */
```

The `pipe` system call creates a pipe, which is a communication channel represented by two file descriptors that are returned in the `pfd` array. Writing to `pfd[1]` puts data in the pipe; reading from `pfd[0]` gets it out. Some I/O system calls act differently on these file descriptors from the way they do on ordinary files, and some do nothing at all, as summarized by this list:

`write`   Data written to a pipe is sequenced in order of arrival. Normally, if the pipe becomes full, `write` will block until enough old data is removed by `read`. There are no partial writes; the entire `write` will be completed. The capacity of a pipe varies with the UNIX implementation, but it is always at least 4096 bytes. If `fcntl` is called to set the `O_NDELAY` flag, `write` will not block on a full pipe and will return a count of 0. The only way to put an end-of-file on a pipe is to close the writing file descriptor.

`read`   Data is read from a pipe in order of arrival, just as it was written. Once read, data can't be reread or put back. Normally, if the pipe is empty, `read` will block until at least one byte of data is available, unless the writing file descriptor is closed, in which case the read will return with a 0 count (the usual end-of-file indication). But the byte count given as the third argument to `read` will not necessarily be satisfied—only as many bytes as are present at that instant will be read, and an appropriate count will be returned. The byte count will never be exceeded, of course; unread bytes will remain for the next `read`. If the `O_NDELAY` flag is set, a `read` on an empty pipe will return with a 0 count. This suffers from the same ambiguity as reads on communication lines (see Sec. 4.3): A 0 count also means end-of-file.

`close`   Means more on a pipe than it does on a file. Not only does it free up the file descriptor for reuse, but when the writing file descriptor is closed it acts as an end-of-file for the reader. If the reading file descriptor is closed, a write on the other file descriptor will cause an error. A fatal signal is also normally generated; see Sec. 8.2.

fcntl This system call sets or clears the O_NDELAY flag, whose effect is described under write and read above.

fstat Not very useful on pipes. The size returned is the number of bytes in the pipe, but this fact is seldom useful. A pipe may be distinguished by a link count of 0, since a pipe is the only source of a file descriptor associated with something not linked into a directory. This distinction might be useful to I/O routines that want to treat pipes specially.

dup This system call is explained in Sec. 6.3.

open Not used with pipes.

creat Not used with pipes.

lseek Not used with pipes. This means that if a pipe contains a sequence of messages, it isn't possible to look through them for the message to be read next. Like toothpaste in a tube, you have to get it out to examine it, and then there's no way to put it back. This is one reason why pipes are awkward for application programs that pass messages between processes.

Pipes use the buffer cache just as ordinary files do. Therefore, the benefits of writing and reading pipes in units of a block (usually 512 bytes) are just as great. A single write execution is atomic, so if 512 bytes are written with a single system call, the corresponding read will return with 512 bytes (if it requests that many). It will not return with less than the full block. However, if the writer is not writing complete blocks, but the reader is trying to read complete blocks, the reader may keep getting partial blocks anyhow. This won't happen if the writer is faster than the reader, since then the writer will be able to fill the pipe with a complete block before the reader gets around to reading anything. Still, it's best to buffer writes and reads on pipes, and this is what the Standard I/O Library does automatically.

Considering a single process only, of what use is a pipe? None. But here's a silly example anyway:

```
pipetest() /* write and read pipe */
{
    int pfd[2], nread;
    char s[100];

    if (pipe(pfd) == -1)
        syserr("pipe");
    if (write(pfd[1], "hello", 6) == -1)
        syserr("write");
```

```
switch (nread = read(pfd[0], s, sizeof(s))) {
case -1:
    syserr("read");
case 0:
    fatal("EOF");
default:
    printf("read %d bytes: %s\n", nread, s);
}
}
```

The output:

```
read 6 bytes: hello
```

We could safely write six bytes into the pipe without worrying about it filling up, since the capacity is at least 4096. But if we wrote more, and did fill the pipe, the w r i t e would block until the r e a d emptied it some. But this could never happen, because the program would never get to the r e a d. We would be stuck in a situation called *deadlock*. You must be careful to avoid deadlock when using pipes, but don't be overly concerned: When you connect processes with single, one-directional pipes (like the shell does), deadlock (due to pipes) is *impossible*. Only the more exotic arrangements can cause deadlock.

Given that we have two processes, how can we connect them so that one can read from a pipe what the other writes? We can't. Once the processes are created they can't be connected, because there's no way for the process that makes the pipe to pass a file descriptor to the other process. It can pass the file descriptor number, of course, but that number won't be valid in the other process. But if we make a pipe in one process *before* creating the other process, it will inherit the pipe file descriptors, and they will be valid in both processes. Thus, two processes communicating over a pipe can be parent and child, or two children, or grandparent and grandchild, and so on, but they must be related, and the pipe must be passed on at birth. In practice, this may be a severe limitation, because if a process dies there's no way to recreate it and reconnect it to its pipes—the survivors must be killed too, and then the whole family has to be recreated.

In the following example one process (running p w r i t e) makes a pipe, creates a child process (running p r e a d) that inherits it, and then writes some data to the pipe for the child to read. Although the child has inherited the necessary reading file descriptor, it still doesn't know its number (there are 20 possibilities), so the number is passed as an argument.

```
pwrite() /* pipe data to pread */
{
    int pfd[2];
    char fdstr[10];
```

```
if (pipe(pfd) == -1)
    syserr("pipe");
switch (fork()) {
case -1:
    syserr("fork");
case 0:
    if (close(pfd[1]) == -1)
        syserr("close");
    sprintf(fdstr, "%d", pfd[0]);
    execlp("./pread", "pread", fdstr, NULL);
    syserr("execlp");
}
if (close(pfd[0]) == -1)
    syserr("close2");
if (write(pfd[1], "hello", 6) == -1)
    syserr("write");
}
```

Here is the code for the the child process:

```
main(argc, argv) /* read data from pwrite */
int argc;
char *argv[];
{
    int fd, nread;
    char s[100];

    fd = atoi(argv[1]);
    printf("reading file descriptor %d\n", fd);
    switch (nread = read(fd, s, sizeof(s))) {
    case -1:
        syserr("read");
    case 0:
        fatal("EOF");
    default:
        printf("read %d bytes: %s\n", nread, s);
    }
}
```

And here is the output:

```
reading file descriptor 3
read 6 bytes: hello
```

Some comments about this example are needed: Since the child will only be reading the pipe, not writing it, it closes the writing end (pfd[1]) right away (the statement after `case 0` in the parent) to conserve file descriptors. `sprintf` converts the reading file descriptor from an integer to a string (UNIX has a standard `atoi` function, but no `itoa`) so it can be used as a program argument. Since we know that the child program is in the current directory, we code its path as `./pread` to stop `execlp` from searching. This saves time, but more importantly, it prevents the accidental execution of some other `pread` instead (no telling what might be in `/usr/bin`). We could have accomplished the same thing by using `execl`, which doesn't search, but we prefer to stick to just two variants of `exec` (the other being `execvp`).

Meanwhile, the parent has no use for the reading end of the pipe, so it closes `pfd[0]`. Then it writes six bytes to the pipe and is free to go on to other processing. We don't bother to wait for the child to terminate; having sent the child some data, we no longer care about it.

The child runs `pread`, which just converts its argument back to an integer and reads from that file descriptor. It prints some messages to show that things really worked.

In general, then, here is how to connect two processes with a pipe:

1. Make the pipe.
2. Fork to create the reading child.
3. In the child close the writing end of the pipe, and do any other preparations that are needed (we'll see what these are in subsequent examples).
4. In the child execute the child program.
5. In the parent close the reading end of the pipe.
6. If a second child is to write on the pipe, create it, make the necessary preparations, and execute its program. If the parent is to write, go ahead and write.

All our examples of one-directional piping will follow this paradigm.

Back in Sec. 5.3 we promised we would justify the separation of `fork` and `exec`: Why not a single system call to do both jobs, to save the overhead of `fork`? We now make good on our promise: The two are separated to allow us to perform step 3 above. We've already discovered some work to do between `fork` and `exec` (closing `pfd[1]`), and further on in this chapter we'll see more. We can't do this work before the `fork`, because we don't want it to affect the parent (the parent must not close the writing end of the pipe). We don't want the child's program to do the work, because we want programs to be oblivious to how they got invoked and how their inputs and outputs are connected (this is a cornerstone of UNIX philosophy). So we do it in the perfect place: in the child, executing code cloned from the parent. An added benefit is that the connection code is localized, making it easier to debug and modify.

To persist: Since there are only a few ways that processes are typically connected, why not have a single fork-exec system call with various options for interprocess connection? After all, there are other system calls with lots of options, so why not here? The answer is simply that the original designers of UNIX, Thompson and Ritchie, have above-average taste. f o r k and e x e c are simple; they allow the caller to arrange a wide variety of customized connections, so why kludge up another system call?

The program p r e a d was specially designed to read from a passed-in file descriptor number. It's a strange program—no standard UNIX command works that way. Many programs do read a particular file descriptor, which they assume to be already open, but that file descriptor is fixed at 0 (the standard input). It doesn't have to be passed as an argument. Similarly, many programs are designed to write to file descriptor 1 (the standard output). To connect commands as the shell does we somehow need to force p i p e to return particular file descriptors in the p f d array: 0 for the reading end and 1 for the writing end. Alas, p i p e offers no such feature. We might try closing 0 and 1 before calling p i p e, to make them available, but this won't work because the manual says nothing about what file descriptors p i p e will use, and we can't usually afford to sacrifice our standard input and output just to make a pipe. So how do we perform the trick? We use d u p.

6.3 dup SYSTEM CALL

```
int dup(fd)                    /* duplicate file descriptor */
int fd;                        /* existing file descriptor */
/* returns new file descriptor or -1 on error */
```

d u p duplicates an existing file descriptor, giving a new file descriptor that is open to the same file or pipe. The two share the same file pointer, just as an inherited file descriptor shares the file pointer with the corresponding file descriptor in the parent. The call fails if the argument is bad (not open) or if 20 file descriptors are already open.

Since the file pointer is shared, there is only one benefit to having a second file descriptor: Its number is different and perhaps better suited to the caller's purposes. It is guaranteed that the lowest-numbered available file descriptor will be used. This rule may be exploited to get a file descriptor numbered 0 that is the reading end of a pipe: Close file descriptor 0 and d u p the pipe's reading file descriptor. Since 0 is the lowest possible number, and since we just made it available, d u p will return a file descriptor numbered 0. If we then e x e c a program designed to read file descriptor 0, it will have been tricked into reading the pipe. A similar algorithm can be used to force file descriptor 1 to be the writing end of a pipe. In fact, c l o s e and d u p may be used to get a file descriptor with any number we like, although 0 and 1 are usually the only ones we care to manipulate in this way.

Instead of using d u p, we can use f c n t l with the command F _ D U P F D (see Sec. 3.13). The returned file descriptor is a duplicate of the first argument, but it is guaranteed to be greater than or equal to the third argument. For example, to make file descriptor 6 a duplicate of file descriptor fd:

```
(void)close(6); /* ignore error */
if ((newfd = fcntl(fd, F_DUPFD, 6)) == -1)
    syserr("fcntl");
```

We closed 6 to make it available, just in case it was in use.

Without fcntl this task would be much harder. Not only would we have to make 6 available, but we would have to ensure that 0 through 5 were unavailable, or else one of them would be chosen by dup. This is the procedure:

1. Call dup repeatedly until the desired number is returned.
2. Close the file descriptors that were duped by mistake.

The labor saved by fcntl is usually irrelevant because 0 and 1 are very low numbers and always unavailable, so one close and one dup suffices. An advantage of not using fcntl is that it is absent from most UNIX systems based on Version 7.

We might as well ask a question we've asked before: Now that we have fcntl, why isn't dup just a subroutine? Answer: tradition.

To illustrate dup, here is an example that makes a pipe, creates a child to read it, arranges for the child's standard input to be the reading end of the pipe, and then invokes the cat command to read the pipe (now that we're able to use the standard input, we don't need a special program like pread):

```
pwrite2() /* pipe data to cat */
{
    int pfd[2];

    if (pipe(pfd) == -1)
        syserr ("pipe");
    switch (fork()) {
    case -1:
        syserr("fork");
    case 0:
        if (close(0) == -1)
            syserr("close");
        if (dup(pfd[0]) != 0)
            fatal("dup");
        if (close(pfd[0]) == -1 || close(pfd[1]) == -1)
            syserr("close2");
        execlp("cat", "cat", NULL);
        syserr("execl");
    }
```

```
        if (close(pfd[0]) == -1)
            syserr("close3");
        if (write(pfd[1], "hello\n", 6) == -1)
            syserr("write");
        if (close(pfd[1]) == -1)
            syserr("close4");
    }
```

We got this unsurprising output:

hello

Note that we tested **dup** against 0 instead of −1. It's impossible for that **dup** to return anything other than 0 unless we've made a coding error or UNIX has gone haywire, so we didn't bother to distinguish the −1 case, for which we could have called **syserr**, from the wrong-number case. Note also that we closed **pfd[0]** immediately after duplicating it, because it was no longer needed. The parent closed **pfd[1]** after writing so that **cat** would get an end-of-file.

Incidentally, we might have been in big trouble if file descriptor 0 had been closed when we issued the call to **pipe**, for then 0 would have been one of the **pfd** numbers. When we then closed file descriptor 0, we would have lost one end of the pipe. The **dup** would have failed. This is one reason why it is vital to keep the standard file descriptors (0, 1, and 2) open at all times and to pass them on to all children. Too many algorithms, like the one we've just shown, assume a standard environment and go berserk when they don't find one.[2]

We don't have to limit ourselves to piping from parent to child. This example implements the equivalent of the shell command line:

who | wc

to see how many users are logged in.

```
who_wc()  /* who | wc */
{
    int pfd[2];

    if (pipe(pfd) == -1)
        syserr("pipe");
```

---

[2]Many years ago I accidentally brought a large UNIX system to its knees by invoking the text editor with too many file descriptors already open. The editor kept failing to open its temporary file and filled the /tmp directory with all the possible temporary file names. It thought the names were taken by another editor process, but actually the problem was that 15 (the number in those days) file descriptors were already open (errno either hadn't yet been invented or else simply wasn't checked). Nobody could edit at all and everyone assumed the system had crashed. Clearing /tmp restored the system's sanity.

```
switch (fork()) {
case -1:
    syserr("fork");
case 0:
    if (close(1) == -1)
        syserr("close");
    if (dup(pfd[1]) != 1)
        fatal("dup");
    if (close(pfd[0]) == -1 || close(pfd[1]) == -1)
        syserr("close2");
    execlp("who", "who", NULL);
    syserr("execl");
}
switch (fork()) {
case -1:
    syserr("fork");
case 0:
    if (close(0) == -1)
        syserr("close3");
    if (dup(pfd[0]) != 0)
        fatal("dup2");
    if (close(pfd[0]) == -1 || close(pfd[1]) == -1)
        syserr("close4");
    execlp("wc", "wc", NULL);
    syserr("execl2");
}
if (close(pfd[0]) == -1 || close(pfd[1]) == -1)
    syserr("close5");
while (wait(NULL) != -1)
    ;
}
```

This is the output:[3]

$$1 \ 5 \ 30$$

Of course, it's much easier to use a shell to set up a command line like this than it is to write a custom program. In the next section we'll code such a shell.

6.4 A REAL SHELL

Our shell is a subset of the standard UNIX shell, s h. It has these features:

- A *simple command* consists of a command name followed by an optional sequence of arguments separated by blanks or tabs, each of which is a single

---

[3]I use a personal computer, so only I am ever logged in.

word or a string surrounded by double quotes ("). If quoted, an argument may include any otherwise special characters (| , ; , &, >, <, blank, tab, and newline). An included quote or backslash must be preceded with a backslash (\ " or \ \ ). A command may have up to 20 arguments, each of which may have up to 200 characters.

- A simple command's standard input (file descriptor 0) may be redirected to come from a file by preceding the file name with <. Similarly, the standard output (file descriptor 1) may be redirected with >, which truncates the output file. If the output redirection symbol is > >, the output is appended to the file. An output file is created if it doesn't exist.

- A *pipeline* consists of a sequence of one or more simple commands separated with bars (|). Each except the last simple command in a pipeline has its standard output connected, via a pipe, to the standard input of its right neighbor.

- A pipeline is terminated with a newline, a semicolon (;), or an ampersand (&). In the first two cases the shell waits for the rightmost simple command to terminate before continuing. In the ampersand case, the shell does not wait. It reports the process number of each simple command in the pipeline, and each simple command is run with interrupt and quit signals ignored.

- Built-in commands are assignment, s e t, e x p o r t, and c d. The first three of these are described in Sec. 5.3. c d works in the familiar way.

The first step is to parse input lines into *tokens*, which are groups of characters that form syntactic units; examples are words, quoted strings, and special symbols such as & and > >. Each token is represented by a symbolic constant, as follows:

T _ W O R D	An argument or file name. If quoted, the quotes are removed after the token is recognized.
T _ B A R	The symbol	.
T _ A M P	The symbol &.
T _ S E M I	The symbol ; .
T _ G T	The symbol >.
T _ G T G T	The symbol > >.
T _ L T	The symbol <.
T _ N L	A newline.
T _ E O F	A special token signifying that the end-of-file has been reached. If the standard input is a terminal, the user has typed an EOT (Control-D).

The job of a *lexical analyzer* is to read the input and assemble the characters into tokens. Each time it is called, one token is returned. If the token is T _ W O R D, a string containing the actual characters composing it is also returned (for the other tokens the actual characters are obvious). The lexical analyzer should bypass irrelevant characters, such as blanks separating arguments, without returning anything.[4]

Our lexical analyzer is a finite-state-machine: As characters are read they are either recognized immediately as tokens or they are accumulated (characters of a word, for example). With each character, the lexical analyzer can switch into a new state which serves to remember what it is doing and how characters are to be interpreted. For example, when accumulating a quoted string, blanks are treated differently than when they appear outside quotes. For our shell we need four states:

NEUTRAL
: The starting state. Blanks and tabs are skipped. The characters |, &, ;, <, and newline are recognized immediately as tokens. The character > causes a switch to state GTGT, which will see if it is followed by another >, since > and >> are two different tokens. A quote causes a switch to state INQUOTE, which gathers a quoted string. Anything else is taken as the beginning of an unquoted word. The character is saved in a buffer and the state is switched to INWORD.

GTGT
: This state means that > was just read. If the next character is also >, the token T_GTGT is returned. Otherwise, T_GT will be returned. But first, we've read one character too many, so we put it back on the input (the Standard I/O Library provides the function ungetc for this purpose).

INQUOTE
: This state means that a starting quote was read. We accumulate characters into a buffer until the closing quote is read. Then we return the token T_WORD and the accumulated string. Special steps must be taken to process the escape character \.

INWORD
: This state means that the first character of a word was read and has been put into the buffer. We keep accumulating characters until a nonword character is read (|, say). We put the gratuitous character back on the input and return the token T_WORD.

With this explanation, the code for our lexical analyzer, gettoken, should be readily understandable:

_____

[4]Most UNIX systems include a command called lex that can automatically generate a lexical analyzer from a description of the tokens it is to recognize. Because lex is complicated to use, and because the lexical analyzers it generates are big and slow, it's usually preferable to code lexical analyzers by hand. They aren't difficult programs to write.

```
typedef enum {T_WORD, T_BAR, T_AMP, T_SEMI, T_GT, T_GTGT, T_LT,
  T_NL, T_EOF} TOKEN;

static TOKEN gettoken(word)  /* collect and classify token */
char *word;
{
    enum {NEUTRAL, GTGT, INQUOTE, INWORD} state = NEUTRAL;
    int c;
    char *w;

    w = word;
    while ((c = getchar()) != EOF) {
        switch (state) {
        case NEUTRAL:
            switch (c) {
            case ';':
                return(T_SEMI);
            case '&':
                return(T_AMP);
            case '|':
                return(T_BAR);
            case '<':
                return(T_LT);
            case '\n':
                return(T_NL);
            case ' ':
            case '\t':
                continue;
            case '>':
                state = GTGT;
                continue;
            case '"':
                state = INQUOTE;
                continue;
            default:
                state = INWORD;
                *w++ = c;
                continue;
            }
        case GTGT:
            if (c == '>')
                return(T_GTGT);
            ungetc(c, stdin);
            return(T_GT);
```

```
    case INQUOTE:
        switch (c) {
        case '\\':
            *w++ = getchar();
            continue;
        case '"':
            *w = '\0';
            return(T_WORD);
        default:
            *w++ = c;
            continue;
        }
    case INWORD:
        switch (c) {
        case ';':
        case '&':
        case '|':
        case '<':
        case '>':
        case '\n':
        case ' ':
        case '\t':
            ungetc(c, stdin);
            *w = '\0';
            return(T_WORD);
        default:
            *w++ = c;
            continue;
        }
    }
}
return(T_EOF);
}
```

When coding a large program, it's convenient to debug it in pieces. This not only provides early feedback, but it makes finding bugs easier since there are fewer lines of code to search. Here is the throwaway program we wrote to test gettoken:

```
main() /* test gettoken */
{
    char word[200];

    while (1)
        switch (gettoken(word)) {
        case T_WORD:
            printf("T_WORD <%s>\n", word);
            break;
```

```
                    case T_BAR:
                        printf("T_BAR\n");
                        break;
                    case T_AMP:
                        printf("T_AMP\n");
                        break;
                    case T_SEMI:
                        printf("T_SEMI\n");
                        break;
                    case T_GT:
                        printf("T_GT\n");
                        break;
                    case T_GTGT:
                        printf("T_GTGT\n");
                        break;
                    case T_LT:
                        printf("T_LT\n");
                        break;
                    case T_NL:
                        printf("T_NL\n");
                        break;
                    case T_EOF:
                        printf("T_EOF\n");
                        exit(0);
                    }
            }
```

When we ran this program and typed this line (followed by an EOT):

```
sort <inf | pr -h "Sept. Results" >>outf&
```

we got this output:

```
                T_WORD <sort>
                T_LT
                T_WORD <inf>
                T_BAR
                T_WORD <pr>
                T_WORD <-h>
                T_WORD <Sept. Results>
                T_GTGT
                T_WORD <outf>
                T_AMP
                T_NL
                T_EOF
```

This test doesn't prove that g e t t o k e n is correct, but it's encouraging enough for us to go on with more of the shell.

The next step is to write a function to process a simple command, which is terminated by |, &, ;, or a newline. We'll call this function c o m m a n d. Arguments are simply entered into an a r g v array for later use in a call to e x e c v p. There are three possibilities for the standard input: the default (file descriptor 0), a file (if < was present), or the reading end of a pipe (if this simple command was *preceded* by |). The standard output has four possibilities: the default (file descriptor 1), a file to be created or truncated (if > was present), a file to be created or appended to (if >> was present), or the writing end of a pipe (if this simple command was *followed* by a |). The tokens received from g e t t o k e n tell us which possibilities obtain.

As c o m m a n d processes the tokens, it uses these variables to record the standard input and output situation for a simple command:

s r c f d	The source file descriptor, initially 0. If input is redirected with <, s r c f d is set to B A D F D (−2) and s r c f i l e records the file name. If the input is a pipe, s r c f d will take on a number greater than 0.
s r c f i l e	The source file. It contains valid data only when the simple command includes a <.
d s t f d	The destination file descriptor, initially 1. If output is redirected with > or >>, it is set to B A D F D and d s t f i l e records the file name. It takes on a number greater than 1 if the output is a pipe.
a p p e n d	This Boolean variable is set to T R U E if output was redirected with >>. It is set to F A L S E if redirected with >. It is uninitialized otherwise.
m a k e p i p e	This is an argument to c o m m a n d. If T R U E, the caller is requesting that c o m m a n d make a pipe, use the reading end as its standard input, and pass the file descriptor for the writing end back to the caller, who will use it for its standard output. This scheme will be explained shortly.

As it goes through the tokens, c o m m a n d also checks for logical errors: two occurrences of < or >, the occurrence of > when the simple command terminates with |, the occurrence of < when the simple command is preceded with |, and so on. It's interesting that the standard UNIX shell doesn't check for some of these anomalies: You can actually run a command line like this:

```
who >outf | wc
```

The function c o m m a n d returns the token that terminated the pipeline, because the type of terminator affects later processing: If the terminator is &, the rightmost simple command is not waited for, and all simple commands in the pipeline are run with interrupt and quit signals ignored. If the rightmost simple command is to be waited for, its process-ID must be returned too, through the argument `waitpid`. If the terminator is a newline, the user is prompted for a new command.

The most subtle thing about `command` is that it calls itself recursively when a simple command is followed by `|`. Recursive calls continue until one of the other terminators (`;`, `&`, or newline) is reached. Each recursive call is responsible for actually making the pipe (with the `pipe` system call), and its argument `makepipe` is therefore set to `TRUE`. The writing pipe file descriptor is passed back (through another argument, `pipefdp`). A simple command is not actually invoked (with the function `invoke`) until after the recursive call returns, since it can't be invoked until the writing end of the pipe is available. Also, as stated above, the pipeline terminator must be known before any of the constituent simple commands can be invoked, so that `invoke` will know what to do about signals. Thus pipelines are processed from left to right, but the simple commands are invoked from right to left. There is one call to `command`, with `makepipe` set to `FALSE`, for the leftmost simple command; and then one more recursive call, with `makepipe` set to `TRUE`, for each additional simple command. As the stack of `command` calls returns, the simple commands are invoked—all needed information is available then.

Here is the code for `command`. It's worth careful study.

```
static TOKEN command(waitpid, makepipe, pipefdp) /* do simple cmd */
int *waitpid, *pipefdp;
BOOLEAN makepipe;
{
    TOKEN token, term, gettoken();
    int argc, srcfd, dstfd, pid, pfd[2];
    char *argv[MAXARG + 1], srcfile[MAXFNAME], dstfile[MAXFNAME];
    char word[MAXWORD], *malloc();
    BOOLEAN append;

    argc = 0;
    srcfd = 0;
    dstfd = 1;
    while (1) {
        switch (token = gettoken(word)) {
        case T_WORD:
            if (argc == MAXARG) {
                fprintf(stderr, "Too many args\n");
                break;
            }
```

```
        if ((argv[argc] = malloc(strlen(word) + 1)) == NULL) {
            fprintf(stderr, "Out of arg memory\n");
            break;
        }
        strcpy(argv[argc], word);
        argc++;
        continue;
    case T_LT:
        if (makepipe) {
            fprintf(stderr, "Extra <\n");
            break;
        }
        if (gettoken(srcfile) != T_WORD) {
            fprintf(stderr, "Illegal <\n");
            break;
        }
        srcfd = BADFD;
        continue;
    case T_GT:
    case T_GTGT:
        if (dstfd != 1) {
            fprintf(stderr, "Extra > or >>\n");
            break;
        }
        if (gettoken(dstfile) != T_WORD) {
            fprintf(stderr, "Illegal > or >>\n");
            break;
        }
        dstfd = BADFD;
        append = token == T_GTGT;
        continue;
    case T_BAR:
    case T_AMP:
    case T_SEMI:
    case T_NL:
        argv[argc] = NULL;
        if (token == T_BAR) {
            if (dstfd != 1) {
                fprintf(stderr, "> or >> conflicts with |\n");
                break;
            }
            term = command(waitpid, TRUE, &dstfd);
        }
        else
            term = token;
        if (makepipe) {
            if (pipe(pfd) == -1)
                syserr("pipe");
```

```
                    *pipefdp = pfd[1];
                    srcfd = pfd[0];
            }
            pid = invoke(argc, argv, srcfd, srcfile, dstfd, dstfile,
                append, term == T_AMP);
            if (token != T_BAR)
                *waitpid = pid;
            if (argc == 0 && (token != T_NL || srcfd > 1))
                fprintf(stderr, "Missing command\n");
            while (--argc >= 0)
                free(argv[argc]);
            return(term);
        case T_EOF:
            exit(0);
        }
    }
}
```

Once command has sensed the need for a pipe by encountering the token T_BAR, why does it ask the next call to command to make the pipe instead of making it itself and just passing on the reading file descriptor? It is to conserve file descriptors. If the pipe system call were called before command, instead of after, each level of recursion—each simple command—would tie up two pipe file descriptors which could not be closed until after the recursive call returned. Since there is a limit of 20 file descriptors, pipelines would be limited to about eight simple commands. By asking the reader to make the pipe, we can call pipe just before we call invoke, if our caller asked us to make one, thereby allowing pipelines to be of any length.

Here's the main program that makes the first call to command. It's modeled on the main program for the one-shot shell in Sec. 5.3.

```
        main() /* real shell */
        {
            char *prompt;
            int pid, fd;
            TOKEN term, command();

            ignoresig();
            if (!EVinit())
                fatal("can't initialize environment");
            if ((prompt = EVget("PS2")) == NULL)
                prompt = "> ";
            printf("%s", prompt);
```

```
    while (1) {
        term = command(&pid, FALSE, NULL);
        if (term != T_AMP && pid != 0)
            waitfor(pid);
        if (term == T_NL)
            printf("%s", prompt);
        for (fd = 3; fd < 20; fd++)
            (void)close(fd);  /* ignore error */
    }
}
```

The call to ignoresig causes interrupt and quit signals to be ignored—we don't want to kill our shell when we hit the interrupt or quit keys. We'll show the code for ignoresig in Sec. 8.3. The pipeline terminator returned by command tells us whether to wait for the rightmost simple command to terminate (we'll see waitfor shortly) and whether to prompt. After each pipeline we close all but the standard file descriptors, just in case an error caused command to leave some open.

command calls invoke to invoke a simple command. It passes on the command arguments (argc and argv) and the source and destination variables described earlier (srcfd, srcfile, dstfd, dstfile, and append). The last argument tells invoke whether the simple command is to be run in the background. The fork and exec scheme used by invoke should by now be familiar (review Sec. 5.4 if it isn't):

```
static int invoke(argc, argv, srcfd, srcfile, dstfd, dstfile,
    append, bckgrnd)                    /* invoke simple command */
int argc, srcfd, dstfd;
char *argv[], *srcfile, *dstfile;
BOOLEAN append, bckgrnd;
{
    int pid;
    BOOLEAN builtin();

    if (argc == 0 || builtin(argc, argv, srcfd, dstfd))
        return(0);
    switch (pid = fork()) {
    case -1:
        fprintf(stderr, "Can't create new process\n");
        return(0);
    case 0:
        if (!bckgrnd)
            entrysig();
        if (!EVupdate())
            fatal("can't update environment");
        redirect(srcfd, srcfile, dstfd, dstfile, append, bckgrnd);
        execvp(argv[0], argv);
```

```
            fprintf(stderr, "Can't execute %s\n", argv[0]);
            exit(0);
        default:
            if (srcfd > 0 && close(srcfd) == -1)
                syserr("close src");
            if (dstfd > 1 && close(dstfd) == -1)
                syserr("close dst");
            if (bckgrnd)
                printf("%d\n", pid);
            return(pid);
        }
}
```

The command to be invoked may be built in. If so, b u i l t i n (to be shown shortly) returns T R U E. If not, a child process is created to run the simple command. Recall that interrupt and quit signals are already ignored. If the command is not to be run in the background, they are restored to the way they were on entry to the shell with a call to e n t r y s i g (detailed in Sec. 8.3).

    i n v o k e calls r e d i r e c t to redirect I/O and to ensure that the source and destination are file descriptors 0 and 1. Here is the code for r e d i r e c t:

```
static void redirect(srcfd, srcfile, dstfd, dstfile, append, bckgrnd)
                                                    /* I/O redirection */
int srcfd, dstfd;
char *srcfile, *dstfile;
BOOLEAN append, bckgrnd;
{
    int flags, fd;
    long lseek();

    if (srcfd == 0 && bckgrnd) {
        strcpy(srcfile, "/dev/null");
        srcfd = BADFD;
    }
    if (srcfd != 0) {
        if (close(0) == -1)
            syserr("close");
        if (srcfd > 0) {
            if (dup(srcfd) != 0)
                fatal("dup");
        }
        else if (open(srcfile, O_RDONLY, 0) == -1) {
            fprintf(stderr, "Can't open %s\n", srcfile);
            exit(0);
        }
    }
```

```
    if (dstfd != 1) {
        if (close(1) == -1)
            syserr("close");
        if (dstfd > 1) {
            if (dup(dstfd) != 1)
                fatal("dup");
        }
        else {
            flags = O_WRONLY | O_CREAT;
            if (!append)
                flags |= O_TRUNC;
            if (open(dstfile, flags, 0666) == -1) {
                fprintf(stderr, "Can't create %s\n", dstfile);
                exit(0);
            }
            if (append)
                if (lseek(1, 0L, 2) == -1)
                    syserr("lseek");
        }
    }
    for (fd = 3; fd < 20; fd++)
        (void)close(fd); /* ignore error */
}
```

If a background command does not have its standard input redirected to come from a file or a pipe, we take the precaution of redirecting it to the special file /dev/null, which gives an immediate end-of-file when read. This prevents the ugly situation of two processes simultaneously reading the user's keyboard. The rest of redirect should be clear. Note that open, like dup, always uses the lowest-numbered available file descriptor.

In all code executed by the child process, we call exit(0) when an error is discovered, rather than the more usual exit(1). This is to distinguish between errors caught directly by the shell, such as a file that can't be opened, and errors committed by the invoked program. In the latter case we want the shell to print the exit code; in the former case a simple message suffices. Indeed, if we printed an exit code when the child terminates without completing the exec, the user would be confused—exit from what? Only UNIX system programmers are supposed to know about the separation of fork and exec.

waitfor (called from the main program) is an extension to code presented in Sec. 5.6 (the function execut3). It is told what process to wait for, but during the wait it may learn of other terminations. If so, it uses statusprt to print their process-IDs and a description of the reason for their termination, if abnormal. When the designated process terminates, waitfor calls statusprt and returns. Here's the code:

```
static void waitfor(pid)  /* wait for child */
int pid;
{
    int wpid, status;

    while ((wpid = wait(&status)) != pid && wpid != -1)
        statusprt(wpid, status);
    if (wpid == pid)
        statusprt(0, status);
}
```

Finally, here is bui lt in. Most of it is taken from Sec. 5.3; we've added code to handle the c d command. c d without arguments changes to the directory whose path is given by the HOME environment variable.

```
static BOOLEAN builtin(argc, argv, srcfd, dstfd)  /* do built-in */
int argc, srcfd, dstfd;
char *argv[];
{
    char *path;

    if (strchr(argv[0], '=') != NULL)
        asg(argc, argv);
    else if (strcmp(argv[0], "export") == 0)
        export(argc, argv);
    else if (strcmp(argv[0], "set") == 0)
        set(argc, argv);
    else if (strcmp(argv[0], "cd") == 0) {
        if (argc > 1)
            path = argv[1];
        else
            if ((path = EVget("HOME")) == NULL)
                path = ".";
        if (chdir(path) == -1)
            fprintf(stderr, "%s: bad directory\n", path);
    }
    else
        return(FALSE);
    if (srcfd != 0 || dstfd != 1)
        fprintf(stderr, "Illegal redirection or pipeline\n");
    return(TRUE);
}
```

You may have observed that some errors discovered by our shell are fatal (calls to syserr and fatal), while others just cause a message to be printed, after which the shell keeps running. We've made the ''impossible'' errors fatal, since if they occur it means that the operating system is mortally wounded. This is a compromise: We certainly don't want to ignore these errors, since the impossible has been known to happen, but we're too lazy to print a message and recover from a situation that will probably never occur. Sometimes we guess wrong—a fatal error keeps occurring because it's not impossible after all. Then we have to revise the code to handle the error differently.

We won't show any example of this shell in use. We don't have to, because it behaves just like the standard shell.

6.5 BIDIRECTIONAL PIPES

Now we want to move beyond one-way pipelines, as used by the shell, to two-way pipelines. The standard shell, s h, offers no notation to set up two-way communication between processes (there are experimental shells that do). Two-way pipelines are set up from C programs.

We'll start with a fairly simple example. From within a program we want to invoke the s o r t command to sort some data. Of course, we could do it like this:

```
system("sort <data >output");
```

Then we could read the contents of out put to access the sorted data. We don't want to do it that way, however—we want to pipe the data to s o r t, and have s o r t pipe the sorted output back to us. Since s o r t can read and write its standard input and output (it's a filter), we should be able to use it the way we want. We already know how to force an arbitrary file descriptor to be the standard input or output of a process.

Just as a baby learns to fall down before learning to walk, we'll begin by doing the job incorrectly. That way we'll learn more about how to do it properly than if we just presented the solution right off the bat.

Since every pipe has both a reading end and a writing end, and since both file descriptors are inherited by a child process, we'll use just one pipe. s o r t will read it to get its input and write it to send back the sorted output. The parent has file descriptors that access the pipe too. It will write the unsorted data to the pipe and read the sorted data from the pipe. Here's a program that reads data from the file d a t a and invokes s o r t to sort it. The sorted data is printed.

```
fsort0() /* sort data file (wrong) */
{
    int pfd[2], fd, nread;
    char buf[512];

    if (pipe(pfd) == -1)
        syserr("pipe");
```

```
switch (fork()) {
case -1:
    syserr("fork");
case 0:
    if (close(0) == -1)
        syserr("close");
    if (dup(pfd[0]) != 0)
        fatal("dup");
    if (close(1) == -1)
        syserr("close");
    if (dup(pfd[1]) != 1)
        fatal("dup");
    if (close(pfd[0]) == -1 || close(pfd[1]) == -1)
        syserr("close");
    execlp("sort", "sort", NULL);
    syserr("execl");
}
if ((fd = open("data", 0)) == -1)
    syserr("open");
while ((nread = read(fd, buf, sizeof(buf))) != 0) {
    if (nread == -1)
        syserr("read");
    if (write(pfd[1], buf, nread) == -1)
        syserr("write");
}
if (close(fd) == -1 || close(pfd[1]) == -1)
    syserr("close");
while ((nread = read(pfd[0], buf, sizeof(buf))) != 0) {
    if (nread == -1)
        syserr("read");
    if (write(1, buf, nread) == -1)
        syserr("write");
}
if (close(pfd[0]) == -1)
    syserr("close");
}
```

This is what's in the file **data**:

```
peach
apple
orange
strawberry
plum
pear
cherry
banana
```

```
apricot
tomato
pineapple
mango
```

When we ran this program it printed the fruits just as they appeared in d a t a—unsorted—and then hung. We had to hit the interrupt key to kill it. What went wrong?

There were two problems with using just one pipe. First of all, after writing the unsorted data to the pipe, the parent immediately began to read the pipe, assuming that it would read the output of s o r t. But it got there before s o r t did, and just read its own output right back! So the data was printed in its unsorted form. This is reminiscent of the first example in Sec. 6.2.

The second problem caused the deadlock. The child process, running s o r t, began to read its standard input, which happened to be empty since its parent had already emptied it. Empty or not, s o r t would have blocked in a r e a d system call waiting for an end-of-file, which would occur only when the writing end was closed. Sure enough, the parent had already closed the writing end. But the *child* still had it open—after all, the child was supposed to write its output there. So the child was stuck. Generally, any filter tricked into reading and writing the same pipe will deadlock.

One might try to fix the first problem by having the parent wait for the child to terminate before reading the pipe. At first, this sounds appealing. It won't work, however, if the child's output fills the pipe, which it might if we're sorting a large amount of data, because the child will block in the w r i t e system call. With the parent blocked in w a i t, we'll have deadlock again.

Next, one might add some semaphores to synchronize things without causing deadlock. There are two disadvantages to this solution. First, until System V, no AT&T version of UNIX offered semaphores, so this solution is unavailable to a large segment of the UNIX population. Second, and more important, the problem goes away completely if one just uses *two* pipes, each of which handles only one-way traffic. One pipe handles data flowing into s o r t, and the other pipe handles data flowing back. Here is a rewrite of f s o r t 0 that works correctly:

```
fsort() /* sort data file (right) */
{
    int pfdout[2], pfdin[2], fd, nread;
    char buf[512];

    if (pipe(pfdout) == -1 || pipe(pfdin) == -1)
        syserr("pipe");
    switch (fork()) {
    case -1:
        syserr("fork");
```

```
    case 0:
        if (close(0) == -1)
            syserr("close");
        if (dup(pfdout[0]) != 0)
            fatal("dup");
        if (close(1) == -1)
            syserr("close");
        if (dup(pfdin[1]) != 1)
            fatal("dup");
        if (close(pfdout[0]) == -1 || close(pfdout[1]) == -1 ||
          close(pfdin[0]) == -1 || close(pfdin[1]) == -1)
            syserr("close");
        execlp("sort", "sort", NULL);
        syserr("execl");
    }
    if (close(pfdout[0]) == -1 || close(pfdin[1]) == -1)
        syserr("close");
    if ((fd = open("data", 0)) == -1)
        syserr("open");
    while ((nread = read(fd, buf, sizeof(buf))) != 0) {
        if (nread == -1)
            syserr("read");
        if (write(pfdout[1], buf, nread) == -1)
            syserr("write");
    }
    if (close(fd) == -1 || close(pfdout[1]) == -1)
        syserr("close");
    while ((nread = read(pfdin[0], buf, sizeof(buf))) != 0) {
        if (nread == -1)
            syserr("read");
        if (write(1, buf, nread) == -1)
            syserr("write");
    }
    if (close(pfdin[0]) == -1)
        syserr("close");
}
```

Here's the output we got this time:

```
                apple
                apricot
                banana
                cherry
                mango
                orange
                peach
```

```
pear
pineapple
plum
strawberry
tomato
```

Not only is it sorted, but the program stopped all by itself! The interesting thing about the correct version is that although it uses one more pipe, no additional file descriptors are consumed. In both versions parent and child need to read and write to each other, so each needs two pipe file descriptors. In the second version the parent can close the reading end of `pfdout` and the writing end of `pfdin`.

In general, deadlock is still possible with two pipes, although not in our example using `sort`. Deadlock would occur if the parent blocks writing its output pipe because it is full, and the child, instead of emptying it, writes enough output back to the parent to block on the other pipe. Each case must be examined carefully to ensure that it is always deadlock free, and not only for small amounts of test data.

There are other ways to get deadlocked. To explore one of these, we'll look at a more complex example of two-way interprocess communication. Here the child is the standard line editor, `ed`. The parent is using the editor as a subroutine,[5] sending editor command lines to it and getting the output back. Such an arrangement might be used by a screen editor, where the parent handles the keyboard and screen, but lets `ed` do the actual editing. We don't have space to show a screen editor, so our example will have to be ridiculously simple. It's an interactive search program, much like `grep`. Here's a sample session:

```
$ search

File? data

Search pattern? ^a
apple
apricot

Search pattern? apple
apple
pineapple

Search pattern? o$
tomato
mango

Search pattern? EOT
$
```

[5]More precisely, *coroutine*.

The fruit data file is from the sorting examples, above.

When we used sort, we knew when to stop reading its output: when we reached an end-of-file. The situation was simple because sort reads all its input, writes all its output, and then terminates. The editor, however, is interactive. It reads some input, may or may not write some output of indeterminate length, and then goes back to read some more input. We can capture its output by making its standard output a pipe, but how do we know how much to read at a time? We can't wait for an end-of-file, for the editor won't close its output file descriptor until it terminates. If we read too far we'll deadlock, and if we don't read far enough we'll lose synchronization between a command and its results.

If we could change the editor, we would have it send an unambiguous line of data whenever it is ready for more input. In fact, the editor does have the ability to prompt the user for input (enabled by the P command), but the prompt character is *—hardly unambiguous. Somehow we need to get the editor to tell us when it's done outputting the results of each command.

We'll use a trick, a kludge if there ever was one: After each command, issue an r (read file) command with a nonexistent file name, and look for the resulting error message. When this message shows up, we know the editor has responded to the bad r command and is ready for another command. The nonexistent file name should be such that the error message is unambiguous. It's probably best to use a name containing ASCII control characters, which rarely appear in text files, but for clarity we'll use the name end-of-file. To see the exact form of the message, we run the editor:

```
$ ed
r end-of-file
?end-of-file
q
$
```

So we have to look for ?end-of-file.

To make things easier, we'll code subroutines to handle interaction with the editor. At the start of processing we call edinvoke to invoke the editor and set up the pipes. Instead of using the file descriptors directly, which would require us to do I/O with read and write, we create Standard I/O Library file pointers instead, using fdopen. We can then write to the editor on sndfp and read from the editor on rcvfp. Here is edinvoke, which is a lot like the first part of fsort:

```
static FILE *sndfp, *rcvfp; /* used by edsnd and edrcv */

static edinvoke() /* invoke editor process */
{
    int pfdout[2], pfdin[2];
```

```
if (pipe(pfdout) == -1 || pipe(pfdin) == -1)
    syserr("pipe");
switch (fork()) {
case -1:
    syserr("fork");
case 0:
    if (close(0) == -1)
        syserr("close");
    if (dup(pfdout[0]) != 0)
        fatal("dup");
    if (close(1) == -1)
        syserr("close");
    if (dup(pfdin[1]) != 1)
        fatal("dup");
    if (close(pfdout[0]) == -1 || close(pfdout[1]) == -1 ||
      close(pfdin[0]) == -1 || close(pfdin[1]) == -1)
        syserr("close");
    execlp("ed", "ed", "-", NULL);
    syserr("execl");
}
if (close(pfdout[0]) == -1 || close(pfdin[1]) == -1)
    syserr("close");
sndfp = fdopen(pfdout[1], "w");
rcvfp = fdopen(pfdin[0], "r");
}
```

To write and read the pipe we use edsnd, edrcv, and turnaround. edrcv returns FALSE when no more editor output is available, which fact it knows because it has found the forced error message. To make sure the error message is there, turnaround must be called to switch from sending to receiving. Here are these three functions:

```
static void edsnd(s)  /* send line to editor */
char *s;
{
    if (fputs(s, sndfp) == EOF)
        fatal("edsnd");
}

static BOOLEAN edrcv(s, max) /* receive line from editor */
char *s;
int max;
{
    if (fgets(s, max, rcvfp) == NULL)
        fatal("edrcv");
    return(strcmp(s, "?end-of-file\n") != 0);
}
```

```
static void turnaround()  /* change from edsnd to edrcv */
{
    edsnd("r end-of-file\n");
    fflush(sndfp);
}
```

We flush `sndfp` so that the editor gets all our output. Remember that the Standard I/O Library normally buffers output to pipes.

Since we'll usually want to display everything the editor has to say, a function to do that will come in handy:

```
static void rcvall()  /* receive and print editor output */
{
    char s[200];

    turnaround();
    while (edrcv(s, sizeof(s)))
        printf("%s", s);
}
```

Last, the main program that conducts the dialogue with the user and communicates with the editor:

```
main()  /* interactive search program */
{
    char s[100], line[100];
    BOOLEAN prompt();

    edinvoke();
    if (!prompt("File", s))
        exit(0);
    sprintf(line, "e %s\n", s);
    edsnd(line);
    rcvall();
    while (prompt("Search pattern", s)) {
        sprintf(line, "g/%s/p\n", s);
        edsnd(line);
        rcvall();
    }
    edsnd("q\n");
    exit(0);
}

static BOOLEAN prompt(msg, result)  /* prompt user */
char *msg, *result;
{
    printf("\n%s? ", msg);
    return(gets(result) != NULL);
}
```

Is this program deadlock free? Since we know that the capacity of a pipe is at least 4096 bytes, the parent will never block while writing to the editor's input pipe, because our editor commands are quite short. The editor will never block, except temporarily, writing back to the parent, because the parent will read everything it has to say. There's no reason why the bad-file message should be missed, unless somebody actually makes a file with that name, which they had better not. Not much of a proof, but at least the obvious pitfalls have been avoided.

6.6 PORTABILITY

Except for nonblocking reads and writes, all of the concepts in this chapter are portable across all versions of UNIX. The portability of fcntl and the O_NDELAY flag is discussed in Sec. 3.14. The use of fcntl instead of dup is unnecessary, and O_NDELAY is seldom needed on pipes, so, to be portable, most software can simply skip these features.

The pipe and dup system calls work the way we've described them in all UNIX versions. Indeed, no system can claim to be UNIX unless these calls work in the standard way.

Version 7 and 4.2 BSD offer a version of dup called dup2, which is similar to fcntl in that you can supply the file descriptor number to be used for the duplicate. A difference is that it is closed first, if necessary, to guarantee that it will be used. However, dup2 is no more essential than is fcntl, and since it is missing from Systems III and V, it should be avoided.[6]

EXERCISES

6.1. Using the standard shell (sh) and/or the Berkeley shell (csh), try typing bad command lines to see what error message you get, if any. Try these examples for starters:

```
echo abc >f1 >f2
echo def | cat <f1
echo ghi >f1 | cat
cat <f1 <f2
echo jkl | | cat
echo jkl | >f1
```

6.2. Program dup in terms of fcntl.

---

[6]The designers of System III were correct in removing dup2 as a system call once the more general fcntl was added. But they should have supplied a dup2 subroutine for upward compatibility with Version 7.

6.3. In the function `gettoken` in Sec. 6.4, in state `INQUOTE`, when `getchar` is called there is no check for an end-of-file. Is this a problem? Why or why not?

6.4. Add parameter replacement (e.g., `echo $PATH`) to the shell in Sec. 6.4.

6.5. Add wild-cards (file-name generation) to the shell in Sec. 6.4. Restrict matching to the last component of path names (i.e., `ls */*.c` is illegal).

6.6. Same as Exercise 6.5, but without the restriction. Hint: Use recursion.

6.7. The shell of Sec. 6.4 makes all processes in a pipeline its children. The standard shell (`sh`) makes each process the child of the process to its right, and only the rightmost process is a child of the shell. Change the shell in Sec. 6.4 to set up parentage as the standard shell does.

6.8. Add a `goto` statement to the shell of Sec. 6.4.

6.9. Add an `if` statement to the shell of Sec. 6.4.

6.10. Design and implement a *menu shell*. Instead of prompting for commands, it displays a menu of choices and the user simply picks one. You'll need menus for command arguments too. Rather than building in the details of various commands, the shell should take its information about commands and their arguments from a database.

6.11. Design and implement a *window* system. You may use `curses` if you have access to it. Divide the terminal screen into two halves (which is easier—a horizontal or vertical split?). Run a shell process in each half. The user presses a function key to select the active window. A command running in the inactive window continues to output to the screen, but when input is requested it blocks until the user activates the window and types a response. A window scrolls when it gets full, but the user can scroll it back to see what disappeared (up to some limit). Hint: The hardest part is keeping one window's data from overwriting the other window. Design question: Should the standard output of a command go directly to the CRT, to a specially designed filter, or back to the window's shell?

6.12. After finishing Exercise 6.11 and polishing it to perfection, turn it over to a software publisher. Use your royalties to buy additional copies of this book.

6.13. Write a program that writes its process-ID to the standard output, and then reads a list of process-IDs from its standard input. If its own process-ID is on the list, it prints out the list (using file descriptor 2). Otherwise, it adds its process-ID to the list and writes the entire list to its standard output. Then it repeats. Arrange five processes running this program into a ring, and let them play a while (this is a computer game for a computer to play by itself).

6.14. Using a scheme similar to that of the interactive search program in Sec. 6.5, write a front-end to the desk calculator `dc` that allows the user to enter expressions in infix notation (`2 + 3`) instead of postfix (`2 3 +`). (This is what the `bc` command does.)

ADVANCED INTERPROCESS COMMUNICATION

7.1 INTRODUCTION

In 1973, only a few years after UNIX was invented, several organizations within Bell Laboratories began to use it as a basis for transaction-processing systems. These systems, built to automate telephone company administration and record keeping, consisted of terminals that accessed a database management system running on a PDP-11 minicomputer. Since then, hundreds of these so-called *operation support systems* have been installed throughout what was formerly known as the Bell System.

From the start, designers of these systems realized that UNIX lacked essential features for database management, mostly in the area of interprocess communication. Since UNIX was even smaller and simpler then than it is today, system programmers working in various application development groups simply added what they wanted to the kernel. Soon, a version of UNIX evolved that was well suited to database management. It included system calls to support interprocess messages, semaphores, and shared memory. This system was called Columbus UNIX, after the city in Ohio where its developers worked (at a branch laboratory). By the late 1970s it had become an internal standard for operation support systems, although it was almost unknown outside of Bell Laboratories. The externally released versions (up through System III) were not used internally for serious database management, and there was little interest in making them suitable for such tasks since Columbus UNIX was the preferred alternative.

156

The developers of System III added FIFOs to UNIX to make its interprocess communication more suitable for database management systems, but this failed to impress operation support system designers. They stuck with Columbus UNIX, which was more familiar and much faster. But with System V, interprocess communication features similar to those in Columbus UNIX were added to the externally released version, making the system viable for high-speed transaction processing for the first time. It is ironic that the outside world has viewed messages, semaphores, and shared memory as coming along about three years after FIFOs, whereas they actually preceded FIFOs by about five years.

We begin our exploration of these advanced interprocess communication facilities by introducing some database management system design issues that concern interprocess communication, since these facilities were originally added for that purpose. We'll next show how to use FIFOs, which are present in all versions of UNIX based on System III (including System V, Xenix 3, and PC/IX). Then we'll consider messages as implemented in System V, semaphores and shared memory as implemented in System V and Xenix 3, and record locking as implemented in Xenix 3 and PC/IX, and as defined in the /usr/group Proposed Standard.

One of our goals in this chapter is to develop a simple set of interprocess-communication primitives that can be implemented on several versions of UNIX, taking advantage of the unique efficiencies of each version. For example, we'll introduce a set of message-sending functions that use FIFOs, and then reimplement them using the message-handling system calls of System V. This scheme won't exploit every feature of the System V system calls (which are quite grandiose), but it will allow database management systems to be freely ported between those versions, while at the same time taking advantage of the increased efficiency of System V.

7.2 DATABASE MANAGEMENT SYSTEM ISSUES

For our purposes, we define a *database management system* (DBMS) as a software module that controls access to and maintains an information model of some enterprise. A DBMS consists of two main pieces: the permanent *database* that is kept in files (divided into records and fields, and indexed for efficient access), and *access primitives* that allow other modules—application programs—to store, retrieve, modify, and delete data. An application program that uses the DBMS is called a *client*.

In a *transaction-processing system* a form is displayed on the screen of a CRT terminal, a human operator fills out the blanks, and then the completed form is processed by an appropriate application program that accesses the DBMS to perform the requested task. The results are displayed on the screen.

Many human operators at many terminals may be accessing the same database simultaneously. Although there may be a separate application process and a separate copy of the access primitives for each operator, there can be only one copy of the data itself, so it must be shared. Hence, one important function of the DBMS is to control concurrent access to the data, so that one operator's actions don't interfere with another's.

We'll postpone a detailed discussion of concurrency control until Sec. 7.8. For now, just assume that there is a part of the DBMS called the *lock manager* that maintains a lock for each data record in use by a process. Another process cannot access a locked record until the first process unlocks it. Just as there is only one copy of the data, there can be only one lock manager. We'll get to the question of where it is shortly. Note, however, that the lock manager cannot be just another shared data file containing the locks, because then that file would be concurrently accessed and there must be some way to lock *it*. In other words, access to the lock manager must be controlled by some mechanism other than the lock manager.

There are two ways to organize the access primitives. In the *decentralized* approach they are simply a subroutine library that is bound into each application program; each application process has a separate copy of them. In the *centralized* approach the access primitives are in a unique DBMS process; an application process exercises a primitive by sending a message to the central DBMS process. A message containing the response (a status code or some data records) is sent back. To achieve good performance with the centralized approach, interprocess communication must be fast.

If it's feasible, the centralized approach is better. There is only one copy of the access primitives, saving memory and swap time. The DBMS, being a separate process, is protected from damage that might result from a faulty or devious application program. It can run with a separate user-ID, so the UNIX permission system can protect the data. Finally, since there is only one process that directly accesses the data, it can easily control concurrent access by keeping a table of locks in its own address space; no kernel locking facility is necessary or desirable. There is no concurrent access to the lock table, since only one process deals with it.

The decentralized approach is somewhat simpler to understand—subroutine libraries are commonplace. There need be no interprocess communication at all, so this approach is potentially faster and more portable. However, the lock manager cannot be decentralized, and that presents a serious obstacle to taking the decentralized approach. There are several solutions:

- Use the "head-in-the-sand" technique: Run the system without locks, and when users complain about strange results either pretend you don't hear them or blame it on the hardware.[1]

- Implement a centralized lock manager process, and use interprocess messages to communicate with it. Of course, if you're going to go to all this trouble you might as well centralize the whole DBMS.

- Implement a phony device driver that acts as a lock manager. This is easier than changing the kernel, and you don't need the kernel source code. Use the `fcntl` system call to set and clear locks.

[1] Don't laugh—this is more common than we'd like to admit!

- Use a version of UNIX that has a lock manager built into the kernel, such as Xenix 3 or PC/IX.

None of these alternatives is entirely satisfactory. Implementing a device driver sounds like a lot of work, and it is. If your version of the UNIX kernel has a lock manager, it's probably easy to use, but your system won't be portable. Moreover, the built-in lock manager may be too slow; for high-performance systems the lock manager often has to be designed along with the rest of the database software.

In summary, I recommend the centralized approach because it saves memory, it provides more reliability and security, it can be implemented with FIFOs *or* with messages, and it doesn't require kernel-provided locking.[2]

Now that we understand some DBMS basics, we can present some advanced interprocess communication primitives and see how they are used in DBMS implementation.

7.3 FIFOS, OR NAMED PIPES

A FIFO combines features of a file and a pipe. Like a file, it has a name, and any process with appropriate permissions may open it for reading or writing. Unlike with a pipe, then, unrelated processes may communicate over a FIFO, since they need not rely on inheritance alone to access it. Once opened, however, a FIFO acts more like a pipe than a file. Written data is read back in first-in-first-out order, and single write and read system calls are guaranteed to be atomic, provided the amount read or written doesn't exceed the capacity of the FIFO, which is the same as the capacity of a pipe (implementation dependent, but at least 4096 bytes). Data once read can't be read again, nor does lseek work.

Normally, when a FIFO is opened for reading, the open waits until it is also opened for writing, usually by another process. Similarly, an open for writing blocks until the FIFO is opened for reading. Hence, whichever process, reader or writer, executes the open first will wait for the other one. This allows the processes to synchronize themselves before the actual data transmission starts.

If the O_NDELAY flag is set on open, an open for reading returns immediately, without waiting for the writer, and an open for writing will return an error

---

[2]A common criticism of UNIX is that it lacks record locking. For example, in a single issue of *Computerworld Extra* (Sept. 26, 1984), one writer stated that "a major contribution of the /usr/group effort is agreement on a standard method for [record] locking. . . . This feature is critically needed in commercial multiuser applications. . . ." and another writer stated that "features such as record and file locking . . . are generally considered necessary for commercial operating systems." This last statement is remarkable in view of the fact that IBM's OS (MVS), surely the most successful commercial operating system, does *not* provide record locking—it is provided by the centralized DBMS, which is usually IMS. Over a dozen years of Bell Laboratories experience implementing very high performance transaction-processing systems has shown record locking to be unnecessary in UNIX too. The kernel needs to provide record locking about as much as it needs to provide trigonometric functions.

if no reader has the FIFO open. This asymmetry implies that O_NDELAY is useful when opening for reading but awkward when opening for writing, since the error has to be processed and then perhaps the open has to be retried. The intent is to prevent a process from putting data into a FIFO that will not be read immediately, because UNIX has no way of storing data in FIFOs permanently. As with a water pipe, you have no business turning on the water until both ends are soldered in. If any data is still in a FIFO when all readers and writers close their file descriptors, the data is discarded with no error indication. This is like a water pipe too: The water leaks out if you disconnect the pipe at both ends.

The O_NDELAY flag affects read and write on FIFOs just as it does on pipes. That is, if the flag is clear then the reader blocks until some data is available, and the writer blocks when the FIFO gets full. If the flag is set then neither blocks, but an error is returned instead.

We showed how to call mknod to make a FIFO in Sec. 3.8, and we showed how to interrogate it with stat and fstat in Sec. 3.12.

An obvious use for a FIFO is as a replacement for a pipe. Instead of using the pipe system call, you make a FIFO instead and then open it twice, to get read and write file descriptors. From then on you can treat it like a pipe. Used this way, however, FIFOs have absolutely no advantages over pipes, and several disadvantages: extra overhead in making the FIFO, two system calls to get file descriptors, and the risk of a name clash (just as with a temporary file).

FIFOs weren't added to UNIX to replace *pipes*—they were added to replace *messages*, which many system programmers inside Bell Laboratories insisted were necessary for efficient DBMS implementation. Actually, the idea of named pipes was well known since the early 1970s, but stayed on the back burner until about 1978, when System III was produced. The developers of System III felt that messages were too awkward to add to UNIX, whereas FIFOs were simple, effective, and elegant. Anyone who reads the System V UNIX manual pages for the message system calls is likely to agree.

7.4 IMPLEMENTING MESSAGES WITH FIFOS

Plain FIFOs don't work well as message carriers—some additional mechanism has to be added. We'll show how to do this by implementing two primitives, send and receive. Then we'll use these primitives in several example applications, culminating with a centralized DBMS that can handle multiple clients.

Here are the send and receive headers:

```
BOOLEAN send(dstkey, buf, nbytes)   /* send message */
    long dstkey;                    /* destination key */
    char *buf;                      /* pointer to message data */
    int nbytes;                     /* number of bytes in message */
    /* returns TRUE on success or FALSE on error */
```

```
BOOLEAN receive(srckey, buf, nbytes)    /* receive message */
long srckey;                            /* source key */
char *buf;
int nbytes;
/* returns TRUE on success or FALSE on error */
```

Messages are sent to a *queue*, identified by a long integer called the *key*. buf points to the message, which is nbytes bytes in length. Note that the arguments resemble those of read and write. This is intentional.

Messages sent to a queue are deposited there in order of arrival. A message may consist of any arbitrary data, but it must begin with a long integer that is unused. That is, a message might be structured like this:

```
struct msgdata {
    long unused;
    char data[100];
};
```

This allows room for 100 bytes of message data. The long integer at the beginning will be used in Sec. 7.5 when we reimplement send and receive to use System V messages; we have no need for it now. The header declares buf as a pointer to a char instead of a pointer to a struct msgdata because the actual structure will vary with the application, as we shall see.

The queue can get full. If it does, send blocks until it empties enough to hold the message being sent.

receive takes the oldest message off the queue and copies it to storage pointed to by buf. At most, nbytes of data are copied. The extra bytes may either be left on the queue or discarded, at the discretion of the implementor (again, we're hedging so we can implement things differently later on). Either way, it is a serious error if the nbytes argument to receive does not exactly equal the corresponding argument to the call to send that deposited the message. You must either make all messages the same size (recommended) or else arrange for the receiver to know the size of the message at the head of the queue.

In order for two processes to communicate with send and receive they must know each other's receiving queue keys. Each can then send messages to the other's queue. They could communicate with only one queue, but they then have to synchronize themselves to avoid the same problems we saw in Sec. 6.5, which we avoided by using two pipes instead of one for two-way communication. In the case of a centralized DBMS and its clients, the DBMS's queue key should be established in advance and told to each client; an environment variable (DBMSKEY, say) is ideal for this. Each client makes up its own key, which can simply be its process number, since that guarantees uniqueness. A client passes its key to the DBMS with each request for service so the DBMS knows on which queue to respond. This is analogous to ordering something from a mail-order catalog: The catalog company's address is prominently advertised so anyone can send it mail, but it can mail your order back to you only if you include a return address.

Here's how to implement send and receive with FIFOs: A queue is a FIFO. We'll construct its name by converting the key to a string and prefixing it with /tmp/fifo. For example, the queue corresponding to key 12345 would be /tmp/fifo12345.

Our implementation must avoid two major problems. First, we don't want a sender to block permanently if the expected receiver never opens its FIFO for reading. This might hang the DBMS if a client terminates abnormally, which would deny service to all clients. But we also don't want the sender to give up too soon if the receiver isn't ready, because in starting the application system we have to create several processes (the DBMS and its initial clients), and it might take a few seconds for every participant to get rolling. So a sender sets O_NDELAY when opening a FIFO for writing, and, if it fails because no reader had the FIFO open, it sleeps for a while and tries again. After a few times it gives up. The symbolic constant NAPTIME is equal to the number of seconds to sleep; MAXTRIES is equal to the number of tries (this is the same approach we used back in Sec. 2.5).

We care a lot less about whether the receiver blocks. We expect the DBMS to wait patiently if it has no clients—either one will shortly show up or else there's no work to be done, in which case blocking doesn't matter. A client can safely block waiting for the DBMS to respond—if the DBMS isn't working right it will be fixed by its caretakers, and the clients are useless without it anyhow. Of course, these assumptions may not apply in every situation. If you like, you can easily change receive to use the same short-term-blocking technique that send uses.

The second major problem is that a DBMS with many clients can easily run out of file descriptors (20 per process). It has three standard file descriptors (0, 1, and 2), one for its receiving queue, one for each client's queue, and one for each data file. DBMSs with more than a dozen data files and with dozens of clients are common. Since all client FIFOs can't be open at once, the obvious solution is to open a FIFO, write the message, and then close it to free the file descriptor. But open takes too long, so this would slow down communication too much. After all, it's when the DBMS has many clients that efficiency matters most.

A good solution is to use a scheme analogous to that used by virtual memory systems. Keep a limited number of FIFOs open, say seven. When an eighth is needed, close an open one and use its file descriptor. The best one to close is the one that will be needed furthest in the future (this can be proven), but unfortunately, the DBMS can't predict the future. (If it could, it might as well give each client all its data at once!) So a reasonable compromise is to close the FIFO that was least recently used, on the theory that a FIFO that hasn't been used for a while won't be used for a while yet. If the clients make DBMS requests in round-robin order, our scheme will fail, since the least-recently-used FIFO is precisely the wrong one to close. But if each client tends to bunch its requests, the scheme will work well. In a transaction-processing system, a client remains idle while the operator is filling out the form, and then makes several DBMS requests in rapid succession, followed by another idle period while the operator ponders the results and starts on the next form. So we can expect that a least-recently-used approach will work well.

We can keep a table of the open file descriptors like this:

```
static struct {
    long key;
    int fd;
    int time;
} fifos[MAXOPEN];
```

Whenever we read or write a FIFO, we record the current time in the time member of the corresponding fifo element. If we need to usurp a file descriptor, we just go through the array looking for the element with the oldest time. We close its fd member, open the new FIFO, and store the key, file descriptor, and current time in that element.

Since we are using the time member only to record relative times, we don't need to actually interrogate the computer's clock to store the current time. We can increment a local variable (clock) each time send or receive is called, and then store the current value of clock in the time member. If the clock has only 16 bits it will overflow after 32,767 ticks. Then there will be a brief period of sub-optimal selection, followed quickly by restored sanity. This is perfectly acceptable, since the least-recently-used scheme is rough to begin with. A clock with more bits would be overkill.

Here's the code for send and receive. We've added another call, rmqueue, to dispose of a queue when it's no longer needed (before a client terminates). The function openfifo uses the least-recently-used scheme to find an unused file descriptor and opens it with the short-term wait discussed above.

```
#define MAXOPEN 7
#define MAXTRIES 3
#define NAPTIME 5

static char *fifoname(key)   /* construct fifo name from key */
long key;
{
    static char fifo[20];

    sprintf(fifo, "/tmp/fifo%ld", key);
    return(fifo);
}

static int openfifo(key, flags)   /* return fifo fd */
long key;
int flags;
{
```

```
static struct {
    long key;
    int fd;
    int time;
} fifos[MAXOPEN];
static int clock;
int i, avail, oldest, fd, tries;
char *fifo;
extern int errno;

clock++;
avail = -1;
for (i = 0; i < MAXOPEN; i++) {
    if (fifos[i].key == key) {
        fifos[i].time = clock;
        return(fifos[i].fd);
    }
    if (fifos[i].key == 0 && avail == -1)
        avail = i;
}
if (avail == -1) { /* all fds in use; find oldest */
    oldest = -1;
    for (i = 0; i < MAXOPEN; i++)
        if (oldest == -1 || fifos[i].time < oldest) {
            oldest = fifos[i].time;
            avail = i;
        }
    if (close(fifos[avail].fd) == -1)
        return(-1);
}
fifo = fifoname(key);
if (mkfifo(fifo) == -1 && errno != EEXIST)
    return(-1);
for (tries = 1; tries <= MAXTRIES; tries++) { /* await writer */
    if ((fd = open(fifo, flags | O_NDELAY)) != -1)
        break;
    if (errno != ENXIO)
        return(-1);
    sleep(NAPTIME);
}
if (fd == -1) {
    errno = ENXIO; /* sleep may have messed it up */
    return(-1);
}
if (fcntl(fd, F_SETFL, flags) == -1) /* clear O_NDELAY */
    return(-1);
fifos[avail].key = key;
fifos[avail].fd = fd;
```

```
        fifos[avail].time = clock;
        return(fd);
}

BOOLEAN send(dstkey, buf, nbytes) /* send message */
long dstkey;
char *buf;
int nbytes;
{
    int fd;

    if ((fd = openfifo(dstkey, O_WRONLY)) == -1)
        return(FALSE);
    return(write(fd, buf, nbytes) != -1);
}

BOOLEAN receive(srckey, buf, nbytes)  /* receive message */
long srckey;
char *buf;
int nbytes;
{
    int fd, nread;

    if ((fd = openfifo(srckey, O_RDONLY)) == -1)
        return(FALSE);
    while ((nread = read(fd, buf, nbytes)) == 0)
        sleep(NAPTIME);
    return(nread != -1);
}

void rmqueue(key) /* remove message queue fifo */
long key;
{
    int errno;

    if (unlink(fifoname(key)) == -1 && errno != ENOENT)
        syserr("unlink");
}
```

We coded mkfifo in Sec. 3.8.

To see these functions in action, here is a simple example consisting of a program that sends messages and another program to receive them. The message structure is defined in a header file (message.h) so both programs can include it:

```
            typedef struct {
                    long unused;
                    int pid;
                    int number;
            } MESSAGE;
```

The first member is the required unused long integer that was explained earlier in this section. The second member, p i d, is the sender's process-ID. The receiver can use it as the queue key to send replies back to the sender, although our first example doesn't do so. The last member, n u m b e r, is the message itself, which is just a number in this simple example.

Here is the sender:

```
#include "message.h"

main() /* sender */
{
    MESSAGE m;

    m.pid = getpid();
    for (m.number = 1; m.number <= 4; m.number++) {
        sleep(1);
        if (!send(1000L, &m, sizeof(m)))
            syserr("send");
    }
    exit(0);
}
```

And here is the receiver:

```
#include "message.h"

main() /* receiver */
{
    MESSAGE m;

    setbuf(stdout, NULL);
    while (receive(1000L, &m, sizeof(m)))
        printf("Received %d from %d\n", m.number, m.pid);
    syserr("receive");

}
```

Note that the queue key is fixed at 1000—not a very good idea in general, but adequate for now.

When we typed this command line:

```
receiver & sender & sender & sender &
```

we got this output:

```
Received 1 from 3723
Received 1 from 3724
Received 2 from 3724
Received 2 from 3723
Received 3 from 3723
Received 3 from 3724
Received 1 from 3725
Received 4 from 3723
Received 4 from 3724
Received 2 from 3725
Received 3 from 3725
Received 4 from 3725
```

Now for a slightly more complex example, this time with two-way communication. Our centralized service is a process that can add two numbers and send the result back. Here is the message structure, in the header file addmsg.h:

```
typedef struct {
    long unused;
    long clientkey;
    int x;
    int y;
    int sum;
} MESSAGE;

#define ADDERKEY 1000L
```

The member clientkey is used by the central adder to send responses back to its clients. x and y are the numbers to add; sum is their sum. Rather than have different messages for the service request and the result, we've included all three members in the structure so we can use it for both directions. Also, the header file defines a symbolic constant for the adder's queue key.

Here is the adder program, which just receives a request, adds x and y, and sends the sum back:

```
#include "addmsg.h"

main() /* adder service */
{
    MESSAGE m;
    extern int errno;

    while (receive(ADDERKEY, &m, sizeof(m))) {
        m.sum = m.x + m.y;
        if (!send(m.clientkey, &m, sizeof(m)))
            printf("can't send to %ld; errno = %d\n", m.clientkey,
                errno);
    }
    syserr("receive");
}
```

This is a client program that sends a request to the adder, receives a message in reply, and checks the arithmetic to ensure that things worked OK:

```
#include "addmsg.h"

main() /* adder client */
{
    MESSAGE m;
    int x, y;

    m.clientkey = getpid();
    for (x = 1; x <= 5; x++)
        for (y = 1; y <= 5; y++) {
            m.x = x;
            m.y = y;
            if (!send(ADDERKEY, &m, sizeof(m)))
                syserr("send");
            if (!receive(m.clientkey, &m, sizeof(m)))
                syserr("receive");
            if (x + y != m.sum) {
                printf("Addition error!\n");
                exit(1);
            }
        }
    rmqueue(m.clientkey);
    printf("%ld worked OK\n", m.clientkey);
    exit(0);
}
```

With this command line:

```
adder & addclient & addclient &
```

we got this output:

```
3757 worked OK
3758 worked OK
```

Now that we've shown two trivial examples, we're ready to present a multi-user DBMS. We don't have space for a good DBMS, so we'll have to resign ourselves to a bad one. But the main point is that the interprocess communication is good enough even for a good DBMS.

Our example breaks down into three parts:

1. The DBMS proper, accessed via direct function calls from its own address space. This is the part that's not so good.

2. The interprocess communication mechanism, consisting of code on the DBMS side that accesses Part 1 via function calls, the message primitives themselves (send, receive, and rmqueue), and a library of functions on the client side that composes request messages and receives replies.

3. The application program, which is a DBMS client. It calls the library of functions that comprise Part 2, which then communicates with the DBMS on its behalf.

We'll start with Part 1, the heart of the DBMS. It can store one kind of record in a single file. Each record is of type RCD:

```
typedef struct {
    char name[20];
    char street[15];
    char city[10];
    char state[3];
    char zip[6];
    char tel[15];
} RCD;
```

The data file is a sequence of RCD objects. A new record is just added onto the end of the file—there's no attempt to keep records in order. An existing record is deleted by making its name member the null string. An existing record can be modified by overwriting it.

All of the database functions return a value of type STATUS:

```
typedef enum {OK, NOTFOUND, ERROR} STATUS;
```

The NOTFOUND return value isn't used by some functions, so their return value is effectively a Boolean value, but STATUS is used anyhow for uniformity. The type definitions for RCD and STATUS are in the header file dbms.h.

A new database is created with Dcreate; an old one is opened with Dopen. These functions just put the file descriptor in a global variable (fd), since only one database can be open at a time. Dclose closes the database. Here are these three functions:

```
#include "dbms.h"

static int fd = -1;

static STATUS Dopen(file)    /* open database */
char *file;
{
    if ((fd = open(file, O_RDWR, 0)) == -1)
        return(ERROR);
    return(OK);
}
```

```
static STATUS Dcreate(file)  /* create database */
char *file;
{
    if ((fd = open(file, O_RDWR | O_CREAT | O_TRUNC, 0666)) == -1)
        return(ERROR);
    return(OK);
}

static STATUS Dclose()  /* close database */
{
    if (close(fd) == -1)
        return(ERROR);
    return(OK);
}
```

A particular record is retrieved with **Dget**; the arguments are the value of the **name** member and a pointer to a **RCD** that is to receive the retrieved record:

```
long lseek();
extern int errno;

static STATUS Dtop()  /* go to top of database */
{
    if (lseek(fd, 0L, 0) == -1)
        return(ERROR);
    return(OK);
}

static STATUS Dget(name, r)  /* retrieve record by name */
char *name;
RCD *r;
{
    int nread;

    if (Dtop() != OK)
        return(ERROR);
    while ((nread = read(fd, r, sizeof(RCD))) == sizeof(RCD))
        if (strcmp(r->name, name) == 0) {
            if (lseek(fd, -(long)sizeof(RCD), 1) == -1) /* go back */
                return(ERROR);
            return(OK);
        }
    switch (nread) {
    case 0:
        return(NOTFOUND);
```

```
case -1:
    return(ERROR);
default:
    errno = 0;
    return(ERROR);
}

}
```

Dtop is called to position the data file to the beginning, since **Dget** searches sequentially to find the requested record. After finding a record, **Dget** seeks back to the beginning of it so that it can be overwritten if it is to be modified.

To generate reports, a client might want to retrieve all records. First, **Dtop** is called to seek to the start of the data file, and then **Dgetnext** retrieves the next record each time it is called. It returns **NOTFOUND** when it gets to the end.

```
static STATUS Dgetnext(r)  /* retrieve next record */
RCD *r;
{
    while (1)
        switch (read(fd, r, sizeof(RCD))) {
        case sizeof(RCD):
            if (r->name[0] == '\0')
                continue;
            return(OK);
        case 0:
            return(NOTFOUND);
        case -1:
            return(ERROR);
        default:
            errno = 0;
            return(ERROR);
        }
}
```

A record is inserted with **Dput**. It first calls **Dget** to see if a record with the same name already exists. If so, it is overwritten; if not, the new record is placed at the end.

```
static STATUS Dput(r)  /* insert record */
RCD *r;
{
    RCD rcd;
```

```
switch (Dget(r->name, &rcd)) {
case NOTFOUND:
    if (lseek(fd, OL, 2) == -1) /* seek to end */
        return(ERROR);
    break;
case ERROR:
    return(ERROR);
}
switch (write(fd, r, sizeof(RCD))) {
case sizeof(RCD):
    return(OK);
case -1:
    return(ERROR);
default:
    errno = 0;
    return(ERROR);
}
}
```

Finally, D de l e t e deletes a record by overwriting it (if it exists) with a record with a null name. No attempt is made to reuse the old space.

```
static STATUS Ddelete(name)  /* delete record */
char *name;
{
    RCD rcd;

    switch (Dget(name, &rcd)) {
    case NOTFOUND:
        return(OK);
    case ERROR:
        return(ERROR);
    }
    rcd.name[0] = '\0';
    switch (write(fd, &rcd, sizeof(RCD))) {
    case sizeof(RCD):
        return(OK);
    case -1:
        return(ERROR);
    default:
        errno = 0;
        return(ERROR);
    }
}
```

Note that deleting a nonexistent record is OK.

That's it—what is surely one of the world's most compact database management systems! It lacks only flexibility, robustness, and efficiency.

We could use these database access functions directly, in the manner of the decentralized approach described in Sec. 7.2. However, we instead want to use them in a centralized DBMS, and communicate via messages. For that we need to add a main program that receives a message from a client, processes it by calling the appropriate access function, and then sends the results back. Here is the message structure we'll use (defined in dbms.h):

```
typedef struct {
    long mtype;
    long clientkey;
    char cmd;
    char file[20];
    RCD rcd;
    STATUS status;
    int errno;
} MESSAGE;
```

The first two members are the same as in the adder example. cmd is a single letter that indicates the requested command. If a file name is required, it is put into file. rcd is used both to send records to the DBMS and to get records back. The status from each request is sent back in status, and so is the errno (meaningful only when status is ERROR). Again, we've used the same message structure for both requests and responses, even though some fields are sometimes unused.

Here's the DBMS process's main program:

```
main() /* receive requests and send responses */
{
    MESSAGE m;
    char *dbmsval, name[30], *getenv();
    long dbmskey, atol();

    if ((dbmsval = getenv("DBMSKEY")) == NULL)
        fatal("missing DBMSKEY environment variable");
    dbmskey = atol(dbmsval);
    while (receive(dbmskey, &m, sizeof(m))) {
        switch (m.cmd) {
        case 'o':
            m.status = Dopen(m.file);
            break;
        case 'c':
            m.status = Dcreate(m.file);
            break;
        case 'q':
            m.status = Dclose();
            rmqueue(dbmskey);
            break;
```

```
    case 'g':
        strcpy(name, m.rcd.name);
        m.status = Dget(name, &m.rcd);
        break;
    case 'n':
        m.status = Dgetnext(&m.rcd);
        break;
    case 'p':
        m.status = Dput(&m.rcd);
        break;
    case 'd':
        m.status = Ddelete(m.rcd.name);
        break;
    case 't':
        m.status = Dtop();
        break;
    default:
        errno = EINVAL;
        m.status = ERROR;
    }
    m.errno = errno;
    if (!send(m.clientkey, &m, sizeof(m)))
        printf("can't send to %ld; errno = %d\n", m.clientkey,
            errno);
    if (m.cmd == 'q')
        exit(0);
}
syserr("receive");
}
```

The DBMS receiving queue key is taken from the environment variable **DBMSKEY**. It's preassigned from the shell.

A client does not send messages directly to the DBMS. Instead, a library of functions mimics the direct DBMS function calls described above. In fact, an application programmer need not even know that the DBMS is centralized; he or she uses the same functions that would be used if it were decentralized. Here is the DBMS library:

```
#include "dbms.h"

extern int errno;
static MESSAGE m;

static STATUS dbmscall(r)  /* "call" DBMS */
RCD *r;
```

```
{
    char *dbmsval, *getenv();
    static long dbmskey;
    long atol();

    if (dbmskey == 0) {
        if ((dbmsval = getenv("DBMSKEY")) == NULL)
            fatal("missing DBMSKEY environment variable");
        dbmskey = atol(dbmsval);
    }
    if (m.clientkey == 0)
        m.clientkey = getpid();
    if (!send(dbmskey, &m, sizeof(m)))
        return(ERROR);
    if (!receive(m.clientkey, &m, sizeof(m)))
        return(ERROR);
    if (r != NULL)
        *r = m.rcd;
    if (m.status == ERROR)
        errno = m.errno;
    else
        errno = 0;
    return(m.status);
}

STATUS Dopen(file)  /* open database */
char *file;
{
    m.cmd = 'o';
    strcpy(m.file, file);
    return(dbmscall(NULL));
}

STATUS Dcreate(file)  /* create database */
char *file;
{
    m.cmd = 'c';
    strcpy(m.file, file);
    return(dbmscall(NULL));
}

STATUS Dclose()  /* close database */
{
    STATUS status;

    m.cmd = 'q';
    status = dbmscall(NULL);
    rmqueue(m.clientkey);
    return(status);
}
```

```
STATUS Dtop() /* go to top of database */
{
    m.cmd = 't';
    return(dbmscall(NULL));
}

STATUS Dget(name, r) /* retrieve record by name */
char *name;
RCD *r;
{
    m.cmd = 'g';
    strcpy(m.rcd.name, name);
    return(dbmscall(r));
}

STATUS Dgetnext(r) /* retrieve next record */
RCD *r;
{
    m.cmd = 'n';
    return(dbmscall(r));
}

STATUS Dput(r) /* insert record */
RCD *r;
{
    m.cmd = 'p';
    m.rcd = *r;
    return(dbmscall(NULL));
}

STATUS Ddelete(name) /* delete record */
char *name;
{
    m.cmd = 'd';
    strcpy(m.rcd.name, name);
    return(dbmscall(NULL));
}
```

The function **dbmscall** represents the message-based equivalent of the normal subroutine call-return paradigm. Not only do **send** and **receive** hide the fact that we're using FIFOs, but **dbmscall** hides the fact that we're using messages. This is desirable because a hidden design decision is one that can easily be changed later. If we decide to replace FIFOs with messages (which we will do shortly), we can do so by changing only **send**, **receive**, and **rmqueue**, because the rest of our program never knew that we were using FIFOs in the first place. Similarly, if we decide to change to a decentralized approach, we can do it by changing only the DBMS library, because our application programs were oblivious to the fact that we were centralized.

Finally, we need an application program to act as a test client. Here's an interactive utility that allows a user to exercise each DBMS function:

```
#include "dbms.h"

main()  /* DBMS interactive utility */
{
    char cmd[5], file[50], name[30];
    RCD rcd;
    extern int errno;

    while (1) {
        prompt("Command (? for help)", cmd, sizeof(cmd), TRUE);
        if (strlen(cmd) != 1) {
            printf("One letter only\n");
            continue;
        }
        switch (cmd[0]) {
        case '?':
            printf("o   open database\n");
            printf("c   create database\n");
            printf("p   put record\n");
            printf("d   delete record\n");
            printf("g   get record by key\n");
            printf("n   get next record\n");
            printf("t   rewind to top of database\n");
            printf("q   quit\n");
            continue;
        case 'o':
            prompt("File to open", file, sizeof(file), TRUE);
            if (Dopen(file) == OK)
                printf("OK\n");
            else
                printf("FAILED; errno = %d\n", errno);
            continue;
        case 'c':
            prompt("File to create", file, sizeof(file), TRUE);
            if (Dcreate(file) == OK)
                printf("OK\n");
            else
                printf("FAILED; errno = %d\n", errno);
            continue;
        case 'q':
            if (Dclose() == OK)
                printf("OK\n");
            else
                printf("FAILED; errno = %d\n", errno);
            exit(0);
```

```
case 'g':
    prompt("Name", name, sizeof(name), TRUE);
    switch (Dget(name, &rcd)) {
    case OK:
        rcdprint(&rcd);
        continue;
    case NOTFOUND:
        printf("NOT FOUND\n");
        continue;
    case ERROR:
        printf("FAILED; errno = %d\n", errno);
        continue;
    }
case 'n':
    switch (Dgetnext(&rcd)) {
    case OK:
        rcdprint(&rcd);
        continue;
    case NOTFOUND:
        printf("NOT FOUND\n");
        continue;
    case ERROR:
        printf("FAILED; errno = %d\n", errno);
        continue;
    }

case 'p':
    prompt("Name", rcd.name, sizeof(rcd.name), TRUE);
    prompt("Street", rcd.street, sizeof(rcd.street),FALSE);
    prompt("City", rcd.city, sizeof(rcd.city), FALSE);
    prompt("State",rcd.state,sizeof(rcd.state),FALSE);
    prompt("ZIP", rcd.zip, sizeof(rcd.zip), FALSE);
    prompt("Tel", rcd.tel, sizeof(rcd.tel), FALSE);
    if (Dput(&rcd) == OK)
        printf("OK\n");
    else
        printf("FAILED; errno = %d\n", errno);
    continue;
case 'd':
    prompt("Name", name, sizeof(name), TRUE);
    if (Ddelete(name) == OK)
        printf("OK\n");
    else
        printf("FAILED; errno = %d\n", errno);
    continue;
case 't':
    if (Dtop() == OK)
        printf("OK\n");
```

```
            else
                printf("FAILED; errno = %d\n", errno);
            continue;
        default:
            printf("Unknown command - use ? for help\n");
        }
    }
}

static void prompt(msg, result, max, required) /* prompt user */
char *msg, *result;
{
    char s[200];
    int len;

    while (1) {
        printf("\n%s? ", msg);
        if (gets(s) == NULL)
            exit(0);
        len = strlen(s);
        if (len >= max) {
            printf("Response too long\n");
            continue;
        }
        if (len == 0 && required) {
            printf("Value required\n");
            continue;
        }
        strcpy(result, s);
        return;
    }
}

static void rcdprint(r)  /* print record */
RCD *r;
{
    printf("Name\t%s\n", r->name);
    printf("Street\t%s\n", r->street);
    printf("City\t%s\n", r->city);
    printf("State\t%s\n", r->state)
    printf("ZIP\t%s\n", r->zip);
    printf("Tel\t%s\n", r->tel);
}
```

This program is pretty easy to follow, especially since the DBMS library hides so many details. As an experiment, see if you can find anything in it that indicates it is communicating to a centralized DBMS via messages, rather than to a decentralized DBMS using function calls. If you can't, it means that once interprocess communication is dealt with, the centralized approach is just as easy to use by application programmers as the more familiar decentralized approach.

Here's a sample session to show our test program in action. Before we invoke the utility (dbmstest), we must assign a value to DBMSKEY and run the DBMS (program dbms) in the background.

```
$ DBMSKEY=5000
$ dbms &
3789
$ dbmstest


Command (? for help)? ?
o       open database
c       create database
p       put record
d       delete record
g       get record by key
n       get next record
t       rewind to top of database
q       quit


Command (? for help)? c


File to create? tstdb
OK


Command (? for help)? p

Name? Mary Smith

Street? 123 Main St

City? Cityville

State? MD

ZIP? 20964

Tel? 301 345-9876
OK
```

```
Command (? for help)? p

Name? John Jones

Street? 222 Maple Dr

City? Hometown

State? OK

ZIP? 73112

Tel? 405 878-1445
OK

Command (? for help)? g

Name? Mary Smith
Name      Mary Smith
Street    123 Main St
City      Cityville
State     MD
ZIP       20964
Tel       301 345-9876

Command (? for help)? t
OK

Command (? for help)? n
Name      Mary Smith
Street    123 Main St
City      Cityville
State     MD
ZIP       20964
Tel       301 345-9876

Command (? for help)? n
Name      John Jones
Street    222 Maple Dr
City      Hometown
State     OK
ZIP       73112
Tel       405 878-1445

Command (? for help)? q
OK
$
```

7.5 MESSAGE SYSTEM CALLS (SYSTEM V)

```
#include <sys/types.h>
#include <sys/ipc.h>
#include <sys/msg.h>

int msgget(key, flags)                  /* get message queue-ID */
key_t key;                              /* queue key (long)*/
int flags;                              /* option flags */
/* returns queue-ID or -1 on error */

int msgsnd(qid, buf, nbytes, flags)     /* send message to queue */
int qid;                                /* queue-ID */
struct msgbuf *buf;                     /* pointer to message */
int nbytes;                             /* size of message */
int flags;
/* returns 0 on success or -1 on error */

int msgrcv(qid, buf, nbytes, mtype, flags)      /* receive message */
int qid;
struct msgbuf *buf;
int nbytes;
long mtype;                             /* type of message */
int flags;
/* returns number of bytes received or -1 on error */

int msgctl(qid, cmd, sbuf)              /* control message queue */
int qid;
int cmd;                                /* command */
struct msqid_ds *sbuf;                  /* pointer to status buffer */
/* returns 0 on success or -1 on error */
```

These system calls, available only in System V, handle messages analogously to send and receive, which were implemented in the previous section with FIFOs. The System V scheme is much more elaborate, however, and has many more options than anyone is likely to ever need. One can almost picture a committee designing these system calls, afraid to adjourn without including every possible feature, lest someone accuse them of oversimplifying.

We'll explain most of what these system calls do. We'll skip the more esoteric details, however, and concentrate on presenting the essentials that will enable us to reprogram send and receive.

To use messages you start with msgget, which is analogous to open. It takes a key, which must be a long integer, and returns an integer called the *queue-ID*. A queue-ID is like a file descriptor, except that any process that knows its value may use it—it does not have to be inherited to be valid. Like a file descriptor, a queue-ID is an index into a table inside the kernel. By translating external keys to queue-IDs, a time-consuming lookup can be avoided when the queue has to be referenced.

The f l a g s argument to m s g g e t is similar to the second and third arguments to o p e n combined. If the I P C _ C R E A T bit is on, the queue is created if it doesn't already exist. In this case the rightmost nine bits of f l a g s become the permissions for the queue, and are used similarly to the way they are used with files. Write permission allows a message to be sent; read permission allows one to be received. If the I P C _ C R E A T bit is off, the queue must already exist. In this case m s g g e t is being used just to translate from a key to a queue-ID.

If the k e y argument is equal to I P C _ P R I V A T E, a queue is created regardless of whether f l a g s has the I P C _ C R E A T bit on. This avoids a clash with an existing queue, which would be possible were an actual key to be used. Without this feature one could still program an algorithm to create a private queue, using techniques similar to those used to create temporary files with unique names. In our examples we'll use the process-ID as the key for a private queue.

Once you have a queue-ID, you can call m s g s n d to put a message on it. The second argument, b u f, points to an arbitrary structure that must begin with a long integer greater than zero, called the *message type*. All of the **MESSAGE** objects defined in the header files of the previous section qualify. Message types allow the receiver to choose a message from the queue by type, or to wait for a message of a particular type. n b y t e s is the number of bytes in the message exclusive of the message type. The last argument, f l a g s, is normally 0, causing m s g s n d to block if the queue is full. If it is set instead to I P C _ N O W A I T, then m s g s n d returns immediately with an error if the queue is full. This flag acts much like O _ N D E L A Y on FIFOs. (It probably should have been called I P C _ N D E L A Y.)

Message types effectively multiplex a single message queue to allow it to handle a set of subqueues, one for each type. Unless the number of different types is large—an unusual situation—several separate queues, each handling messages of only one type, could be used instead.

The receiver calls m s g r c v. n b y t e s is set to the size of the largest message that will fit in the storage area pointed to by b u f, again exclusive of the message type member. Since the size of the actual message received can be less than n b y t e s, it is returned as the value of m s g r c v (analogously to r e a d). If the receiver wants messages only of a certain type, m t y p e is set to the type number. Otherwise, it should be zero, in which case the oldest message on the queue, regardless of type, will be received. If no appropriate message is on the queue, the receiver blocks if f l a g s is zero. If the I P C _ N O W A I T flag is on, the receiver returns with an error instead of blocking.

m s g c t l interrogates or controls various properties of the queue such as access permissions, ownership, and capacity. We'll skip the details except to mention that the command I P C _ R M I D destroys a message queue. Any processes blocked in m s g s n d or m s g r c v at that time will receive an error return.

Here is a rewrite of s e n d, r e c e i v e, and r m q u e u e using System V messages; you'll want to compare it to the version using FIFOs in the previous section.

All messages are of type 1 and sender or receiver blocks if the queue is, respectively, full or empty. This is OK because, unlike with FIFOs, the sender can put messages on the queue without waiting for the receiver—there's no concept of "open for reading."

```c
#include <sys/types.h>
#include <sys/ipc.h>
#include <sys/msg.h>

#define MAXOPEN 20

static int openqueue(key)  /* return queue ID; create if necessary */
long key;
{
    static struct {
        long key;
        int qid;
    } queues[MAXOPEN];
    int i, avail, qid;
    extern int errno;

    avail = -1;
    for (i = 0; i < MAXOPEN; i++) {
        if (queues[i].key == key)
            return(queues[i].qid);
        if (queues[i].key == 0 && avail == -1)
            avail = i;
    }
    if (avail == -1) {
        errno = 0;
        return(-1);
    }
    if ((qid = msgget(key, 0666 | IPC_CREAT)) == -1)
        return(-1);
    queues[avail].key = key;
    queues[avail].qid = qid;
    return(qid);
}

BOOLEAN send(dstkey, buf, nbytes)  /* send message */
long dstkey;
struct msgbuf *buf;
int nbytes;
{
    int qid;
```

```
    if ((qid = openqueue(dstkey)) == -1)
        return(FALSE);
    buf->mtype = 1;
    return(msgsnd(qid, buf, nbytes - sizeof(buf->mtype), 0) != -1);
}


BOOLEAN receive(srckey, buf, nbytes)  /* receive message */
long srckey;
struct msgbuf *buf;
int nbytes;
{
    int qid;

    if ((qid = openqueue(srckey)) == -1)
        return(FALSE);
    return(msgrcv(qid, buf, nbytes - sizeof(buf->mtype), 0L, 0) != - 1);

}

void rmqueue(key)  /* remove queue */
long key;
{
    int qid;

    if ((qid = openqueue(key)) == -1 || msgctl(qid, IPC_RMID, NULL)
      == -1)
        syserr("rmqueue");
}
```

Note that we allow 20 message queues, and we don't remove any of them to make room for more. They're not as scarce a resource as file descriptors.

Why choose System V messages over FIFOs? They're faster, but possibly not enough to warrant their use in an application unless message-passing time is a problem. They do offer lots of nifty features (very few of which are used by s e n d or r e c e i v e), but these aren't needed in most applications either. They're complex, incompletely documented, and nonportable. *Avoid them if at all possible*!

7.6 SEMAPHORES

7.6.1 Basic Semaphore Usage

A semaphore is a mechanism that prevents two or more processes from accessing a shared resource simultaneously. On the railroads a semaphore prevents two trains from crashing on a shared section of track. On railroads and computers, semaphores are advisory: If a train engineer doesn't observe and obey it, the semaphore won't prevent a crash, and if a process doesn't check a semaphore before accessing a shared resource, chaos might result.

A *binary* semaphore has only two states: locked and unlocked. A *general* semaphore has an infinite (or, at least, very large) number of states. It's a counter that decreases by one when it is acquired ("locked") and increases by one when it is released ("unlocked"). If it's zero, a process trying to acquire it must wait for another process to increase its value—it can't ever get negative. (If a semaphore can take on only two values, 0 and 1, it is a binary semaphore.) General semaphores are usually accessed with two operations, P (acquire) and V (release).[3] We can try to write these in C like this:

```
void P(sem)  /* acquire semaphore */
int *sem;
{
    while (*sem <= 0)
        ; /* do nothing */
    (*sem)--;
}

void V(sem)  /* release semaphore */
int *sem;
{
    (*sem)++;
}
```

The semaphore must be initialized by calling V; otherwise it starts out with nothing to acquire. For example, if the semaphore counts the number of free buffers, and there are initially five buffers, we would start out by calling V five times. Alternatively, we can just set the semaphore variable to five.

Having gone to the trouble of programming P and V, we now have to say that they won't work, for three reasons:

- The semaphore variable pointed to by sem cannot be shared among processes, which have distinct data segments.
- The functions do not execute atomically—the kernel can interrupt a process at any time. The following scenario could occur: Process 1 completes the while loop in P and is interrupted before it can decrement the semaphore; process 2 enters P, finds the semaphore equal to 1, completes its while loop, and decrements the semaphore to 0; process 1 resumes and decrements the semaphore to −1 (an illegal value).

---

[3]P and V are abbreviations for the Dutch words for "wait" and "signal." We use "acquire" and "release" instead because "wait" and "signal" have other meanings in UNIX. Besides, I don't speak Dutch.

- P does what's called a *busy-wait* if s e m is zero. This is a dumb way to use a CPU.

Therefore, P and V can't just be programmed in user space. Semaphores have to be supplied by the kernel, which can share data between processes, can execute atomic operations, and can give the CPU to a ready process when a process blocks.

7.6.2 Implementing Semaphores With Messages

Back in Sec. 2.5 we showed how to use c r e a t to make a crude binary semaphore, and in Sec. 2.6 we improved on this technique by using the O_EXCL flag with open. Those methods are OK for a process that accesses a shared resource only a few times, such as a mail program that's writing into a mailbox file, but the overhead is far too great for heavy-duty use. We want a semaphore that takes less time to check and set.

A message queue can be used as a semaphore: s e n d adds a message to the queue, and is equivalent to V; and r e c e i v e removes a message from the queue, and is equivalent to P. r e c e i v e blocks when the queue is empty, which is equivalent to the semaphore being zero.

Here are P and V implemented using s e n d and r e c e i v e:

```
void P(sem)  /* acquire semaphore */
int sem;
{
      long type;

      if (!receive((long)sem, &type, sizeof(type)))
          syserr("receive");
}

void V(sem)  /* release semaphore */
int sem;
{
      long type;

      if (!send((long)sem, &type, sizeof(type)))
          syserr("send");
}
```

We've changed the argument s e m from an integer pointer to an integer. Since the message has no contents, we've simply made it a long integer, which just meets the requirement of having a message type at the beginning of the message. Either of the two implementations for s e n d and r e c e i v e will work, FIFOs or System V messages.

7.6.3 Semaphores in System V

Using messages for semaphores is much faster than creating files, but there's still a lot more overhead adding and removing a message to and from a queue than there is just incrementing or decrementing a variable. So both System V and Xenix 3 have a group of system calls specifically for managing semaphores. Alas, neither system just uses P and V. Their semaphores are more elaborate.

We'll start with System V. These system calls are too complex for us to describe completely.[4] We'll make sure, however, that we explain enough to allow us to implement P and V.

```
#include <sys/types.h>
#include <sys/ipc.h>
#include <sys/sem.h>

int semget(key, nsems, flags)      /* get semaphore-set-ID */
key_t key;                         /* semaphore-set key */
int nsems;                         /* number of semaphores */
int flags;                         /* option flags */
/* returns semaphore-set-ID or -1 on error */

int semop(sid, ops, nops)          /* operate on semaphore-set */
int sid;                           /* semaphore-set-ID */
struct sembuf (*ops)[];            /* ptr to array of operations */
int nops;                          /* number of operations */
/* returns semaphore value prior to last operation or -1 on error */

int semctl(sid, snum, cmd, arg)    /* control semaphore */
int sid;
int snum;                          /* semaphore number */
int cmd;                           /* command */
char *arg;                         /* argument */
/* returns value depending on command or -1 on error */
```

These system calls appear to have been designed by someone fond of the programming language APL: semget gets an *array* of semaphores, and they're operated on all at once—atomically—by an array of operations given to semop.

System V semaphores are too complicated. In any program using semaphores it's essential to be able to demonstrate that access to shared resources is exclusive, that deadlock does not occur, and that starvation (never getting access) does not occur. Testing alone can't usually suffice because things are so timing-dependent; analysis must be used. This is difficult enough with plain P and V. With the System V system calls, used in their full glory, analysis is probably impossible.

---

[4]To be honest, I must admit that I don't *understand* them completely.

Briefly, here's how these calls work. s e m g e t translates a key to an ID representing a set of semaphores. If the **I P C _ C R E A T** bit of f l a g s is on, the set is created if it doesn't already exist. There are n s e m s semaphores in the set, numbered starting with zero. It makes a lot of sense to have just one semaphore in the set if at all possible. For simplicity we'll assume this is true in the remainder of this description; that is, a semaphore operation or control command applies to a single semaphore, and a semaphore-set-ID may as well be called a semaphore-ID.

s e m o p is used to acquire or release the semaphore. o p s points to a structure of three short integers:

```
struct sembuf {
    short sem_num;      /* semaphore number */
    short sem_op;       /* operation */
    short sem_flg;      /* operation options */
};
```

The operation can be a negative, positive, or zero integer. Unlike a **P** operation, which waits until a semaphore can be decremented by 1, it is possible to wait until it can be decremented by an arbitrary amount. Again, this is a feature we'll stay away from by dealing only with two values of o p, −1 and 1, which correspond nicely to **P** and **V**. If o p is −1, the process blocks until the semaphore value can be decremented by 1 without going negative. If o p is 1, the semaphore is incremented by 1. For both operations, f l a g s may be equal to **SEM_UNDO**, which causes Ps and Vs to be balanced automatically when the process exits.

s e m c t l can be used to interrogate or change a semaphore's owner, permissions, or last-change time. It's also possible to find out how many processes are waiting on a semaphore and the process-ID of the last process that changed it.

Here are **P** and **V** implemented with s e m g e t and s e m o p. We've added a call to translate a key to a semaphore-set-ID. In general, s e m t r a n will be called once at the beginning of each process that uses the semaphore.

```
#include <sys/types.h>
#include <sys/ipc.h>
#include <sys/sem.h>

int semtran(key) /* translate semaphore key to ID */
int key;
{
    int sid;

    if ((sid = semget ((key_t)key, 1, 0666 | IPC_CREAT)) == -1)
        syserr("semget");
    return(sid);
}
```

```
static void semcall(sid, op)  /* call semop */
int sid;
int op;
{
    struct sembuf sb;

    sb.sem_num = 0;
    sb.sem_op = op;
    sb.sem_flg = 0;
    if (semop(sid, &sb, 1) == -1)
        syserr ("semop");
}

void P(sid)  /* acquire semaphore */
int sid;
{
    semcall(sid, -1);
}

void V(sid)  /* release semaphore */
int sid;
{
    semcall(sid, 1);
}
```

This implementation of P and V is much faster than the ones using FIFOs or messages.

We didn't need s e m t r a n when we implemented P and V to use s e nd and r e c e i v e, but we can add an identity function to that implementation to make applications using semaphores more portable:

```
int semtran(key)  /* translate semaphore key to ID */
int key;
{
    return(key);
}
```

7.6.4 Semaphores in Xenix 3

A different semaphore mechanism is used by Xenix 3, to handle binary semaphores only. It's wonderfully simple.

```
int creatsem(path, perms)              /* create semaphore file */
char *path;                            /* path name */
int perms;                             /* permission bits */
/* returns semaphore-ID or -1 on error */
```

```
int opensem(path)                /* open existing semaphore file */
char *path;
/* returns semaphore-ID or -1 on error */

int waitsem(sid)                 /* acquire semaphore */
int sid;                         /* semaphore-ID */
/* returns 0 on success or -1 on error */

int nbwaitsem(sid)               /* check on semaphore */
int sid;
/* returns 0 on success or -1 on error */

int sigsem(sid)                  /* release semaphore */
int sid;
/* returns 0 on success or -1 on error */
```

In Xenix 3 a semaphore is a new kind of file with an i-node but no data. Its mode is marked with bit 050000, which is fortunately unused by System V and 4.2 BSD. Only read permission is used—if a process has it, it can open, acquire, and release the semaphore.

creatsem and opensem work much like creat and open. Once you have a semaphore-ID, you can call waitsem to acquire the semaphore and sigsem to release it (that is, to signal a process that may be waiting for it). If several processes are waiting for a semaphore, the oldest one gets it first—it is a first-in-first-out (FIFO) queue (not to be confused with a FIFO). nbwaitsem is a nonblocking form of waitsem. If the semaphore is locked it returns immediately with an errno of ENAVAIL (a new error code added to Xenix 3).

It's very easy to reimplement semtran, P, and V in terms of the Xenix 3 semaphores:

```
int semtran(key)  /* translate semaphore key to ID */
int key;
{
    int sid;
    char sname[20];
    extern int errno;

    sprintf(sname, "/tmp/sem%d\n", key);
    if ((sid = opensem(sname)) != -1)
        return(sid);
    if (errno == ENOENT)
        if ((sid = creatsem(sname, 0444)) != -1)
            return(sid);
    syserr("semtran");
}
```

```
void P(sid)   /* acquire binary semaphore */
int sid;
{
    if (waitsem(sid) == -1)
        syserr("waitsem");
}
void V(sid)   /* release binary semaphore */
int sid;
{
    if (sigsem(sid) == -1)
        syserr("sigsem");
}
```

Don't forget that this implementation supports binary semaphores only. If you call **V** twice in a row you'll get an error return from **s i g s e m**. It would have been just as straightforward for the developers of Xenix 3 to have supported general semaphores. However, in view of our harsh criticism of the System V semaphore offering, we should compliment the people at Microsoft for their restraint.

Deadlock is always a possibility when you use two or more semaphores. Neither System V nor Xenix 3 checks for deadlock, and our FIFO implementation doesn't check either. If possible, you should always design your application to be deadlock-free; the fewer semaphores you use, the easier this is. The best solution—not always feasible—is to use no semaphores at all. For example, with a centralized DBMS that communicates with messages, the only semaphores are the record locks inside the DBMS. In this special case the DBMS is never a participant in a deadlock—only its clients are. So the DBMS can be programmed to detect the deadlock and then remove it, usually by terminating one of the deadlocked clients.

7.7 SHARED MEMORY

7.7.1 Basic Shared Memory Usage

The fastest way to move data between two processes is not to move it at all. The sender and receiver share some memory, and when the data is placed there by the sender it is instantly available to the receiver. A semaphore or a message is used to prevent the receiver from reading the data too soon and to prevent the sender from writing new data until the reader has finished.

Both System V and Xenix 3 support shared memory, between any number of processes. The shared memory is called a *segment*. There may be several shared segments, each shared between a subset of the active processes. A process may access several shared segments.

In both implementations a segment is first created outside the address space of any process, and then each process that wants to access it executes a system call to map it into its own address space. On modern computers there are several hardware segmentation registers used to address data segments. By keeping one or more of these free, the mapping to a shared segment is very fast. Subsequent access to the shared memory is via normal machine instructions that store and fetch data. Since the shared segment is within the process's address space, access to it is just as fast as access to local variables.

Hardware constraints may limit the number of shared segments that can be simultaneously accessed by a process. For portability across computers it's best to map in only one segment at a time. The hardware may also limit the size of a segment. For example, on a PDP-11 a segmentation register can address only 8192 bytes, so this is the maximum size of a segment (it's plenty big enough for most purposes).

There is one major difference between the System V and Xenix 3 implementations. On System V a process may map a shared segment in and leave it mapped for a long time. This is efficient because, while the mapping is faster than most system calls, it's thousands of times slower than accessing the segment with direct machine instructions. On Xenix 3, however, a process must map and unmap the segment each time it needs to use it. This is because it is forbidden to execute any system calls while the segment is mapped in. So on Xenix 3 shared memory may, depending on the application, be many times slower than it is on System V, although in both systems shared memory is much faster than any other method of interprocess communication.

7.7.2 Shared Memory in System V

The System V shared memory system calls resemble those for messages and semaphores:

```
#include <sys/types.h>
#include <sys/ipc.h>
#include <sys/shm.h>


int shmget(key, nbytes, flags)      /* get shared memory segment-ID */
key_t key;                          /* queue key (long) */
int nbytes;                         /* size of segment */
int flags;                          /* option flags */
/* returns segment-ID or -1 on error */


char *shmat(segid, addr, flags)     /* attach segment */
int segid;                          /* segment-ID */
char *addr;                         /* desired address */
int flags;
/* returns segment address or -1 on error */


int shmdt(addr)                     /* detach segment */
char *addr;                         /* segment address */
/* returns 0 on success or -1 on error */
```

```
int shmctl(segid, cmd, sbuf)      /* control segment */
int segid;
int cmd;                          /* command */
struct shmid_ds *sbuf;            /* pointer to status buffer */
/* returns 0 on success or -1 on error */
```

You translate a shared memory segment key to a segment-ID with shmget. If flags is IPC_CREAT the segment is created if necessary. The rightmost nine bits of flags are the permissions; read permission allows fetching data from the segment only, whereas write permission allows both storing and fetching. Since the actual storing and fetching is done outside the kernel, permissions are only enforced if the hardware provides appropriate facilities (such as the ability to designate a data segment read-only).

You map (attach) a segment to your address space with shmat. You can request a particular address by setting the addr argument appropriately. This is important if you are also allocating memory dynamically with the brk or sbrk system calls (see Sec. 9.3), because they won't go beyond an attached shared segment. Unfortunately, in many applications this constraint requires you to know exactly how memory is to be used, and to carefully assign regions to shared segments and dynamic allocation subroutines (such as malloc). This makes programs buggy, hard to maintain, and nonportable. If you don't care where the memory is mapped (lucky you!), you can use zero for addr and let the kernel pick an address. Don't expect to be able to use brk or sbrk again, however. If you've already called them, the kernel will respect their work and allocate the shared segment out of harm's way.

shmat gives you a honest-to-goodness pointer to the number of bytes you requested. You can store and fetch data using ordinary C operators. Presumably another process has mapped, or will map, this same segment (identified by key) to its address space. The two processes can then share data freely.

When you're done with a segment, or if you need the segmentation register it uses for another segment, you call shmdt to unmap (detach) it. The actual memory stays undisturbed and you can map it in later, although its address in your data space may be different then. Eventually you destroy the segment by calling shmctl with a command of IPC_RMID. It's a serious error to destroy a segment that is mapped into a process's address space.

On a machine with limited address space, it's possible for a process to use shared memory segments to increase its effective address space. For example, if the data space is limited to 64K (eight segments of 8K each), you might save one segmentation register (giving you 56K of data) and use it to access one of several shared segments, created with shmget. If you have, say, five of these, your program can then address 106K of RAM by moving among the shared segments with shmat and shmdt. You have to be pretty desperate to try this, but in special circumstances—such as a DBMS with a large appetite for buffers—it can be a lifesaver. It can be a lifetaker too, so be careful.

The kernel only gives you access to shared memory; it doesn't help you use it effectively. There is a wide variety of ways to use shared memory, but perhaps the most common is as a message-passing medium. Passing messages through shared memory is faster than with kernel-provided message system calls for two main reasons:

- During the transmission, the kernel is involved only in handling semaphores, a very quick operation. The overhead of a message queue is avoided.
- Data need not be copied from a process's data space to the kernel and back to the other process. If it is copied at all, it is copied entirely within user space, using ordinary machine instructions. On most computers this is much faster than intercontext copies. Because of this efficiency, it is feasible to pass much larger messages with shared memory than with kernel-provided messages. Many DBMSs need this increased capacity.

We'll show how to pass messages with shared memory and semaphores by reimplementing send and receive. The basic scheme is this: One shared memory segment acts like a message queue of length 1. For each such queue, there are two semaphores, one for sending (sndsid) and one for receiving (rcvsid). To send a message, a process acquires the sending semaphore (P(sndsid)) and, when it's available, copies the message to the shared segment. It then releases the receiving semaphore (V(rcvsid)). To receive, a process acquires the receiving semaphore, copies the message from the shared segment, and then releases the sending semaphore.

Since these activities are supposed to be fast, we have to avoid calling semget and shmget more times than necessary. We keep a local lookup table of the active queues to translate from a message queue key to the values of the semaphore-set-IDs, the shared segment address, and the shared segment-ID, in a manner similar to what we did in the previous section to avoid calling msgget too often (the function openqueue). We keep the segment mapped to our address space throughout the entire conversation.

Here's the code:

```
#include <sys/types.h>
#include <sys/ipc.h>
#include <sys/sem.h>
#include <sys/shm.h>

#define MAXMSG 4096
#define MAXOPEN 20
#define BADADDR (char *)(-1)

static BOOLEAN findinfo(key, sndsidp, rcvsidp, addrp, segidp)
                                        /* find msg info */
```

```
int key;
int *sndsidp, *rcvsidp, *segidp;
char **addrp;
{
    static struct {
        int key;                /* message queue key */
        int sndsid;             /* semaphore-ID for sending */
        int rcvsid;             /* semaphore-ID for receiving */
        char *addr;             /* address of shared memory segment */
        int segid;              /* shared memory ID */
    } sems[MAXOPEN];
    int i, avail;
    extern int errno;
    char *shmat();

    avail = -1;
    for (i = 0; i < MAXOPEN; i++) {
        if (sems[i].key == key) {
            *sndsidp = sems[i].sndsid;
            *rcvsidp = sems[i].rcvsid;
            *segidp = sems[i].segid;
            *addrp = sems[i].addr;
            return(TRUE);
        }
        if (sems[i].key == 0 && avail == -1)
            avail = i;
    }
    if (avail == -1) {
        errno = 0;
        return(FALSE);
    }
    sems[avail].key = key;
    *sndsidp = sems[avail].sndsid = semtran(key);
    *rcvsidp = sems[avail].rcvsid = semtran(key + 10000);
    if ((*segidp = sems[avail].segid = shmget((key_t)key, MAXMSG,
      0666 | IPC_CREAT)) == -1)
        return(FALSE);
    if ((*addrp = sems[avail].addr = shmat(*segidp, 0, 0)) == BADADDR)
        return(FALSE);
    return(TRUE);
}

BOOLEAN send(dstkey, buf, nbytes)  /* send message */
int dstkey;
char *buf;
int nbytes;
{
```

```
    int sndsid, rcvsid, segid;
    char *addr;


    if (!findinfo(dstkey, &sndsid, &rcvsid, &addr, &segid))
        return(FALSE);
    if (nbytes > MAXMSG)
        nbytes = MAXMSG;
    P(sndsid);
    memcpy(addr, buf, nbytes);
    V(rcvsid);
    return(TRUE);
}


BOOLEAN receive(srckey, buf, nbytes) /* receive message */
int srckey;
char *buf;
int nbytes;
{
    int sndsid, rcvsid, segid;
    char *addr;


    if (!findinfo(srckey, &sndsid, &rcvsid, &addr, &segid))
        return(FALSE);
    if (nbytes > MAXMSG)
        nbytes = MAXMSG;
    P(rcvsid);
    memcpy(buf, addr, nbytes);
    V(sndsid);
    return(TRUE);
}


void rmqueue(key) /* remove semaphores and segment */
int key;
{
    int sndsid, rcvsid, segid;
    char *addr;


    if (!findinfo(key, &sndsid, &rcvsid, &addr, &segid))
        syserr("findinfo");
    (void)semctl(sndsid, 0, IPC_RMID, 0); /* ignore error */
    (void)semctl(rcvsid, 0, IPC_RMID, 0); /* ignore error */
    (void)shmdt(addr); /* ignore error */
    (void)shmctl(segid, IPC_RMID, 0); /* ignore error */
}
```

m e m c p y is a standard System V subroutine that copies data from the area pointed to by its second argument to the area pointed to by its first. The third argument is the number of bytes to copy.

If this implementation isn't fast enough, there are a few things that can be done, although they may not help very much. One idea is to avoid the table lookup in f i n d i n f o entirely by making the user of s e n d and r e c e i v e deal with an index into the s e m s table instead of with an abstract key. The user gets the index through an initial call, analogous to s e m t r a n for semaphores.

For even more speed, the sender or the receiver can actually compute or process the message directly in the shared segment, without copying it in and out with m e m c p y. This keeps the semaphores locked for a much longer time, of course, so a bottleneck results if many processes are using the same message queue. This would happen if a DBMS has a single request queue and processes data directly in the shared segment. No other process could send a message until the DBMS finished with the previous one. Response time would increase, but the time to service a single request (considering only message-passing overhead, that is) would decrease.

You can have your cake and eat it too by designing the DBMS to work with several shared memory segments, one per client. More changes have to be made to bring this off. For one thing, the DBMS must do a nonblocking r e c e i v e since it has several queues to service; it doesn't know which one will have a message first. Also, there should be another (general, not binary) semaphore to tell the DBMS when it has work to do so it doesn't busy-wait when all the queues are empty. If you take this approach, make sure you don't go too far and end up with a monolithic system with the DBMS and all the clients joined into what is effectively a giant process, with half of physical memory wired down for shared message buffers. You're supposed to let the operating system do what it was designed for, not code your own operating system in user space!

Another alternative is to dispense with semaphores entirely (always a pleasant thought). Database requests and status responses are handled with messages, but the actual data is passed through shared memory. When the DBMS receives a request message it knows that the supplied data, if any, is available in the shared segment; when a client receives a response message it knows that the requested data, if any, is in the segment. No process ever accesses shared memory out of turn. A scheme like this was used at Bell Laboratories to implement an extremely high performance DBMS application.[5] On a single PDP-11/70 computer this application processes thousands of transactions an hour from a network of hundreds of terminals. This is as fast as a PDP-11/70 can go.

7.7.3 Shared Memory in Xenix 3

Now we'll move on to the shared-memory system calls in Xenix 3. As usual, they're simpler than those in System V.

---

[5]See R. F. Bergeron and M. J. Rochkind, "Automated Repair Service Bureau: Software Tools and Components," *Bell System Technical Journal* 61, no. 6 (July-August 1982), 1177-95.

```
#include <sd.h>

char *sdget(path, flags, nbytes, perms) /* attach shared segment */
char *path;                             /* path name */
int flags;                              /* option flags */
long nbytes;                            /* size of segment */
int perms;                              /* permission bits */
/* returns segment address or -1 on error */

int sdfree(addr)                        /* detach segment */
char *addr;                             /* segment address */
/* returns 0 on success or -1 on error */

int sdenter(addr, flags)                /* begin access to segment */
char *addr;
int flags;
/* returns 0 on success or -1 on error */

int sdleave(addr)                       /* end access to segment */
char *addr;
/* returns 0 on success or -1 on error */

int sdgetv(addr)                        /* get segment version number */
char *addr;
/* returns current version number or -1 on error */

int sdwaitv(addr, vnum)                 /* wait for version number */
char *addr;
int vnum;                               /* version number */
/* returns current version number or -1 on error */
```

Xenix 3 shared memory is like semaphores in that a zero-length file is used to represent the shared memory segment; this takes the place of the key used in System V. You start by making a call to sdget to map a shared segment of size nbytes to your address space. flags is used similarly to the second argument of open. These bits are defined:

SD_RDONLY   Allow reading only from the segment.

SD_WRITE   Allow reading and writing.

SD_CREAT   Create the segment if necessary. Use perms for the permission bits. As with System V, write permission allows both reading and writing.

SD_UNLOCK   Allow multiple processes to access the segment simultaneously. The Xenix 3 manual warns that this may slow access down considerably on computers without appropriate segmentation hardware (we'll see why shortly). When

shared memory is used for message passing this option is
undesirable anyway.

The `size` and `mode` arguments are used only with `SD_CREAT`.

Unlike with System V, you can't go ahead and use the segment even though
it is mapped into your address space. You have to call `sdenter` first. You should
call `sdleave` as soon thereafter as possible, and certainly before you make any
other system call. If you don't, data in the shared segment may be corrupted. There
are two `flags` bits: `SD_NOWAIT` makes `sdenter` return with an error instead
of blocking if another process is accessing the segment (and if `SD_UNLOCK` isn't
set). `SD_WRITE` allows the entering process to modify the segment; this is a
stronger statement than merely having permission to do so.

If you don't set the `SD_UNLOCK` flag on `sdget`, there is an apparent benefit in that `sdenter` and `sdleave` then act as semaphores, since only one
process at a time can access the segment. Unfortunately, this is no benefit at all
since it doesn't eliminate the need to call `P` and `V` on the sending and receiving
semaphores, as we did in the implementation of `send` and `receive` above.
Senders and receivers still have to alternate. `sdenter` and `sdleave` only guarantee that no two of them access the memory concurrently; it does not prevent a
sender from receiving its own data, or one sender overwriting another's message,
or a receiver receiving the same message twice. The semaphores do prevent these
atrocities.

In truth, the real purpose of `sdenter` and `sdleave` is to allow an implementor to handle Xenix 3 shared memory by copying data from the kernel to
the accessor's address space upon `sdenter`, and then to copy it back upon
`sdleave`. Without enough hardware segmentation registers, there's no other
choice. You might be using shared memory to simulate messages while the kernel
is using messages to simulate shared memory!

The last two system calls are very strange. Each time `sdleave` is executed
on a segment, its version number is incremented. `sdgetv` retrieves the current
version number. `sdwaitv` blocks until it attains a certain value. You could use
these to make the sender of a message wait for a response from the receiver: The
sender gets the version number (N, say) with `sdgetv`, calls `sdleave`, and then
waits on `sdwaitv` for the version number to become N + 2. A clever idea, but
it won't work for multiple senders or multiple receivers.

Here's `send` and `receive` implemented again, for the fourth and last time
(in this book, anyway):

```
#include <sd.h>

#define MAXMSG 4096
#define MAXOPEN 20
#define BADADDR (char *)(-1)
```

```
static BOOLEAN findinfo(key, sndsidp, rcvsidp, addrp)
                                            /* find msg info */
int key;
int *sndsidp, *rcvsidp;
char **addrp;
{
    static struct {
        int key;              /* message queue key */
        int sndsid;           /* semaphore-ID for sending */
        int rcvsid;           /* semaphore-ID for receiving */
        char *addr;           /* address of shared memory segment */
    } sems[MAXOPEN];
    int i, avail;
    char sname[20];
    extern int errno;
    char *sdget();

    avail = -1;
    for (i = 0; i < MAXOPEN; i++) {
        if (sems[i].key == key) {
            *sndsidp = sems[i].sndsid;
            *rcvsidp = sems[i].rcvsid;
            *addrp = sems[i].addr;
            return(TRUE);
        }
        if(sems[i].key == 0 && avail == -1)
            avail = i;
    }
    if (avail == -1) {
        errno = 0;
        return(FALSE);
    }
    sems[avail].key = key;
    *sndsidp = sems[avail].sndsid = semtran(key);
    *rcvsidp = sems[avail].rcvsid = semtran(key + 10000);
    sprintf(sname, "/tmp/sd%d\n", key);
    if ((*addrp = sems[avail].addr = sdget(sname, SD_CREAT, MAXMSG,
      0666)) == BADADDR)
        return(FALSE);
    return(TRUE);
}

BOOLEAN send(dstkey, buf, nbytes) /* send message */
int dstkey;
char *buf;
int nbytes;
{
```

```
    int sndsid, rcvsid;
    char *addr;


    if (!findinfo(dstkey, &sndsid, &rcvsid, &addr))
        return(FALSE);
    if (nbytes > MAXMSG)
        nbytes = MAXMSG;
    P(sndsid);
    if (sdenter(addr, SD_WRITE) == -1) {
        V(sndsid);
        return(FALSE);
    }
    memcpy(addr, buf, nbytes);
    if (sdleave(addr) == -1) {
        V(sndsid);
        return(FALSE);
    }
    V(rcvsid);
    return(TRUE);
}


BOOLEAN receive(srckey, buf, nbytes)  /* receive message */
int srckey;
char *buf;
int nbytes;
{
    int sndsid, rcvsid;
    char *addr;


    if (!findinfo(srckey, &sndsid, &rcvsid, &addr))
        return(FALSE);
    if (nbytes > MAXMSG)
        nbytes = MAXMSG;
    P(rcvsid);
    if (sdenter(addr, 0) == -1) {
        V(rcvsid);
        return(FALSE);
    }
    memcpy(buf, addr, nbytes);
    if (sdleave(addr) == -1) {
        V(rcvsid);
        return(FALSE);
    }
    V(sndsid);
    return(TRUE);
}
```

```
void rmqueue(key) /* un-map segment */
int key;
{
    int sndsid, rcvsid;
    char *addr;

    if (!findinfo(key, &sndsid, &rcvsid, &addr))
        syserr("findinfo");
    (void)sdfree(addr); /* ignore error */
}
```

memcpy isn't available in Xenix 3, but it can easily be coded in C. In send and receive we clear the sndsid and rcvsid semaphores if an error occurs. Just because we failed to accomplish our purpose doesn't mean we can't at least allow someone else to try. rmqueue doesn't remove the special files created for the semaphores and the shared memory segment. If desired, appropriate calls to unlink can be added.

7.8 RECORD LOCKING IN XENIX 3

Record locking is the tip of a rather large iceberg. After surveying the submerged part, we'll show how the tip is implemented in Xenix 3.

In a DBMS-based application a *transaction* is a small computation that changes a database in a consistent way. By consistent we mean that the database obeys certain structural rules before and after the transaction executes, but not necessarily while it is executing. For example, one rule may be that an employee may be in only one department. A transaction to transfer an employee may have to perform two distinct operations: removal from one department's record and insertion in another department's record. During the transaction the employee may be in no department or in two departments, but when the transaction completes the employee is in exactly one department.

To guarantee that a transaction leaves the database in a consistent state, it must be *atomic*, which means that it must be executed in its entirety or not at all, and it must be *serializable*, which means that if several transactions are executed concurrently, their effect must be the same as if they were run one at a time, in any order.

Atomicity is typically achieved by saving the old copy of each updated record on an *undo log* while the transaction executes. If the transaction aborts, the database can be restored to the way it was by undoing each updated record. When the transaction completes, the undo log can be discarded.

Serializability is typically achieved by locking records as the transaction accesses them. There are two kinds of locks: *share* and *exclusive*. A share lock is placed when a transaction reads a record; it is allowed if the record is unlocked or share-locked by another transaction. An exclusive lock is placed when a transaction writes a record; it is allowed only if the record is unlocked. Locks may *not* be released when the read or write activity is complete—they must be held until the transaction completes. This is because until the transaction completes there is the possibility that it may be undone, which can occur safely only if all the records it touched are still locked. For example, consider the following scenario:

1. Transaction A locks record 1, saves a copy on the undo log, modifies it, and then unlocks it.
2. Transaction B similarly modifies record 1 (with different data).
3. Transaction B completes.
4. Transaction A aborts and restores record 1 from the undo log, wiping out transaction B's modification.

This sort of lost update is prevented if transaction A holds its lock on record 1 until it completes. That forces transaction B to wait in step 2. Not having an undo log would be just as bad, because then the effects of a half-completed transaction, which is allowed to put the database in an inconsistent state, would remain after it aborts. There would be no way of undoing the damage.

So there's little point in using record locking without an undo log unless you can ensure that all transactions complete normally, which is impossible. An aborted transaction that simply releases its locks without undoing its updates can cause just as much inconsistency as a transaction that updates the database without locking at all. Record locking is not a concurrency-control solution—it's just part of one.

Two transactions attempting to lock the same records can deadlock. In this case one of them must be aborted to allow the other to proceed. The use of the undo log allows the aborted process to back out its updates smoothly. It is somewhat time-consuming to do the computation necessary to detect deadlock: The lock table must be examined to create a graph of dependencies, and then loops have to be found. The process of *victim selection*—deciding which deadlocked transaction to abort—may also be complex. For example, it may be best to abort the transaction that has the least already invested in database processing, or the transaction with the lowest priority, or the transaction that is tying up the most records. How often deadlock detection and victim selection occur, how fast they are done, and how well the victim is selected may have a major impact on the performance of the DBMS.

Some versions of UNIX have implemented record locking in the kernel as a system call. The similar approaches taken by Xenix 3, PC/IX, and the /usr/group Proposed Standard have these defects:

- There is no undo log. When deadlock is discovered, the process receiving the error must undo things for itself. Because this is a complex operation, designers will usually elect to use a centralized DBMS design. As we stressed in Sec. 7.2, with a centralized approach there is no need for the kernel to do record locking, since it can be done just as effectively in user space.
- Deadlock detection is done on *every* lock request and on *every* read and write to a database file.

- Victim selection is naive. The first process to request a lock that would, if granted, cause deadlock is given an error return.
- In Xenix 3 there can be only 200 locks.
- In some designs, such as those in PC/IX and the /usr/group Proposed Standard, there are no share locks, only exclusive locks. In many applications this reduces concurrency significantly.

Having thoroughly discouraged you from using kernel record locking, we'll now explain how it works in Xenix 3. The PC/IX and /usr/group system calls (both named lockf) work similarly.

```
#include <sys/locking.h>

int locking(fd, flags, nbytes)      /* lock or unlock record */
int fd;                             /* file descriptor */
int flags;                          /* option flags */
long nbytes;                        /* number of bytes to lock */
/* returns 0 on success or −1 on error */
```

Since a UNIX file consists only of a sequence of bytes, with no concept of records, this system call deals with an arbitrary region of a file defined as the nbytes bytes located at the current file pointer. To lock or unlock a region, the file must first be opened and the file pointer positioned with lseek. Special files, pipes, FIFOs, and directories may not be locked. The size of the region to lock or unlock is given by nbytes; if it is 0, the entire file is locked or unlocked. The region need not exist yet; that is, nbytes may define a region that goes beyond the current end-of-file. The flags argument can have these values:

LK_UNLCK	Unlock the region.
LK_LOCK	Set an exclusive lock on the region. If it is currently locked (share or exclusive), wait for it to become free.
LK_NBLCK	Similar to LK_LOCK but return with error code EACCES if the region is locked.
LK_RLCK	Set a share lock on the region. If it currently has an exclusive lock, wait for it to become free.
LK_NBRLCK	Similar to LK_RLCK but return with error code EACCES if the region has an exclusive lock.

Deadlock detection is performed on every call to set a lock. If granting the lock would cause deadlock, error code EDEADLOCK is returned. Note that this scheme is based on the assumption that a process waiting on a lock will wait for it to be freed. Since locking can be interrupted by a signal, an apparent deadlock could be resolved by the processes involved even if the deadlocking lock were granted. This is not a defect of the Xenix 3 implementation, however, since a centralized DBMS with its own lock manager would undoubtedly make the same assumption—what other choice is there?

Regions to be locked or unlocked can overlap; the Xenix 3 manual page describes in detail how overlap is handled. In practice, regions are distinct records and no overlap occurs. Handling overlap at all is a waste because it slows down processing, it is incompatible with most undo-logging designs, and it isn't used by DBMSs.

Here's a naive example that illustrates how `locking` is called (don't take it as a recommendation). We open a file, lock a record, read it, modify it, write it back, and unlock it.

```
void locktest() /* test locking */
{
    int fd, nread;
    char buf[RECSIZE];
    long lseek();

    if ((fd = open("dbfile", O_RDWR, 0)) == -1)
        syserr("open");
    if (lseek(fd, POS, 0) == -1)
        syserr("lseek");
    if (locking(fd, LK_LOCK, RECSIZE) == -1)
        syserr("locking");
    switch (read(fd, buf, RECSIZE)) {
    case -1:
        syserr("read");
    case RECSIZE:
        break;
    default:
        fatal("read");
    }
    process(buf); /* perform application-defined processing */
    if (write(fd, buf, RECSIZE) == -1)
        syserr("write");
    if (lseek(fd, POS, 0) == -1)
        syserr("lseek");
    if (locking(fd, LK_UNLCK, RECSIZE) == -1)
        syserr("locking");
}
```

7.9 PORTABILITY

Nothing in this chapter works on UNIX systems based on Version 7 or 4.2 BSD, although `send`, `receive`, P, and V can be implemented on 4.2 BSD using system calls unique to that version of UNIX. Efficient and reliable DBMSs can't be implemented on an unadulterated Version 7 UNIX.[6]

[6]For evidence of this, see Michael Stonebraker, "Retrospection on a Database System," *ACM Transactions on Database Systems*" 5, no. 2 (June 1980), 225–40. Stonebraker tried to implement a multiple-process DBMS on a UNIX system without FIFOs or messages.

As for systems based on System III, the best approach is to use high-level functions like s e n d, r e c e i v e, P, and V to the extent possible, rather than to use direct system calls. If necessary, minor changes can be made to the functions as we have presented them. For instance, a nonblocking option can easily be added.

Initially, stick with FIFOs for both messages and semaphores. When your application is running, measure its performance to see if an alternative implementation is needed. If so, change the implementation of your high-level functions, but don't change the interface. This will allow you to port your system to other System III-based environments, with a loss in efficiency but not in function.

Many commercial developers are concerned with porting only between System V and Xenix 3. We've shown high-performance implementations for messages and semaphores on both systems in this chapter. If shared memory is needed, high-level functions can be designed for that too, since both System V and Xenix 3 support shared memory explicitly. However, if shared memory is to be used only for messages, it should be subsumed into the implementation of s e n d and r e c e i v e.

There's much more to implementing DBMSs and other related applications on UNIX besides interprocess communication, of course. We've given it so much attention primarily because it's been the area in which UNIX has been least adequate. In areas such as access to files and devices, UNIX has always been more open-ended. While the UNIX file system may not be suitable for DBMSs, at least you can go around it with raw I/O (see Sec. 3.3). And no matter what devices you need to handle, you can always add a device driver (assuming the kernel has space for one more). Indeed, it's fair to say now that modern UNIX systems like System V or Xenix 3 are excellent bases for DBMS implementation. This doesn't mean that the job is easy, only that it's possible, and that the results can be outstanding.

EXERCISES

7.1. Change the shell in Sec. 6.4 to use FIFOs instead of pipes.

7.2. If you have access to one or more UNIX versions with messages or shared memory (System V, Xenix 3, or 4.2 BSD), conduct an experiment to compare the efficiency of messages implemented using different mechanisms (FIFOs, kernel-provided messages, and shared memory). Does the message length affect which mechanism is most efficient? Prepare a table that summarizes your results.

7.3. Redefine r e c e i v e to take a fourth Boolean argument that tells it whether to block if the queue is empty. Change each implementation (FIFO, message, and both shared memory versions) appropriately.

7.4. Redesign the System V message system calls so they are simpler to use but still retain most of the important features. Try to implement your design in terms of the existing system calls. The complexity of your new system calls should be between s e n d/ r e c e i v e and the existing system calls.

7.5. Same as Exercise 7.4, but for semaphores.

7.6. Same as Exercise 7.4, but for shared memory.

7.7. Design and implement a lock manager for the centralized DBMS in Sec. 7.4.

8
SIGNALS

8.1 INTRODUCTION

Signals are a little like messages, but not so much like them that they deserve to be in either of our chapters on interprocess communication. In fact, as we shall see in this chapter, signals are awkward as mechanisms for interprocess communication. Signals differ from messages in these ways:

- A signal can be sent at any time, occasionally from another process, but more often from the kernel as a result of some exceptional event (such as a hangup or a floating-point error).
- A signal isn't necessarily received and acted on. By default most signals cause the receiving process to terminate. Alternatively, the process can arrange to ignore signals of a given type. Even if a process tries to receive a signal, it might slip through and terminate the process anyhow.
- Signals have no information content. In particular, the receiver can't find out the identity of the sender.
- Signals can be sent only to processes, not to a message queue. Therefore a signal can't be used as a semaphore.

With these limitations, why bother dealing with signals at all? It's primarily a question of defense. The kernel sends signals whether you like it or not—you have to arrange to ignore them or catch them, or your process will terminate. But signals should be used only for exceptional events, never for normal communications. The facilities described in Chaps. 6 and 7 should be used for that.

We'll begin, in the next section, with a listing of the different signals that can be sent, why they are sent, and what effect they have on a process. Then we'll discuss the `signal` system call, which is used to specify the action that occurs when a signal is received. Next we'll go into the related system calls `kill`, `pause`, and `alarm`. We'll close with our customary section on portability, but there won't be much to say because almost everything in this chapter is common to all modern UNIX versions except 4.2 BSD.

8.2 TYPES OF SIGNALS

Systems III and V define 19 types of signals, the first 15 of which are in Version 7 as well. While these break down into a few related groups, they're really just a miscellaneous assortment of events for which the signal mechanism is useful. Some signals are widely used, while others are extremely obscure and used by only one or two programs. For example, the trace-trap signal is used only by the debuggers `adb` and `sdb`.

The following list gives a brief explanation of each signal. Except for the last two signals listed, which are ignored, the default action upon receipt of a signal is for the process to terminate. Each signal's number is given in parentheses after its symbolic name, which is defined in the header file `/usr/include/signal.h`. You should always use the name instead of the number.

SIGHUP   (1)   *Hangup.* Sent when a terminal is hung up to every process for which it is the control terminal (see Sec. 1.5). Also sent to each process in a process group when the group leader terminates for any reason. This simulates hanging up on terminals that can't be physically hung up, such as a personal computer.

SIGINT   (2)   *Interrupt.* Sent to every process associated with a control terminal when the interrupt key is hit. This action of the interrupt key may be suppressed or the interrupt key may be changed via the `ioctl` system call (see Sec. 4.4.6). Note that suppressing the interrupt key is completely different from ignoring the signal, although the effect (or lack of it) on the process is the same.

SIGQUIT   (3)   *Quit.* Similar to SIGINT, but sent when the quit key (normally Control-\) is hit. Commonly sent in order to get a core dump.[1]

---

[1]Dumps of semiconductor memory are still called *core* dumps, and they always will be.

SIGILL   (4)   *Illegal instruction.* Sent when the hardware detects an illegal instruction. On some computers, notably the PDP-11, this fault occurs when a process executes a floating-point instruction on a computer without hardware floating point. A library package catches this signal and interprets the instruction with software. Sometimes a process using floating point aborts with this signal when it is accidentally linked without the −f option on the cc command. Since C programs are in general unable to modify their instructions, this signal rarely indicates a genuine program bug.

SIGTRAP   (5)   *Trace trap.* Sent after every instruction when a process is run with tracing turned on with ptrace (see Sec. 9.9).

SIGIOT   (6)   *I/O trap instruction.*[2] Sent when a hardware fault occurs, the exact nature of which is up to the implementor and is machine-dependent. In practice, this signal is preempted by the standard subroutine abort, which a process calls to commit suicide in a way that will produce a core dump.

SIGEMT   (7)   *Emulator trap instruction.* Sent when an implementation-dependent hardware fault occurs. Extremely rare.

SIGFPE   (8)   *Floating-point exception.* Sent when the hardware detects a floating-point error, such as a floating point number with an illegal format. Almost always indicates a program bug.

SIGKILL   (9)   *Kill.* The one and only sure way to kill a process, since this signal is always fatal (can't be ignored or caught). To be used only in emergencies; SIGTERM (see next page) is preferred.

SIGBUS   (10)   *Bus error.* Sent when an implementation-dependent hardware fault occurs. Usually means that the process referenced at an odd address data that should have been word-aligned.

SIGSEGV   (11)   *Segmentation violation.* Sent when an implementation-dependent hardware fault occurs. Usually means that the process referenced data outside its address space.

SIGSYS   (12)   *Bad argument to system call.* Not used.

SIGPIPE   (13)   *Write on a pipe not opened for reading.* Sent to a process when it writes on a pipe that has no reader. Usually

---

[2]IOT and EMT are PDP-11 instruction mnemonics.

this means that the reader was another process that terminated abnormally. This signal acts to terminate all processes in a pipeline: When a process terminates abnormally, all processes to its right receive an end-of-file and all processes to its left receive this signal. Note that the standard shell (s h) makes each process in a pipeline the parent of the process to its left. Hence, the writer is not the reader's parent (it's the other way around), and would otherwise not be notified of the reader's death.

SIGALRM   (14)   *Alarm clock.* Sent when a process's alarm clock goes off. The alarm clock is set with the a l a r m system call (see Sec. 8.7).

SIGTERM   (15)   *Software termination.* The standard termination signal. It's the default signal sent by the k i l l command, and is also used during system shutdown to terminate all active processes. A program should be coded to either let this signal default or else to clean up quickly (e.g., remove temporary files) and call e x i t.

SIGUSR1   (16)   *User defined signal 1.* This signal may be used by application programs for interprocess communication. This is not recommended, however, and consequently this signal is rarely used.

SIGUSR2   (17)   *User defined signal 2.* Similar to SIGUSR1.

SIGCLD   (18)   *Death of a child.* Sent to the parent when a child process terminates. Acts differently from any other signal (discussed in detail later in this section).

SIGPWR   (19)   *Power-fail restart.* Exact meaning is implementation-dependent. One possibility is for it to be sent when power is about to fail (voltage has passed, say, 100 volts and is falling). The process has a very brief time to execute. It should normally clean up and exit (as with SIGTERM). If the process wishes to survive the failure (which might only be a momentary voltage drop), it can clean up and then sleep for a few seconds. If it wakes up it can assume that the disaster was only a dream and resume processing. If it doesn't wake up, no further action is necessary.

Programs that need to clean up before terminating should arrange to catch signals SIGHUP, SIGINT, and SIGTERM. Until the program is solid, SIGQUIT should be left alone so there will be a way to terminate the program (with a core dump) from the keyboard. Arrangements for the other signals are made much less often; usually they are left to terminate the process. But a really polished program will want to catch everything it can, to clean up, possibly log the error, and print a nice error message. Psychologically, a message like "Internal error 53: contact customer support" is more acceptable than the message "Bus error—core dumped" from the shell.

For some signals, the default action of termination is accompanied by a core dump. These are `SIGQUIT`, `SIGILL`, `SIGTRAP`, `SIGIOT`, `SIGEMT`, `SIGFPE`, `SIGBUS`, `SIGSEGV`, and `SIGSYS`.

8.3 signal SYSTEM CALL

```
#include <signal.h>

int (*signal(sig, fcn))()      /* specify handling for signal */
int sig;                        /* signal number */
int (*fcn)();                   /* action on receipt */
/* returns previous action or -1 on error */
```

The declarations here baffle practically everyone at first sight. All they mean is that the second argument to `signal` is a pointer to a function, and that a pointer to a function is returned.[3] That the pointer is to a function returning an `int` is vestigial; the function returns nothing and might better be declared:

```
void (*fcn)();
```

(`void` is a relatively new addition to the C language.)

The first argument, `sig`, is a signal number. The second argument, `fcn`, can be one of three things:

1. `SIG_DFL`. This sets the default action for the signal. `SIGCLD` and `SIGPWR` are ignored; all others terminate the receiving process. A parent waiting on its child with `wait` is notified via the exit status that its child met this fate rather than normally exiting with `exit` (see Sec. 5.6).

2. `SIG_IGN`. This sets the signal to be ignored; the process becomes immune to it. The signal `SIGKILL` can't be ignored. Generally, only `SIGHUP`, `SIGINT`, and `SIGQUIT` should ever be permanently ignored. The receipt of other signals should at least be logged, since they indicate that something exceptional has occurred. `SIG_IGN` has an additional meaning for `SIGCLD` that is explained below.

3. *A pointer to a function.* This arranges to catch the signal; every signal but `SIGKILL` may be caught. The function is called when the signal arrives.

---

[3]See Sec. 8.4 of the "C Reference Manual" (Appendix A of *The C Programming Language*).

A parent's action for a signal is inherited by a child process. Actions
S I G _ D F L and S I G _ I G N are preserved across an e x e c, but caught signals are
reset to S I G _ D F L. This is essential because the catching function will be overwritten by new code. Of course, the new program can set its own signals.

With one exception, S I G C L D, arriving signals are not queued. They are either
ignored, they terminate the process, or they are caught. This is the main reason why
signals are inappropriate for interprocess communication—a message in the form
of a signal might be lost if it arrives when that type of signal is temporarily ignored.
Another problem is that arriving signals are rather rude. They interrupt whatever
is currently going on, which is complicated to deal with properly, as we'll see shortly.

s i g n a l returns the previous action for the signal. This is used if it's necessary to restore it to the way it was. By way of example, we'll now show the code
for the functions i g n o r e s i g and e n t r y s i g that were used in the shell of
Sec. 6.4. Recall that i g n o r e s i g sets interrupt and quit to be ignored, and
e n t r y s i g restores them to the way they were on program entry, which is how
we want them set when we run a command from the shell. The first time it is called,
i g n o r e s i g must save the old signals for use by e n t r y s i g. The external declarations in this example are fascinating:

```
#include <signal.h>

static int (*entryint)(), (*entryquit)();
#define BADSIG (int (*)())-1 /* -1 cast to ptr to int fcn */

void ignoresig() /* ignore interrupt and quit */
{
    static BOOLEAN first = TRUE;

    if (first) {
        first = FALSE;
        entryint = signal(SIGINT, SIG_IGN);
        entryquit = signal(SIGQUIT, SIG_IGN);
        if (entryint == BADSIG || entryquit == BADSIG)
            syserr("signal");
    }
    else if (signal(SIGINT, SIG_IGN) == BADSIG ||
        signal(SIGQUIT, SIG_IGN) == BADSIG)
        syserr("signal");
}

void entrysig() /* restore interrupt and quit */
{
    if (signal(SIGINT, entryint) == BADSIG ||
        signal(SIGQUIT, entryquit) == BADSIG)
        syserr("signal");
}
```

In checking the error return we cast -1 to a function pointer rather than casting the return value from `signal` to an `int`, because some versions of the `lint` command complain about the latter but not the former. The business of using -1 as an error return for functions returning pointers (also used by `shmat` in Sec. 7.7.2) is questionable to begin with—we're lucky it works at all. Standard subroutines like `malloc` use `NULL` instead, which is the proper thing to do.

Defaulting and ignoring signals is easy; the hard part is catching them. To catch a signal you supply a pointer to a function as the second argument to `signal`. When the signal arrives two things happen, in this order:

1. The signal is reset to its default action, which is usually termination. Exceptions are `SIGILL` and `SIGTRAP`, which are not reset because they are signaled too often.

2. The designated function is called with a single integer argument equal to the number of the signal that it caught. When and if the function returns, processing resumes from the point where it was interrupted.

If the signal arrives while the process is waiting for any event at all, and if the signal-catching function returns, the interrupted system call returns with an error return of `EINTR`—it is not restarted automatically. You must distinguish this return from a legitimate error. Nothing is wrong—a signal just happened to arrive. System calls that can wait include `open`, `read`, `write`, `wait`, `ioctl`, `pause`, and certain interprocess communication system calls described in Chapter 7 (such as `semop` and `msgrcv`). I/O on files is immune to interruption since it never blocks.

When a parent process that catches interrupts and quits waits for a child to terminate, there is the danger that an interrupt or quit will bounce the parent out of `wait` before the child has terminated, since pressing either key sends a signal to both processes. There are several ways to avoid this, but the simplest is for the parent to ignore interrupts and quits while executing `wait`. In the shell of Sec. 6.4 this was the case because the parent ran all the time with interrupts and quits ignored.

It's extremely difficult to take interrupted system calls into account when programming. You either have to program to restart every system call that can wait or else temporarily ignore signals when executing such a system call. Both approaches are awkward, and the second runs the additional risk of losing a signal during the interval when it's ignored. We therefore offer this rule: *Never return from a signal-catching function.* Either terminate processing entirely or terminate the current operation by executing a global jump (see the next section). The text editor `ed`, for example, catches interrupts and jumps directly to its main loop. It doesn't care at all about resuming interrupted system calls. (Catching an alarm clock signal is an exception to this rule; see Sec. 8.7.)

Occasionally a UNIX programmer violates this rule with the clever trick of just setting a flag when a signal arrives instead of processing it right away. Then, when the program is ready, it checks the flag to see if the signal arrived. This is a bad technique unless it is known for certain that a waiting system call won't be interrupted. Even if that is true initially, subsequent modifications to the program may introduce new system calls. You can imagine the plight of another programmer trying to figure out why system calls keep failing, unaware of the signal-catching function that may be in an entirely different module.[4]

Since the first thing that happens when a caught signal arrives is to change its action to the default (termination), another signal of the same type arriving immediately after the first can terminate the process before it has a chance to even begin the catching function. This is rare but possible, especially on a busy system. The situation is like tossing a raw egg around your living room: Even though it will be caught almost every time, the odds of messing up the carpet are still too high. It's the *miss* you'll remember, not the *catches*.

This loophole can be tightened, but not eliminated, by setting the signal to be ignored immediately upon entering the catching function, before doing anything else. Since we're not using signals as messages, we don't care if an arriving signal is thereby missed. We're concerned only with processing the first one correctly and with not terminating prematurely. Here is a function that arranges to catch hangup, interrupt, quit, and termination signals so that a temporary file can be removed before the process terminates. Note that we only bother to catch a signal if it is not already being ignored; otherwise, a process run in the background from the shell (command line terminated with &) with interrupts ignored would terminate (after cleanup) when we hit the interrupt key.

```
#include <signal.h>

#define BADSIG (int (*)())-1

void catchsigs()    /* catch signals */
{
    void cleanup();

    setsig(SIGHUP, cleanup);
    setsig(SIGINT, cleanup);
    setsig(SIGQUIT, cleanup);
    setsig(SIGTERM, cleanup);
}
```

---

[4]If you make it a habit to always print out the value of errno when a system call fails (by calling syserr, for example), you won't be mystified for long, since the EINTR error code will clarify what's going on.

```
static void setsig(sig, fcn) /* set signal if defaulted */
int sig;
void (*fcn)();
{
    switch (signal(sig, SIG_IGN)) {
    case BADSIG:
        syserr("signal");
    case SIG_IGN:
        return;
    case SIG_DFL:
        break;
    default:
        fatal("signal already caught!");
    }
    if (signal(sig, fcn) == BADSIG)
        syserr("signal");
}

void cleanup(sig)    /* clean up and terminate */
int sig;
{
    if (signal(sig, SIG_IGN) == BADSIG)
        syserr("signal");
    if (unlink(TEMPFILE) == -1)
        syserr("unlink");
    switch (sig) {
    case SIGHUP:
        fprintf(stderr, "Hangup.\n");
        break;
    case SIGINT:
        fprintf(stderr, "Interrupt.\n");
        break;
    case SIGQUIT:
        fprintf(stderr, "Quit.\n");
    }
    exit(1);
}
```

The first call to **signal** in **setsig** actually serves two purposes:

- If the signal was already ignored, it makes sure it stays that way.
- If the signal wasn't ignored, it sets it to be ignored so we have some breathing room in which to set it to be caught.

catchsig is a handy function to keep around. You call it at the front of any program that needs to clean up before terminating. You can supply a different definition for **cleanup** in each application.

The signal S I G C L D behaves differently from the other signals. It allows children to be waited for more efficiently in cases where the child terminates before the parent can execute w a i t (see Sec. 5.6), or when the parent doesn't care to ever execute w a i t. Ordinarily such children continue to occupy a process-table slot as zombie processes; when they are finally waited for, the slot is freed. But if S I G C L D is set to S I G _ I G N in the parent, the effects of e x i t and w a i t are changed: When the child calls e x i t, no zombie process is retained—the process-table slot is freed immediately. When the parent executes w a i t, it waits for *all* children and then returns the error code E C H I L D. The exit codes of the children are unavailable to the parent. This saves considerable overhead when a parent invokes many children that may terminate at various times, provided the parent doesn't care about their error codes.

S I G C L D can also be caught. But since there is no way to determine the exit code, this makes little sense.

The System III and V manuals warn that S I G P W R and S I G C L D may be changed in future versions of UNIX and therefore should not be used in new programs. Sounds like excellent advice.

8.4 GLOBAL JUMPS

In interactive programs you often want a signal like S I G I N T to just terminate the current activity, not terminate the whole program. Somehow the catching function must jump to the main loop, or wherever execution is to resume. This is what e d does when you hit the interrupt key during an editing session.

Once again, we'll start off by doing things wrong. In the interactive status utility shown in Sec. 3.12, the function m a i n l o o p contains the infinite loop that handles commands. Suppose we want to reexecute m a i n l o o p when the user hits the interrupt key. Here's how *not* to do it:

```
...
void mainloop();

...
if (signal(SIGINT, mainloop) == BADSIG)
    syserr("signal");
mainloop();
...
```

After arranging to catch interrupts, we call m a i n l o o p. When an interrupt occurs, we call m a i n l o o p again, this time as the signal-catching function. Everything might appear to work OK for a while, but this approach has two serious defects:

- Every time the interrupt key is hit we stay in the catching function, nesting ourselves deeper and deeper, with more and more return locations and local variables pushed onto the stack.

- If **mainloop** ever returns we'll pop back to the previous invocation—the one that was interrupted. This will totally mystify the user, and probably the programmer as well.

The solution is to resume execution by calling **mainloop** with the stack restored to the way it was when **mainloop** was called the first time. Two standard subroutines (*not* system calls) are designed to do exactly that:

```
#include <setjmp.h>

int setjmp(jmpenv)                    /* set target for longjmp */
jmp_buf jmpenv;                       /* saved environment */
/* returns 0 or value supplied by longjmp */

void longjmp(jmpenv, val)             /* jump to target set by setjmp */
jmp_buf jmpenv;
int val;                              /* value for setjmp to return */
```

You call **setjmp** at the place to which you want **longjmp** to return; **setjmp** returns 0. The current state of the stack is saved in **jmpenv**. When **longjmp** is called it restores the stack to the way it was when **setjmp** was called, erasing the evidence of any functions called after **setjmp**. Then **setjmp** returns (even though it wasn't called) with the value supplied by the **val** argument to **longjmp**. When used with **signal**, **setjmp** is usually called just before the signal is set to be caught, and **longjmp** is called from inside the catching function. When **setjmp** makes its **longjmp**-caused return, **signal** will be called again to recatch the signal (recall that a caught signal is restored to **SIG_DFL**).

Here is the top part of **statutil**, rewritten to handle interrupt signals properly:

```
#include <signal.h>
#include <setjmp.h>

static jmp_buf jmpbuf;
#define BADSIG (int (*)())-1

main()    /* statutil */
{
    void jumper();
    BOOLEAN catchint;

    catchint = signal(SIGINT, SIG_IGN) != SIG_IGN;
    setbuf(stdout, NULL);
    help();
```

```
        if (catchint) {
            if (setjmp(jmpbuf) != 0)
                printf(" ... INTERRUPT\n");
            if (signal(SIGINT, jumper) == BADSIG)
                syserr("signal");
        }
        mainloop();
    }

    static void jumper() /* go to main loop on interrupt */
    {
        longjmp(jmpbuf, 1);
        fatal("longjmp returned");
    }
```

Note the call to `fatal` in `jumper`. It's impossible for it to be called, but during debugging the impossible often occurs. You can always take it out later.

It's good programming practice to use `setjmp` and `longjmp` sparingly, since they impose a nonhierarchical program structure; if a "goto" is bad, `longjmp` is even worse. On the other hand, perhaps two wrongs make a right: `signals` are nonhierarchical to begin with and `longjmp` really just patches things up.

8.5 kill SYSTEM CALL

```
int kill(pid, sig)              /* send signal */
int pid;                        /* receiving process-ID */
int sig;                        /* signal number */
/* returns 0 on success or -1 on error */
```

In the previous sections we mainly discussed signals generated by the kernal as a result of some exceptional event. It is also possible for one process to send a signal of any type to another process. `pid` is the process-ID of the process to receive the signal; `sig` is the signal number. The effective user-IDs of the sending and receiving processes must be the same, or else the effective user-ID of the sending process must be the superuser. This rule applies to all the cases enumerated in the following paragraphs.

If `pid` is equal to zero, the signal is sent to every process in the same process group as the sender (see Sec. 1.5). This feature is frequently used with the `kill` command (`kill 0`) to kill all background processes without referring to their process-IDs. Processes in other process groups (such as a DBMS you happened to have started) won't receive the signal.

If `pid` is equal to −1, the signal is sent to all processes whose real user-ID is equal to the effective user-ID of the sender. This is a handy way to kill all processes you own, regardless of process group. If the superuser executes `kill` with p i d equal to −1, *all* processes are killed except for the two special processes with process-IDs 0 and 1 (the swapper and i n i t). This is used to send S I G T E R M to all processes at system shutdown.

Finally, if p i d is negative but not −1, the signal will be sent to all processes whose process-group-ID is equal to the absolute value of p i d. This is a good way to terminate a subsystem such as a DBMS, a communication handler, or a print spooler, all of which are likely to be in their own process groups.

In practice, k i l l is used 99% of the time for one of these purposes:

- To *terminate* one or more processes, usually with S I G T E R M, but sometimes with S I G Q U I T or S I G I O T so that a core dump will be obtained.
- To *test* the error-handling code of a new program by simulating signals such as S I G F P E (floating-point exception).

k i l l is almost never used simply to inform one or more processes of something (i.e., for interprocess communication), for the reasons outlined in the previous sections.

Note also that the k i l l system call is most often executed via the k i l l command. It isn't usually built into application programs.

8.6 pause SYSTEM CALL

```
void pause()    /* wait for a signal */
```

We've already encountered several system calls that block waiting for an event before they complete some activity. For example, when reading a terminal, r e a d waits for a full line to be typed. p a u s e is pure wait: It doesn't do anything, and it's not waiting for anything in particular. However, since an arriving signal interrupts any system call that's blocked, we might as well say that p a u s e waits for a signal. If the signal-catching function returns, p a u s e returns with e r r n o set to E I N T R, but since that's the only way p a u s e ever returns there's no point testing for it.

Most often the signal that p a u s e is waiting for is the alarm clock. It's difficult to think of other uses, since other situations that require waiting have waiting automatically built into their operation. Examples are waiting for input (r e a d), waiting for a message (m s g r c v), and waiting for a child to terminate (w a i t).

8.7 alarm SYSTEM CALL

```
unsigned alarm(secs)              /* set alarm clock */
unsigned secs;                    /* number of seconds */
/* returns seconds of time previously remaining */
```

Every process has an alarm clock stored in its system-data segment. When the alarm goes off, signal S I G A L R M is sent. A child inherits its parent's alarm clock value, but the actual clock isn't shared. The alarm clock remains set across an e x e c.

a l a r m sets the clock to the number of seconds given by s e c s. The previous setting is returned; it will be 0 if no time remained on the clock previously. The previous setting is used to restore the clock to the way it was before a l a r m was called. This is done by the s l e e p subroutine.

If s e c s is 0, the alarm clock is turned off. This must be done if the alarm clock is set but p a u s e or some other waiting system call returns before the alarm goes off, which might happen if another signal arrives or if the event waited for occurs. If the alarm clock is not turned off it will go off later, when you least expect it to.[5]

Here's a brief history of a l a r m: For many years a serious problem with UNIX was that a process could get stuck reading the terminal—there were no non-blocking reads. A standard trick was to create another process to sleep for a second and then send a signal back to the reading process to interrupt the r e a d. The a l a r m system call was invented to cure this problem; it provided a simple way to break out of r e a d after a decent interval without using another process. Simultaneously, p a u s e was added so that s l e e p could be demoted from a system call to a subroutine. Later, with System III, the O _ N D E L A Y was added to provide a smoother way to make r e a d nonblocking.

To show how a l a r m works with p a u s e, here's a version of s l e e p (much simpler than the real one):

```
void sleep2(secs)    /* sleep for secs seconds */
int secs;
{
    void nullfcn();

    if (signal(SIGALRM, nullfcn) == BADSIG)
        syserr("signal");
    alarm(secs);
    pause();
}

static void nullfcn() /* do nothing */
{
}
```

The only purpose of n u l l f c n is to ensure that alarm signals aren't defaulted or ignored, so that p a u s e will be interrupted.

---

[5]This caused one of the most difficult bugs I ever had. Reads from the terminal were returning garbage at random times. I was at my wits' end—almost ready to attach a diagnostic monitor to the terminal's communication line! Finally I found the alarm I forgot to turn off.

There's one other common use for a l a r m. Ordinarily we would consider the scheme we are about to present too harebrained to be included in a sober book like this one, but because it's used in the popular text editor v i (from Berkeley), we'll describe it anyhow.

The problem this scheme solves is this: Many CRT terminals transmit an escape sequence when a function key like HOME or END is pressed. Such a sequence consists of the escape character (octal 33) followed by a series of additional characters that indicate which key was pressed. For example, on one kind of terminal these sequences are generated (ESC stands for the escape character):

Key	*Escape Sequence*
HOME	ESC [H
END	ESC [Y

It is easy to code an input routine that uses a finite-state machine to recognize function keys. Special symbols can be defined to distinguish them from normal characters. But what if the application uses the escape key too? When the user presses escape, how does the input routine know whether to pass it back right away or to continue reading for the rest of an escape sequence? The input stream is ambiguous.

This is the solution adopted by v i: When an escape is read, the alarm clock is set to one second and then a r e a d is issued for the next character. If r e a d returns before the alarm goes off, it is assumed that characters could have been transmitted that quickly only if they were generated by the keyboard as a function key was pressed; if the alarm goes off (interrupting r e a d), it is assumed that the characters were typed slowly by a human—that is, the escape itself was actually pressed.

The glitch is that if a human types fast enough, the input routine might be fooled into thinking a function key was hit; and if the system gets overloaded, the escape sequence generated by a function key might be transmitted so slowly that the input routine will think that each key was typed explicitly. The problem of the fast typist is ameliorated if all escape sequences have an uncommon character, like [, after the escape, since the input routine can then be designed to treat all other combinations—no matter how fast they are typed—as separate keystrokes. Only when the typist types a [quickly after an escape is a misinterpretation possible. The overloading problem is more severe; users of v i are familiar with how poorly it performs on a busy computer (function-key recognition is only one of the irritants). A perfect and obvious solution is for the application simply to not use the escape key. Then no alarms are needed and a fast, unambiguous finite-state machine can recognize escape sequences.

To see how the v i scheme works, here's a sample input routine and a calling program used to test it out. Only two function keys, HOME and END, are recognized, but extensions to handle an entire keyboard are straightforward.

```
#define HOMEKEY -2
#define ENDKEY -3
#define ESC '\33'

main()  /* test getkey */
{
    int c;

    setraw();
    while (c = getkey())
        switch (c) {
        case ESC:
            printf("ESCAPE\r\n");
            continue;
        case HOMEKEY:
            printf("HOME\r\n");
            continue;
        case ENDKEY:
            printf("END\r\n");
            continue;
        case 'q':
            restore();
            exit(0);
        default:
            printf("%c\r\n", c);
        }
}

int getkey()    /* get character or function key from terminal */
{
    static BOOLEAN first = TRUE;
    static char savec = '\0';
    char c;
    enum {NEUTRAL, FINDLB, FINDLTR} state = NEUTRAL;
    extern int errno;

    if (first) {
        first = FALSE;
        catchsig();
    }
    if (savec != '\0') {
        c = savec;
        savec = '\0';
        return(c);
    }
```

```
    while (1)
        switch (read(0, &c, 1)) {
        case -1:
            if (errno == EINTR)
                return(ESC);
            syserr("read");
        case 0:
            fatal("Mysterious EOF");
        default:
            switch (state) {
            case NEUTRAL:
                if (c == ESC) {
                    state = FINDLB;
                    alarm(1);
                    continue;
                }
                else
                    return(c);
            case FINDLB:
                alarm(0);
                if (c == '[') {
                    state = FINDLTR;
                    continue;
                }
                else {
                    savec = c;
                    return(ESC);
                }
            case FINDLTR:
                switch (c) {
                case 'H':
                    return(HOMEKEY);
                case 'Y':
                    return(ENDKEY);
                }
                state = NEUTRAL;
            }
        }
}


static void catchsig()    /* catch alarm */
{
    if (signal(SIGALRM, catchsig) == BADSIG)
        syserr("signal");
}
```

setraw and restore were shown in Sec. 4.5 and Sec. 4.4.8. We've changed MIN and TIME to zero so as to get more punctual response, which is absolutely critical here.

It's important to arrange things so that an uncaught alarm signal never arrives. To make sure this can't happen, we reset SIGALRM within the signal-catching function itself. Since no time remains on the alarm clock while we're in this function, the short interval in which SIGALRM is set to SIG_DFL is harmless.

In an earlier version of this program the signal was recaught only after read was interrupted:

```
switch (read(0, &c, 1)) {
case -1:
    if (errno == EINTR) {
        if (signal(SIGALRM, catchsig) == BADSIG)
            syserr("signal");
        return(ESC);
    }
```

The problem with this was that on a loaded system the alarm could go off before read was even called—fairly amazing when you consider how few instructions intervene between the call alarm(1) and the call to read. The premature alarm would restore SIGALRM to SIG_DFL, but would otherwise be transparent. Then the next time the alarm went off the process would terminate. I was actually able to kill the process by pounding rapidly on the HOME, END, and ESCAPE keys, but only when I loaded things down by running a high-priority background process to hog the CPU. When the loophole was closed by moving the call to signal, the problem went away. This dramatizes how tricky signals can be.

We turn off the alarm (alarm(0)) as soon as a character following an escape is read, but there's no emergency this time. If it goes off accidentally before we get a chance to turn it off, nothing bad happens, since no system calls are issued between read and alarm.

If you try this example you'll discover that it works pretty well. Still, timing-sensitive algorithms should be avoided on a time-shared computer. The escape key is something we can all learn to live without.

8.8 PORTABILITY

You can write portable programs that use signals by following these guidelines: Stay away from the implementation-dependent signals SIGIOT, SIGEMT, SIGBUS, and SIGSEGV. It's OK to catch them to print a message, but don't try to attach any meaning to them. Avoid SIGCLD and SIGPWR also, because the manual warns that they may not be available in future UNIX versions, and because they're not in Version 7.

The Version 7 k i l l is less fancy than later versions—there are no process groups in Version 7. This shouldn't be a problem because k i l l is usually executed via the k i l l command (which isn't any more portable, but at least isn't wired into C programs).

Don't build timing dependencies into your programs. In a sense v i isn't portable because it works acceptably on some systems but not on others, depending on load and specifics of the terminal device driver. Any use of a l a r m should be viewed with suspicion. One justifiable use is in conjunction with r e a d so as to make terminal input nonblocking. This is actually *more* portable than using O _ N D E L A Y because that flag is unavailable in Version 7. However, if you're only concerned with versions based on System III, then you're better off with O _ N D E L A Y.

If you're porting between 4.2 BSD and the other versions, you have big troubles, because signals have been changed substantially in 4.2 BSD. The system call is s i g v e c and, as usual, it's much fancier than the AT&T versions (pending signals are queued, arriving signals are blocked while the catching function is executing, and interrupted system calls are automatically restarted). The only solution is to consolidate all code related to signals into a separate module, as we did with terminal settings in Chapter 4 and with interprocess communication in Chapter 7.

EXERCISES

8.1. Change the shell in Sec. 6.4 to set S I G C L D to be ignored and to use the simplified w a i t described at the end of Sec. 8.3.

8.2. Choose one or more computers with which you are familiar and list the information that must be saved in the j m p _ b u f environment by s e t j m p.

8.3. l o n g j m p only cleans up the stack; it doesn't deal with memory allocated dynamically by m a l l o c and r e a l l o c. Discuss the ramifications of this. Is an automatic solution possible? Is it desirable? Suggest a possible design change to (at least) s e t j m p, l o n g j m p, m a l l o c, r e a l l o c, and f r e e that handles the problem.

8.4. Can the shared-memory implementation of s e n d and r e c e i v e in Sec. 7.7.2 be changed to use s i g n a l, k i l l, and p a u s e instead of P and V? Discuss the advantages and disadvantages of this change. If the change is possible, implement it.

8.5. Implement the standard function s l e e p. (It's much more complex than s l e e p 2 in Sec. 8.7.)

MISCELLANEOUS SYSTEM CALLS

9.1 INTRODUCTION

This chapter describes system calls for administration, memory management, and other miscellaneous purposes that don't fit neatly into any of the preceding chapters. These system calls have one common property: They are practically never called directly from an application program. Some of them, such as mount and sync, are issued by running commands from the shell; others, such as sbrk, are issued through standard subroutines, such as malloc.

We'll first discuss the system calls usable by everyone, and then the superuser-only system calls.

9.2 ulimit SYSTEM CALL

```
long ulimit(cmd, newlimit)      /* get or set user limits */
int cmd;                        /* command */
long newlimit;                  /* new limit */
/* returns current limit or -1 on error */
```

Every process has a file-size limit and a user-data-segment-size limit. ulimit gets and sets these limits, according to the value of cmd.

If `cmd` is 1, the file-size limit is returned, in units of 512-byte blocks. The initial limit is set when the system is configured; a typical value is 2048, which allows files up to a megabyte in size.

If `cmd` is 2, the file-size limit is set equal to `newlimit`. Any process may reduce its limit, but only the superuser may increase it. The ultimate limit to which it may be increased is implementation-dependent; theoretically it is about one billion bytes (somewhat larger than most disks). Reducing the file-size limit may be useful in a student environment; increasing it may be useful to a database management system. Files of any size can be read even if they are bigger than the limit.

If `cmd` is 3, the data-segment-size limit is returned, in units of bytes. This limit can't be changed, but the data-segment size itself can be changed with `brk` or `sbrk` (see the next section).

By way of example, here is a function to print out both limits:

```
void prtlimits()   /* print limits */
{
    long ulimit();

    printf("File-size limit = %ld\n", ulimit(1, 0L));
    printf("Data-segment limit = %ld\n", ulimit(3, 0L));
}
```

The output on my system was:

```
File-size limit = 2048
Data-segment limit = 65142
```

A process has additional limits other than file size and data-segment size, such as number of open files, and users have limits, such as number of processes. There are also system-wide limits. However, none of these other limits may be changed except by reconfiguring the system. Some limits, such as number of processes or number of open files, can't be determined from a program—the system administrator must be consulted. Hence, any use of such limits is nonportable.[1]

9.3 brk AND sbrk SYSTEM CALLS

```
int brk(newbrk)                    /* set break value */
char *newbrk;                      /* new break value */
/* returns 0 on success or -1 on error */
```

---

[1]The /usr/group Proposed Standard has attempted to improve this situation by printing a list of all limits along with minimum required values. Although the standard is too new to have any adherents, the minimum values are a good guide to how Version 7, System III, and System V are normally configured.

```
char *sbrk(incr)              /* change break value */
int incr;                     /* increment */
/* returns old break value or -1 on error */
```

A process starts with a data segment large enough to hold static data allocated by the linker (ld). The first address beyond the data segment is called the *break value*. The linker defines the C external variable end, which it locates just above the data segment. Hence, the address of end is the initial break value.

A process may stretch or shrink its data segment by calling brk with an argument equal to the desired new break value. The data-segment-size limit determines the maximum possible break value and is implementation-dependent. It ranges from about 64K bytes on a 16-bit computer to megabytes on a 32-bit virtual-memory computer.

Probably the only UNIX program that actually calls brk to set its break value to a specific location is the text editor ed, which calls it to expand or shrink an incore array of line pointers.

Much easier to work with is sbrk. Its argument is just an increment to be added to the break value. The old break value (the address of the new space) is returned. sbrk is used by the standard heap-allocation subroutine malloc. The subroutine free doesn't call brk to give space back; it just adds the space to a free list. malloc calls sbrk to get more memory only when it can't find a large enough block on the free list.

Since the location of end is fixed by the loader, it can't be used to determine the break value once brk or sbrk has been called. Instead, sbrk may be called with an increment of 0 to return the current break value but leave it unchanged.

To find out how much space is available for expanding the data segment, you can simply subtract the current break value from the limit. Here's a handy function to return the number of available bytes:

```
long avail()    /* return number of available bytes */
{
    char *sbrk();
    long ulimit();

    return(ulimit(3, 0L)-(long)sbrk(0));
}
```

brk and sbrk return with an error (**ENOMEM**) if the data segment has reached its limit. Experience has shown that on some UNIX implementations this check is unreliable, particularly on simple computers without hardware memory management. A storage allocator should instead call ulimit to get the limit and then keep track of the data-segment size for itself, so as to avoid ever calling sbrk with a request that can't be honored.

9.4 umask SYSTEM CALL

```
int umask(mask)          /* set/get creation mask */
int mask;                /* new mask */
/* returns previous mask */
```

To improve security, UNIX has a safety feature called the *file mode creation mask*. It is a nine-bit number that is used to clear the corresponding bits in the permission arguments of the system calls `creat`, `open`, and `mknod`. Fortunately, the mask doesn't affect `chmod`, so processes have a way of setting permissions to the way they want regardless of the mask.

The effect of the file mode creation mask is best explained by a simple example:

```
void masktest()   /* test umask */
{
    int fd;

    umask(022);
    if ((fd = creat("temp", 0666)) == -1)
        syserr("creat");
    system("Ls -l temp");
}
```

Here is the output:

```
-rw-r-r-  1 marc   staff     0 Oct 12 12:34 temp
```

You can see that even though `creat` was given permissions allowing for reading and writing by everyone, the group and public write bits were cleared.

All users are given a default file mode creation mask at login, which is octal 22 on most systems. The shell has a built-in command called `umask` (what else?) that changes the mask. This is typically done in the user's login command file (`.profile`) if the system default isn't suitable.

Note that `umask` has to be built into the shell for the same reason `cd` does. The file mode creation mask is inherited by child processes, but the mask itself is unique to each process. If `umask` were a conventional command it would be ineffective, because the shell would create a child process to execute it.

Since every process has a mask, and since every combination of nine bits is legal, `umask` can never give an error return. It returns the old mask. To find out what the old mask is without changing it requires *two* calls to `umask`: one to get the old value, with an argument of anything at all, and a second call to restore the mask to the way it was.

9.5 ustat SYSTEM CALL

```
#include <sys/types.h>
#include <ustat.h>


int ustat(dev, ubuf)                    /* get file system statistics */
int dev;                                /* device number */
struct ustat *ubuf;                     /* pointer to info buffer */
/* returns 0 on success or -1 on error */
```

ustat pulls four items of data from a file system's super block and places them into the supplied ustat structure, which looks like this:

```
struct ustat {
    daddr_t f_tfree;        /* free blocks (long) */
    ino_t f_tinode;         /* free i-nodes (short) */
    char f_fname[6];        /* file system label */
    char f_fpack[6];        /* disk pack label */
};
```

We explained in Sec. 3.3 how to read the super block, so why have ustat? The answer is that disk special files are normally readable only by the superuser, whereas everyone has the right to know a file system's labels and the amount of space remaining. A database management system should monitor the free space closely, since a sequence of updates aborted in midstream for lack of space may be awkward to handle. Subsystems that write huge files, such as data-acquisition programs, will also need to monitor free space so as not to hog the file system.

The file system and volume labels aren't related to any other names. They are recorded in the super block when the file system is mounted. How they are used is up to each UNIX site, so no portable program should make use of them.

Here's a program to print the data supplied by ustat:

```
#include <sys/types.h>
#include <sys/stat.h>
#include <ustat.h>


prtustat()    /* print file system statistics */
{
    struct stat sbuf;
    struct ustat ubuf;
    char name[7];
```

```
        if (stat("/dev/hd0", &sbuf) == -1)
            syserr("stat");
        if (ustat(sbuf.st_rdev, &ubuf) == -1)
            syserr("ustat");
        printf("Free blocks = %ld\n", ubuf.f_tfree);
        printf("Free i-nodes = %ld\n", ubuf.f_tinode);
        name[6] = '\0';
        strncpy(name, ubuf.f_fname, 6);
        printf("File system label = %s\n", name);
        strncpy(name, ubuf.f_fpack, 6);
        printf("Pack label = %s\n", name);
    }
```

The output for my system was:

```
        Free blocks = 6539
        Free i-nodes = 3072
        File system label = usr
        Pack label = usr001
```

ustat requires a device number, which we got by calling stat (see Sec. 3.12). Note that the label fields have just enough room to accommodate the six-character label. We had to copy the labels to a local string in order to ensure that they were null-terminated. This is the same problem we had with directory entries in Sec. 3.2.

9.6 uname SYSTEM CALL

```
#include <sys/utsname.h>

int uname(utsbuf)                       /* get system name */
struct utsname *utsbuf;                 /* pointer to info buffer */
/* returns non-negative value on success or -1 on error */
```

uname returns the name and version of the local UNIX system in the buffer pointed to by utsbuf, which has this structure:

```
struct utsname {
    char sysname[9];        /* system name */
    char nodename[9];       /* uucp node name */
    char release[9];        /* release number */
    char version[9];        /* version number */
    char machine[9];        /* computer model */
};
```

Here's a program to print out the uname information:

```
#include <sys/utsname.h>

prtuname()   /* print system name and version */
{
    struct utsname utsbuf;

    if (uname(&utsbuf) == -1)
        syserr("uname");
    printf("System name = %s\n", utsbuf.sysname);
    printf("Node name = %s\n", utsbuf.nodename);
    printf("Release = %s\n", utsbuf.release);
    printf("Version = %s\n", utsbuf.version);
    printf("Machine = %s\n", utsbuf.machine);
}
```

Note that all character strings in the utsname structure are null-terminated. This is the output I got on my low-budget system:

```
System name = PC/IX
Node name = SELF
Release = 1.0
Version = std
Machine = ibmpc-xt
```

The release and version information can, in theory, be used to achieve portability between System III and System V by varying execution at runtime, depending on the version being executed. One possible application is to implement send and receive (see Chap. 7) with FIFOs on System III and with messages on System V. But uname can't be used to achieve portability to and from Version 7, because it doesn't exist in that version. Another serious problem is that the information returned by uname isn't standardized, so implementors are free to use their own release and version designations. In the example above, although PC/IX is a superset of System III, neither the release nor version tells us so.

9.7 sync SYSTEM CALL

```
void sync()   /* flush dirty buffers */
```

Recall from Sec. 2.7 that the kernel doesn't immediately flush to disk the data written to the buffer cache. Data is automatically flushed only when the kernel needs the buffer for another disk block. The sync system call flushes all dirty buffers to disk.

It's a bad idea to leave dirty buffers around too long. On most UNIX systems the background process cron does a sync every minute or so. That way a CPU crash will lose at most a minute's worth of data. If the system administrator needs to patch the file system without interference, he or she can just kill c r o n first. s y n c is also executed during system shutdown just before the system is halted.

Any user can execute s y n c at any time; superuser permission isn't required.

In Sec. 2.7 I pointed out several problems with delayed writes, such as the inability to ensure that a database log is physically written before the database itself is updated. s y n c can't be used to solve these problems for three reasons:

- It doesn't write anything—it only schedules it to be written. The disk hardware will write the data sometime after s y n c returns.
- It flushes *all* dirty buffers, not just the ones written by the process issuing the s y n c. Indeed, buffers are owned by the kernel, not by any process.
- There is still no way to get reports of physical write errors when a buffer is flushed.

For these reasons, s y n c is rarely called from an application program.

9.8 profil SYSTEM CALL

```
void profil(buf, nbytes, offset, scale)   /* capture profile */
char *buf;                        /* pointer to count buffer */
int nbytes;                       /* size of buffer */
int offset;                       /* program counter offset */
int scale;                        /* scale factor */
```

p r o f i l turns on process profiling, which helps in improving performance by identifying where a program spends its time. Each time the clock ticks (60 or 100 times per second), the value of the program counter is obtained and used to increment a word in the b u f array. o f f s e t and s c a l e are used to determine which word to increment, but we'll not go into those details. A s c a l e of 0 or 1 or an e x e c turns profiling off.

Users rarely, if ever, call p r o f i l directly—it is used only by a special C start-up routine linked into a program when the - p option is specified on the c c command.

9.9 ptrace SYSTEM CALL

```
int ptrace(cmd, pid, addr, data)   /* trace process */
int cmd;                           /* command */
int pid;                           /* process-ID of child */
int addr;                          /* address of child */
int data;                          /* data to write */
/* returns value read or -1 on error */
```

p t r a c e allows a parent process to trace the child process whose process-ID is
p i d. To turn tracing on, the child executes **p t r a c e** with **c m d** equal to 0. This
is almost always done between **f o r k** and **e x e c**. Thereafter, whenever the child
receives a signal or does an **e x e c**, it stops and the parent gets a return from **w a i t**
with a special exit code. The parent can then obtain data from the child's address
space, modify the child's address space, or put the child into single-step mode, which
causes the child to receive a trace-trap (**S I G T R A P**) signal after every instruction.

     p t r a c e is supplied for the exclusive use of the debuggers **a d b** and **s d b**.
It's much too complex for any other use. In particular, it shouldn't be considered
as a method of interprocess communication.

9.10 times SYSTEM CALL

```
#include <sys/types.h>          /* available in System V only */
#include <sys/times.h>

struct tms {                    /* needed for System III only */
    time_t tms_utime;           /* user CPU time for process */
    time_t tms_stime;           /* system CPU time for process */
    time_t tms_cutime;          /* user CPU time for children */
    time_t tms_cstime;          /* system CPU time for children */
};

long times(tbuf)                /* get CPU times */
struct tms *tbuf;               /* pointer to info buffer */
/* returns elapsed real time or −1 on error */
```

t i m e s reports the four times that are maintained automatically for each process:

user CPU	Time spent executing instructions from the process's instruction segment.
system CPU	Time spent executing system calls on behalf of the process.
children's user CPU	Total of user CPU times for all the process's child processes that have terminated and for which the parent has issued a **w a i t**.
children's system CPU	Total of system CPU times for terminated child processes.

The elapsed real (wall clock) time since a point in the past (normally, boot time) is
returned.

     All times are in units of clock ticks, which are usually sixtieths of a second.
However, on some computers—notably, the AT&T 3B series—a clock tick is one
hundredth of a second. This discrepancy makes printing of times nonportable.

The header file /usr/include/times.h was added to System V so that you don't have to include the definition for the tms structure in your programs. For portability between System III and System V, however, you shouldn't include that header file. Alternatively, you can add an equivalent header file to your System III /usr/include directory.

The time command is frequently used to time a UNIX command. However, it's easy to build calls to times itself into a program to time various parts of it. We did this back in Sec. 2.10 using two functions, timestart and timestop. To see how these are used, here's a program that times 1000 calls to getpid (probably the fastest system call):

```
void tmgetpid()   /* time getpid */
{
    int i;

    timestart();
    for (i = 0; i < 1000; i++)
        getpid();
    timestop("1000 getpids");
}
```

This is the output:

```
1000 getpids: real 1.55; user 0.12; sys 1.43
```

Here is the code for timestart and timestop:

```
#include <sys/types.h>

struct tms {
    time_t tms_utime;
    time_t tms_stime;
    time_t tms_cutime;
    time_t tms_cstime;
};
long times();
#define TICKS 60.

static struct tms tbuf1;
static long real1;

void timestart()   /* start timer */
{
    real1 = times(&tbuf1);
}
```

```
void timestop(msg)    /* stop timer */
char *msg;
{
    struct tms tbuf2;
    long real2;


    (real 2 - real1) / TICKS,
    fprintf(stderr, "%s: real %.2f; user %.2f; sys %.2f\n", msg,
        (real 2 - real1) / TICKS,
        (tbuf2.tms_utime - tbuf1.tms_utime) / TICKS,
        (tbuf2.tms_stime - tbuf1.tms_stime) / TICKS);
}
```

9.11 time SYSTEM CALL

```
long time(timep)                    /* get system time */
long *timep;                        /* pointer to time */
/* returns current time or -1 on error */
```

t i m e returns the time, in seconds, since January 1, 1970. A full discussion of how UNIX stores times is in Sec. 3.4.

If the argument t i m e p is not NULL, the current time is stored into the long integer to which it points. This is a carry-over from the days before the C language supported long integers. It is of no use now that a simple assignment statement can be used to capture the return value. The argument to t i m e can always be NULL.

9.12 stime SYSTEM CALL

```
int stime(timep)                    /* set system time */
long *timep;                        /* pointer to time */
/* returns 0 on success or -1 on error */
```

s t i m e is the opposite of t i m e: It is used, by the superuser only, to set the system time. It is normally called only at boot time, and seldom directly, since the time is easily set with the date command (which calls s t i m e). If you call s t i m e directly, the argument has to be converted to the number of seconds since January 1, 1970, which isn't easy. The details (and a sample program) are in Sec. 3.4.

9.13 plock SYSTEM CALL (SYSTEM V)

```
#include <sys/lock.h>

int plock(op)                      /* lock process in memory */
int op;                            /* option */
/* returns 0 on success or -1 on error */
```

UNIX normally swaps out a process to make room for another process. Before a swapped-out process can run, it must be swapped back in. If a swapped-out process is blocked waiting for an event, this will substantially delay the response time to the event. System V has added the call plock to lock a process into memory so that it won't be swapped out. It then can be scheduled to be run as soon as its state changes from blocked to ready.

plock can be executed only by the superuser. The argument op can have one of four values:

PROCLOCK   Lock the entire process, both instruction and data segments.
TXTLOCK   Lock only the instruction (text) segment.
DATLOCK   Lock only the data segment.
UNLOCK   Unlock whatever is locked.

A lock is preserved across an exec, but it is not inherited by a child. To prevent memory fragmentation, those processes to be locked should be the first ones executed after a boot. Clearly, only a few processes can be locked, since each locked process reduces the memory available to run ordinary processes.

Xenix 3 and Version 7 have a similar system call named lock.

9.14 mount SYSTEM CALL

```
int mount(spcl, path, rwflag)      /* mount file system */
char *spcl;                        /* path of block special file */
char *path;                        /* path of directory */
int rwflag;                        /* read/write flag */
/* returns 0 on success or -1 on error */
```

A UNIX file system, or logical volume, may be mounted and unmounted. When mounted, the file system becomes part of the directory hierarchy, and users of it are unaware that its directories are actually on a different volume (except that they can't create a link across volumes with link). When unmounted, the directories on the volume disappear without a trace.

To understand mount, it's necessary to understand the structure of a file system, which was explained in Sec. 3.3. Recall that the root directory of a file system always has i-number 2. When a file system is mounted, the existing directory given by `path` becomes synonymous with its root directory. To perform this trick, the i-node currently assigned to `path` is changed so that all references to it become references to i-node 2 on the mounted volume. From there, paths are treated normally.

The first argument, `spcl`, is the path name of the block special file that is to be mounted. It must already be formatted to look like a file system, with a super block, i-nodes, a free list, and so on. The kernel is not involved in this formatting since the special file can be freely read and written without mounting it. Normally the `mkfs` command is used.

If the third argument, `rwflag`, is 1, the mounted file system is read-only; otherwise it is read-write. A backup disk pack is normally mounted read-only so that users can retrieve files from it without disturbing its contents.

`mount` can only be executed by the superuser. There are two important reasons for this. First, the kernel can crash if the format of the file system is faulty. Second, since the block special file has no formal significance until it is mounted, a user who can write on it can create a program owned by the superuser with the set-user-ID bit on (see Sec. 1.6)—the blocks containing the future i-nodes are just ordinary data blocks. When the file system is mounted, the set-user-ID program becomes authentic.

In practice, the `mount` system call is never executed directly; the `mount` command is used. This is important because certain administrative tables must be updated when a volume is mounted, and the `mount` command automatically takes care of this task.

9.15 umount SYSTEM CALL

```
int umount(spcl)                    /* unmount file system */
char *spcl;                         /* path of block special file */
/* returns 0 on success or -1 on error */
```

`umount` undoes the work of `mount`. `umount` checks to make sure that no directory or file is open before unmounting the volume; it fails if this condition is not met. Once `umount` is executed, the directory at which the file system was mounted reverts to its previous state. Since it no longer is synonymous with the root of the unmounted file system, links from it to directories and files on that file system disappear. Only the superuser can execute `umount`.

Normally the `umount` command is used to execute `umount`, for the same reason that the `mount` command is used to execute the `mount` system call.

9.16 acct SYSTEM CALL

```
int acct(path)                    /* turn accounting on or off */
char *path;                       /* path of accounting file */
/* returns 0 on success or -1 on error */
```

When process accounting is turned on, the kernel writes an accounting record to
the file given by **path** whenever a process terminates. The accounting record includes exit status, user-ID, group-ID, control terminal, starting time, elapsed time,
user and system CPU time, memory usage, number of characters and blocks transferred, and program name. A **path** argument of **NULL** turns off accounting.

A large collection of accounting programs are used to reduce the accumulated
accounting data to useful reports. One of these programs (**accton** in System V)
invokes **acct** to turn accounting on or off; **acct** is seldom executed directly.
Only the superuser can turn accounting on or off.

9.17 sys3b SYSTEM CALL (SYSTEM V)[2]

```
void sys3b(cmd, arg1, arg2)       /* 3B-specific action */
int cmd;                          /* command */
int arg1;                         /* first argument */
int arg2;                         /* second argument */
```

AT&T's 3B line of computers requires various hardware options to be set, such
as the maintenance reset function (MRF) and the system status register (SSR). This
is the system call that does the job.

For what must have been good reasons to them, the implementors of UNIX
on the 3B computers elected to set these options via a system call rather than some
other way. Possibly one reason why a stand-alone program wasn't used is that some
of the 3B computers aren't ever supposed to be rebooted, even during hardware
maintenance. But at least they could have generalized the name! Perhaps **setop**,
short for "set option"?

Anyway, no ordinary user has to worry about using **sys3b**, and you can bet
you won't find it ported to any other brand of computer.

9.18 PORTABILITY

Few of the system calls in this chapter are portable. **ptrace** isn't portable because
it can be used to look at specific addresses and at hardware registers. **times** isn't
portable because computers tick at different frequencies. **uname** isn't portable

---

[2]Every book should end with a good joke.

because its output isn't defined. mount isn't portable because special-file names aren't. sys3b isn't portable because not every computer is a 3B. And so on.

The good news is that this lack of portability isn't a serious problem for applications programmers because these system calls are practically never called directly.

EXERCISES

9.1. Implement malloc and free (omit realloc) in terms of sbrk.

9.2. Implement the time command.

A

SYSTEM V PROCESS ATTRIBUTES

This appendix lists each process attribute, tells whether it is preserved across an **e x e c** and whether a copy is inherited by a child process, and indicates what system calls or other events (such as termination) affect the attribute. A child process shares some attributes with its parent, rather than inheriting a distinct copy; this is indicated by the word *shared*. The word *execution* in the *Affected by* column means that the attribute may be changed by normal process execution, without making a system call.

Attribute	Preserved across e x e c?	Copy inherited by child?	Affected by
instruction segment	N	Y (may be shared)	e x e c
data segment	N	Y	e x e c, b r k, s b r k, execution
environment (in data segment)	optional	Y	e x e c, execution
arguments (in data segment)	optional	Y	e x e c, execution

Attribute	Preserved across exec?	Copy inherited by child?	Affected by
real user-ID	Y	Y	setuid
real group-ID	Y	Y	setgid
effective user-ID	Y	Y	setuid
effective group-ID	Y	Y	setgid
process-ID	Y	N	fork
process-group-ID	Y	Y	setpgrp
parent-process-ID	Y	N	fork, termination of parent
current directory	Y	Y	chdir
root directory	Y	Y	chroot
nice value	Y	Y	nice
trace flag	Y	N	ptrace
alarm clock	Y	Y	alarm
file mode creation mask	Y	Y	umask
file size limit	Y	Y	ulimit
defaulted signals	Y	Y	signal
ignored signals	Y	Y	signal
caught signals	N	Y	signal, receipt of signal
user CPU time	Y	N	execution
system CPU time	Y	N	execution
children's user CPU time	Y	N	termination of child
children's system CPU time	Y	N	termination of child
profiling flag	N	Y	profil
file descriptors	Y (N if close-on-exec)	Y	open, creat, close, dup, pipe, fcntl
file pointers	Y	shared	open, creat, read, write, lseek
close-on-exec flags	Y (if off)	Y	fcntl
O_NDELAY flags	Y	shared	open, fcntl

(Continued)

Attribute	Preserved across exec?	Copy inherited by child?	Affected by
status code	–	–	termination
process lock	Y	N	plock
attached shared memory segments	N	Y	shmat, shmdt
semaphore adjustments	Y	N	semop

B

STANDARD SUBROUTINES

This appendix is a quick guide to standard UNIX subroutines used by the example programs in this book. The descriptions here are intended only to jog your memory, not to provide a definitive explanation. Refer to Section 3 of the UNIX manual for the whole story.

The header file /usr/include/stdio.h is required for many of these functions. An #include statement for it doesn't appear explicitly, but assume that one is present.

asctime

```
#include <time.h>

char *asctime(tm)          /* get ASCII time */
struct tm *tm;             /* broken-down time */
/* returns ASCII time */
```

This function takes the time provided by localtime in a tm structure and converts it to an ASCII string for printing.

atoi

```
int atoi(asc)              /* convert ASCII to integer */
char *asc;                 /* ASCII number */
/* returns integer */
```

This function converts a number in the form of an ASCII string to an integer.

atol

```
int atol(asc)                  /* convert ASCII to long */
char *asc;                      /* ASCII number */
/* returns long integer */
```

This function converts a number in the form of an ASCII string to a long integer.

fclose

```
int fclose(stream)             /* close stream */
FILE *stream;                   /* stream pointer */
/* returns 0 on success or EOF on error */
```

This function closes an I/O stream, flushing the buffer if necessary.

fdopen

```
FILE *fdopen(fd, type)         /* associate stream with FD */
int fd;                         /* file descriptor */
char *type;                     /* type of I/O */
/* returns stream pointer or NULL on error */
```

This function initializes an I/O stream to use an already-open file descriptor. t y p e (for the purposes of this book) points to either r or w.

fflush

```
int fflush(stream)             /* flush stream */
FILE *stream;                   /* stream pointer */
/* returns 0 on success or EOF on error */
```

This function flushes an output stream without closing it.

fgets

```
char *fgets(s, n, stream)      /* get line */
char *s;                        /* string to contain line */
int n;                          /* capacity of s */
FILE *stream;                   /* stream pointer */
/* returns first arg, or NULL on error or end-of-file */
```

This function reads a text line, including the newline, from a stream and places it is s, which is null-terminated. At most n − 1 characters are read.

fopen

```
FILE *fopen(path, type)          /* open stream */
char *path;                      /* path name */
char *type;                      /* type of I/O */
/* returns stream pointer or NULL on error */
```

This function opens an I/O stream for reading or writing. `type` (for the purpose of this book) points to either `r` or `w`.

fprintf

```
int fprintf(stream, fmt, arg, ...)  /* write formatted output */
FILE *stream;                       /* stream pointer */
char *fmt;                          /* format */
int arg;                            /* argument (of any type) */
/* returns number of characters output or negative value on error */
```

This function is like `printf`, but the output goes to the named output stream.

fputs

```
int fputs(s, stream)             /* put string */
char *s;                         /* string */
FILE *stream;                    /* stream pointer */
/* returns EOF on error */
```

This function writes a string to an output stream. A newline is not appended.

free

```
void free(ptr)                   /* free storage block */
char *ptr;                       /* pointer to block */
```

This function frees a block of storage allocated by `malloc` or `realloc`.

getc

```
int getc(stream)                 /* get character */
FILE *stream;                    /* stream pointer */
/* returns character, or EOF on error or end-of-file */
```

This macro gets and returns a character from an input stream.

getchar

```
int getchar()                    /* get character */
/* returns character, or EOF on error or end-of-file */
```

This macro gets and returns a character from the standard input stream (stdin).

getenv

```
char *getenv(var)              /* get value from environment */
char *var;                     /* variable name */
/* returns value or NULL if absent */
```

This function returns the value of the environment variable var.

getgrgid

```
#include <grp.h>

struct group *getgrgid (gid)     /* get group file entry */
int gid;                         /* group-ID */
/* returns pointer to group structure or NULL on error */
```

This function searches the group file for the entry corresponding to the given group-ID. The returned structure contains parts of the entry (see UNIX manual for details).

getgrnam

```
#include <grp.h>

struct group *getgrnam (gnm)      /* get group file entry */
char *gnm;                        /* group name */
/* returns pointer to group structure or NULL on error */
```

This function searches the group file for the entry corresponding to the given group name. The returned structure contains parts of the entry (see UNIX manual for details).

getpwnam

```
#include <pwd.h>

struct passwd *getpwnam(unm)      /* get password file entry */
char *unm;                        /* login name */
/* returns pointer to passwd structure or NULL on error */
```

This function searches the password file for the entry corresponding to the given login name. The returned structure contains parts of the entry (see UNIX manual for details).

getpwuid

```
#include <pwd.h>

struct passwd *getpwuid(uid)        /* get password file entry */
int uid;                            /* user-ID */
/* returns pointer to passwd structure or NULL on error */
```

This function searches the password file for the entry corresponding to the given user-ID. The returned structure contains parts of the entry (see UNIX manual for details).

gets

```
char *gets(s)                       /* get line */
char *s;                            /* string to contain line */
/* returns argument, or NULL on error or end-of-file */
```

This function reads a line from the standard input into the string s. The newline is stripped off and the string is null-terminated.

localtime

```
#include <time.h>

struct tm *localtime(timep)         /* convert time to local time */
long *timep;                        /* pointer to time */
/* returns pointer to broken-down time */
```

This function converts a time in terms of the number of seconds since January 1, 1970, GMT, to broken-down local time, for use by asctime.

longjmp

```
#include <setjmp.h>

void longjmp(jmpenv, val)           /* jump to target set by setjmp */
jmp_buf jmpenv;                     /* saved environment */
int val;                            /* value for setjmp to return */
```

This function jumps to the target location established by setjmp. The stack is cleaned up appropriately.

malloc

```
char *malloc(size)                  /* allocate storage block */
unsigned size;                      /* size to allocate */
/* returns pointer to block or NULL on error */
```

This function allocates a block of s i z e bytes dynamically and returns a pointer to it.

memcpy

```
char *memcpy(to, from, nbytes)    /* copy data */
char *to;                         /* destination */
char *from;                       /* source */
int nbytes;                       /* number of bytes to copy */
/* returns first argument */
```

This function copies raw data, without regard to null bytes. It is in System V only.

printf

```
int printf(fmt, arg, ...)         /* print formatted output */
char *fmt;                        /* format */
int arg;                          /* argument (of any type) */
/* returns number of characters output or negative value on error */
```

This function formats its arguments according to the specification given by f m t and writes the resulting string to the standard output.

putc

```
int putc(c, stream)               /* put character */
char c;                           /* character */
FILE *stream;                     /* stream pointer */
/* returns character or EOF on error */
```

This macro writes a character to an output stream.

realloc

```
char *realloc(ptr, size)          /* reallocate storage block */
char *ptr;                        /* pointer to old block */
unsigned size;                    /* size to allocate */
/* returns pointer to new block or NULL on error */
```

This function checks the size of an existing block to ensure that it is at least s i z e bytes. If necessary, the block is enlarged or a new block is allocated and the old data is copied.

setbuf

```
void setbuf(stream, buf)          /* control buffering */
FILE *stream;                     /* stream pointer */
char *buf;                        /* buffer or NULL */
```

This function either assigns a buffer to a stream or turns off buffering if the second argument is **NULL**.

setjmp

```
#include <setjmp.h>

int setjmp(jmpenv)                    /* set target for longjmp */
jmp_buf jmpenv;                       /* saved environment */
/* returns 0 or value supplied by longjmp */
```

This function saves a target location for longjmp in the buffer jmpenv. When a corresponding longjmp is executed, setjmp appears to return with the value supplied by longjmp.

sleep

```
unsigned sleep(secs)                  /* go to sleep */
unsigned secs;                        /* number of seconds */
/* returns unslept time */
```

This function uses system calls alarm and pause to sleep for a number of seconds.

sprintf

```
int sprintf(s, fmt, arg, ...)         /* format output to string */
char *s;                              /* string */
char *fmt;                            /* format */
int arg;                              /* argument (of any type) */
/* returns number of characters output or negative value on error */
```

This function is like printf, but the formatted output is written to the string s.

sscanf

```
int sscanf(s, fmt, varp, ...)         /* scan string using format */
char *s;                              /* string */
char *fmt;                            /* format */
int *varp;                            /* pointer to variable */
/* returns number of items scanned or EOF on error */
```

This function scans the string s according to the format specified by fmt. Items are converted and assigned to variables in the order encountered.

strcat

```
char *strcat(to, from)          /* concatenate strings */
char *to;                       /* destination */
char *from;                     /* source */
/* returns first argument */
```

This function concatenates the second argument onto the end of the first.

strchr

```
char *strchr(s, c)              /* find char in string */
char *s;                        /* string */
char c;                         /* character */
/* returns pointer to first occurrence or NULL if none */
```

This function scans a string for the first occurrence of the given character.

strcmp

```
int strcmp(s1, s2)              /* compare strings */
char *s1;                       /* string */
char *s2;                       /* string */
/* returns integer indicating relationship */
```

This function compares two strings lexically; it returns a number less than 0 if s1 is less than s2, 0 if they are equal, and a number greater than 0 if s1 is greater than s2.

strcpy

```
char *strcpy(to, from)          /* copy string */
char *to;                       /* destination */
char *from;                     /* source */
/* returns first argument */
```

This function copies the null-terminated string from to the location pointed to by to.

strcspn

```
int strcspn(s, set)             /* find prefix */
char *s;                        /* string */
char *set;                      /* set of characters */
/* returns length of prefix */
```

This function returns the length of the longest prefix of s consisting entirely of characters in set.

strlen

```
int strlen(s)              /* get length of string */
char *s;                   /* string */
/* returns length */
```

This function returns the length of a string (not including the null terminator).

strncpy

```
char *strncpy(to, from, n)   /* copy n chars of string */
char *to;                    /* destination */
char *from;                  /* source */
int n;                       /* number of characters */
/* returns first argument */
```

This function copies at most n characters from the null-terminated string from to the location pointed to by to; copying stops if a null byte is encountered. The destination is not necessarily null-terminated.

strrchr

```
char *strrchr(s, c)          /* find char in string */
char *s;                     /* string */
char c;                      /* character */
/* returns pointer to last occurrence or NULL if none */
```

This function scans a string for the last occurrence of the given character.

strtok

```
char *strtok(subj, delim)    /* break string into tokens */
char *subj;                  /* string */
char *delim;                 /* delimiters */
/* returns pointer into subj or NULL if no tokens remain */
```

This function returns a token in subj each time it is called. Tokens are separated by a character from delim. The first call specifies the subject string, which will have null bytes copied into it to terminate the tokens as they are encountered. All but the first call must have NULL as the first argument.

system

```
int system(cmd)              /* execute shell command line */
char *cmd;                   /* command */
/* returns shell exit code */
```

This function creates a child process running the standard shell s h and passes to that shell the specified command line to execute.

ungetc

```
int ungetc(c, stream)               /* un-get character */
char c;                             /* character */
FILE *stream;                       /* stream pointer */
/* returns character or EOF on error */
```

This function pushes a character back onto an input stream for later reading.

SELECTED BIBLIOGRAPHY

Books referred to directly in the text are referenced in footnotes. This bibliography includes selected books that either help prepare the reader for *Advanced UNIX Programming* or provide opportunities for further study.

PREPARATORY BOOKS

Bell Laboratories. *The Bell System Technical Journal* 57, no. 6, pt. 2 (July/August 1978). Over 400 pages of articles by many of the authors of UNIX, UNIX commands, and UNIX-based applications. Provides an excellent background on developments of the early and middle 1970s.

Bourne, S. R. *The UNIX System.* Reading, Mass.: Addison-Wesley Publishing Company, Inc., 1982. An intermediate UNIX introduction, with a little on editing (with ed and vi), a little on the shell (which Bourne designed), a little on programming, and a little on nroff.

Comer, Douglas. *Operating System Design: The XINU Approach.* Englewood Cliffs, N.J.: Prentice-Hall, Inc., 1984. A detailed look at the internals of an operating system somewhat like UNIX. ("XINU" stands for "XINU is not UNIX.") A complete source code listing is included.

Lomuto, Ann Nicols, and Nico Lomuto. *A UNIX Primer.* Englewood Cliffs, N.J.: Prentice-Hall, Inc., 1983. A good introduction to UNIX for beginners. Several dozen introductory books are available—this is one of the best.

Peterson, James L., and Abraham Silberschatz. *Operating System Concepts.* Reading, Mass.: Addison-Wesley Publishing Company, Inc., 1983. A good introduction to operating-system principles, including most of the principles behind UNIX.

BOOKS ON C AND UNIX PROGRAMMING

Kernighan, Brian W., and Rob Pike. *The UNIX Programming Environment.* Englewood Cliffs, N.J.: Prentice-Hall, Inc., 1984. An excellent introduction to programming on UNIX using the shell, C, and related tools such as make and yacc. The best possible preparation for *Advanced UNIX Programming.*

Kernighan, Brian W., and Dennis M. Ritchie. *The C Programming Language.* Englewood Cliffs, N.J.: Prentice-Hall, Inc., 1978. The first—and still the best—textbook on C. Appendix A is the *C Reference Manual,* written by Dennis M. Ritchie, the inventor of C.

Plum, Thomas. *Learning to Program in C.* Cardiff, N.J.: Plum Hall, Inc., 1983. An alternative textbook on C. Some people find it easier to follow than *The C Programming Language.*

UNIX MANUALS

Bell Laboratories. *UNIX Programmer's Manual,* Vol. 1. New York: Holt, Rinehart and Winston, 1979. This book is the most accessible published UNIX manual, but it's the seventh edition (Version 7) and inappropriate for System III, System V, or Xenix 3. *Caveat emptor.*

Bell Laboratories. *UNIX System Administrator's Manual, System V.* Western Electric Company, Inc., 1983. The administrator's part of the manual.

Bell Laboratories. *UNIX System User's Manual, System V.* Western Electric Company, Inc., 1983. This is the UNIX manual to get if you're not a UNIX user. If you are, the manual that goes with your system will serve you better.

/usr/group. *Proposed Standard.* Santa Clara, Calif.: /usr/group, 1984. The proposed UNIX standard written by a committee of the industry association /usr/group. Essentially a subset of System III.

/usr/group. *Reviewer's Guide to the Proposed /usr/group Standard.* Santa Clara, Calif.: /usr/group, 1984. Comments on the thinking behind the *Proposed Standard,* especially why things were kept in or left out.

INDEX

A

Absolute path, 3
Access primitives, 157–58
Access system call, 57–58
Acct system call, 240
Adb, 209
Advanced interprocess communication, 156–207
   database management system issues, 157–59
   implementing messages with FIFOs, 160–81
   message system calls, 182–85
   portability, 206–7
   record locking, 203–6
   semaphores, 185–92
   shared memory, 192–203
   use of FIFOs, 159–60
Advanced I/O (input/output), 42–72
   access system call, 57–58

chmod system call, 60
chown system call, 60–61
dates and times, 49–52
directories, 42–44, 54–57
fcntl system call, 70–71
file modes, 53–54
fstat system call, 62
link system call, 54–57
mknod system call, 58–60
portability, 72–73
special files, 45–49, 58–60
stat system call, 62–70
utime system call, 61–62
Agrc, 142
Alarm system call, 220–25
Append, 138, 142
Argc, 102, 105, 108–9
Arguments, 93–94
Argv, 102, 105, 107–9, 142
Assign, 96–97
Assignment, 107–9, 133
Atomic transaction, 203

B

Bell Laboratories, 156
Bidirectional pipes, 146–54
Binary semaphores, 86
Blocking, 78
Block special files, 3–4
Break value, 229
Brk system call, 194, 228–29
Buf, 161
Buffered I/O, 3, 32–37
Builtin, 143, 145
Busy-wait, 187

C

Calendar time, 49
Cat, 130–31
Catchsig, 216
Cd, 133
Cget, 81–82
Change i-node, 8–9
Character mapping, 84–85
Character special files, 3–4
Chdir system call, 119
Child process, 5
Chmod system call, 60
Chown system call, 60–61
Chroot system call, 119–20
Close system call:
    ordinary files and, 31–32
    pipes and, 124–25
    terminals and, 75, 78
Cmd, 173, 227–28
Columbus UNIX, 156, 157
Command, 138–46
Control characters, 85–86
Control terminal, 6
Copy-on-write, 113
Core, 115
Cready, 81–82
Creatsem, 191

Creat system call:
    ordinary files and, 20–24, 26–27
    terminals and, 75
Ctime subroutine, 49–52
Current directory, 3
Curses, 82, 91

D

Database, 157
Database management system issues,
    157–59
Dates, 49–52
Dbmscall, 176
DBMSKEY, 161, 174, 180
Dbmstest, 180
Dclose, 169–70
Dcreate, 169–70
Ddelete, 172
Ddtfile, 138, 142
Deadlock, 126, 204, 205
Delays, 85
Device, 3
Device driver, 4
Device number, 4, 59
Dget, 170, 171
Directories:
    fundamental concepts, 2–3
    I/O on, 42–44, 54–57
DMA (direct memory access), 4
Dopen, 169
Dput, 171–72
Drone processes, 46
Dstfd, 138, 142
Dtop, 171
Dup system call, 129–32

E

ECHILD, 217
ECHO, 86

ECHOE, 86
ECHOK, 86
Ed, 150, 217
EDEADLOCK, 205
Edinvoke, 151
Edrcv, 152
Edsnd, 152
Effective group-ID, 7, 8
Effective user-ID, 7, 8
EINTR, 214
EINVAL, 40
EIO, 46
EMPTY, 81
ENAVAIL, 191
End-of-file, 151
Entrysig, 213
Enum, 14
Environ, 94, 95, 98
Environment, 93–101
Envp, 94
Errno, 12–13, 26, 36
EVexport, 97–98
EVget, 98
EVinit, 98
EVset, 96–97
EVupdate, 99
Exclusive lock, 203
Exec system calls, 101–10, 128–29
Execute permission, 7–8
Execution time, 49
Exit system call, 113–14
Export, 95–96, 100, 107–9, 133
Exported, 96, 97

F

FALSE, 36
Fcn, 212
Fcntl system call, 70–71, 125, 129–30
Fdopen, 151–52
FIFOs (first-in-first-out queues), 3,
    11, 59–60

disadvantages of, 11
implementing messages with, 160–
    81
use of, 159–60
File descriptors, 9, 19–20, 70–71
File modes, 53–54
File pointers, 2, 78
Files, 1–4 (*See also* Directories;
        Ordinary files; Special files)
File size limit, 9
File system, 45
Find, 96–97
Flags, 183, 199, 205
Flow control, 85
Fork system call, 101, 110–13, 128–29
Fstat system call, 62, 125

G

General semaphore, 186
Getenv, 52, 94
Gettoken, 134–38
Global jumps, 217–19
Group file, 7
Group-IDs, 7–9
Group leader, 6, 7
Groups, 7
GTGT state, 134

I

ICANON, 87–89
ICRNL, 84
IGNCR, 84
Ignoresig, 213
IGNPAR, 84
INLCR, 84
I-nodes, 2–3
INQUOTE state, 134
Instruction segment, 5

Interprocess communication:
  fundamental concepts, 10–12 (*See
    also* Advanced interprocess
    communication; Pipes; Signals)
I-numbers, 2
Invoke, 139, 142, 143
INWORD state, 134
I/O (input/output), terminal (*See*
    Terminal I/O)
I/O (input/output) on FIFOs, 159–81
I/O (input/output) on ordinary files,
    18–41
  buffered, 32–37
  close system call, 31–32
  creat system call, 20–24, 26–27
  file descriptors, 19–20
  implementing semaphores with
    files, 21–24
  lseek system call, 37–40
  open system call, 24–28
  portability, 40–41
  read system call, 31
  unlink system call, 21
  write system call, 28–31
I/O (input/output) on pipes (*See*
    Pipes)
Ioctl system call, 82–88
ISTRIP, 85
IUCLC, 85
IXANY, 85
IXOFF, 85
IXON, 85

J

Jmpenv, 218, 219

K

Kernal buffering, 32
Key, 161

Kill system call, 219–20

L

Lexical analyzer, 133–38
Libraries, 4
Linker, 4
Links, 2–3
Link system call, 54–57
"Loader," 4
Lock, 22–23
Lockf system calls, 205
Locking, record, 203–6
Lock manager, 158, 159
Lockpath, 23
Login, 118
Longjmp, 218, 219
Lseek system call, 37–40, 125

M

Main, 102, 105, 109
Mainloop, 217–19
Major device number, 59
Makepipe, 138, 139
Memcpy, 198, 203
Memory-mapped video, 91
Message queue, 11
Messages, 11
  implementing semaphores with, 187
  implementing with FIFOs, 160–81
Message system calls, 182–85
Message type, 183
Minor device number, 59
Mkdir, 59–60
Mknod system call, 58–60
Mount system call, 238–39
Msgctl, 183
Msgget, 182, 195
Msgrcv, 183

Msgsnd, 183
Mv, 55–57

N

Name, 96, 97
Named pipes (*See* FIFOs)
Nbwaitsem, 191
Nbytes, 161, 183, 205
NEUTRAL state, 134
Newpath, 54
Nice command, 120
Nice system call, 9, 120–21
Nice value, 9
Nonblocking terminal I/O, 78–82
NULL, 36, 96, 97
Number, 166

O

Object file, 4
OLCUC, 85
Oldpath, 51
Openfifo, 163
Openqueue, 195
Opensem, 191
Open system call, 24–28, 159
Operation support systems, 156
Ordinary files:
    fundamental concepts, 2
    I/O on (*See* I/O on ordinary files)
Owner group-ID, 7
Owner user-ID, 7

P

P, 186–90
PARENB, 85
Parent process, 5

Parent-process-ID, 6, 7
PARMRK, 84
Path, 3, 102, 104–6
Pause system call, 220, 221
Permissions, 7–9
Perms, 199
Pfd, 124, 131
Pid, 166, 219–20
Pipefdp, 139
Pipeline, 133
Pipes, 10–11, 123–54
    bidirectional, 146–54
    dup system call, 129–32
    named (*See* FIFOs)
    pipe system call, 124–29
    portability, 154
    real shell, 132–46
Pipe system call, 124–29
Plock system call, 238
Port, 46
Portability, in general, 16–17
Pread, 126–29
Priority, 9
Processes, 93–121
    attributes, 9–10
    chdir system call, 119
    chroot system call, 119–20
    environment, 93–101
    exec system calls, 101–10
    exit system call, 113–14
    fork system call, 101, 110–13
    fundamental concepts, 5
    nice system call, 120–21
    permissions, 7–9
    portability, 121
    vs. programs, 101
    setgid system call, 118
    setpgrp system call, 118
    setuid system call, 118
    system calls to get IDs, 117
    wait system call, 114–16 (*See also*
        Interprocess communication)
Process group, 6–7
Process-group-ID, 6, 7

Process-ID, 6–7, 117
Process tracing, 10
Profit system calls, 234
Programming conventions, 14–16
Programs:
    fundamental concepts, 4–5
    vs. processes, 101
    with sharable instructions, 54
Ptrace system call, 234–35
Punctual input, 86–88
Pure-procedure, 54

Q

Queue, 161, 162
Queue-ID, 182–83

R

R, 151
Raw I/O:
    disk special files, 45–47
    terminal, 88–89
Rcvfp, 151–52
Rcvsid, 195, 203
Readany, 79–80
Read permission, 7, 8
Read system call:
    directories and, 43–44
    FIFOs and, 160
    ordinary files and, 31
    pipes and, 124–29
    special files and, 45–49
    terminals and, 75–82
Real group-ID, 7
Real time, 32, 37
Real user-ID, 7
Receive, 160–81
Record locking, 203–6
Redirect, 143–44

Refresh, 82
Register declaration, 14
Relative path, 3
Rmdir, 44
Rmqueue, 163, 165, 169, 176
Root directory, 3

S

Sane, 89
Sbrk system call, 194, 228, 229
Sdb, 209
Sdenter, 200
Sdget, 199
Sdgetv, 200
Sdleave, 200
Sdwaitv, 200
Segment, 192–93
SEINVAL, 36
Sem, 186, 187
Semaphores, 11, 185–92
    implementing with files, 21–24
Semctl, 189
Semget, 188–89, 195
Semop, 188, 189
Semtran, 189, 190
Send, 160–81, 187
SENOMEM, 36
Serializable transaction, 203
Set, 100, 107–9, 133
Setblock, 78–79
Setgid system call, 118
Set-group-ID, 9
Setjmp, 218
Setpgrp system call, 118
Setraw, 88–89
Setsig, 216
Setuid system call, 118
Set-user-ID, 9
Sh, 95, 146
Sharable instructions, 54
Sharable text, 54

Shared file pointers, 10
Shared memory, 11–12, 192–203
Share lock, 203
Shmat, 194
Shmdt, 194
Shmget, 194, 195
Sig, 212, 219
SIGALARM, 211, 221, 225
SIGBUS, 210, 225
SIGCLD, 213, 217, 225
SIGEMT, 210, 212, 225
SIGFPE, 210, 212, 220
SIGHUP, 209, 211
SIGILL, 210, 212, 214
SIGINT, 209, 211
SIGIOT, 210, 212, 220, 225
Signals, 208–26
   alarm system call, 220–25
   fundamental concepts, 5–6
   global jumps, 217–19
   interprocess communication with,
      10
   kill system call, 219–20
   pause system call, 220, 221
   portability, 225–26
   signal system call, 212–17
   types of, 209–12
Signal system call, 212–17
SIGQUIT, 209, 211, 212, 220
SIGPIPE, 210–11
SIGPWR, 211, 217, 225
SIGSEGV, 210, 212, 225
Sigsem, 192
SIGSYS, 210, 212
SIGTERM, 211, 220
SIGTRAP, 210, 212, 214
SIGUSR1, 211
SIGUSR2, 211
Simple command, 132–33
Sleep, 80, 221
Sndsid, 195, 203
Sort, 146–51
Special files:
   disk, I/O on, 45–49, 58–60

fundamental concepts, 3–4
   terminal, I/O on, 74–89
Sprintf, 128
Srcfd, 138, 142
Srcfile, 138, 142
Standard error output, 19–20
Standard input, 19–20
Standard output, 19–20
Stat system call, 62–70
STATUS, 169, 173
Status code, 114–16
Statusp, 114
Statusprt, 116
Stderr, 78
Stdin, 78
Stdout, 78
Sticky bit, 54
Stime system call, 237
Strchr, 107
Strcspn, 99
Strtok, 108
Stty, 90–91
Subroutines, standard, 245–53
Super block, 47–48
Superuser, 8
Symbol table, 95, 99–101
Sync system call, 233–34
Syserr, 13
Sys-errlist, 13
Sys-nerr, 13
System calls:
   access, 57–58
   acct, 240
   alarm, 220–25
   brk, 194, 228–29
   chdir, 119
   chmod, 60
   chown, 60–61
   chroot, 119–20
   close (*See* Close system call)
   creat (*See* Creat system call)
   dup, 129–32
   exec, 101–10, 128–29
   exit, 113–14

System calls (*cont.*)
   fcntl, 70–71, 129–30
   fork, 101, 110–13, 128–29
   fstat, 62, 125
   ioctl, 82–88
   kill, 219–20
   link, 54–57
   lockf, 205
   lseek, 37–40, 125
   message, 182–85
   mknod, 58–60
   mount, 238–39
   nice, 9, 120–21
   open, 24–28, 159
   pause, 220, 221
   pipe, 124–29
   plock, 238
   profit, 234
   ptrace, 234–35
   read (*See* Read system call)
   sbrk, 194, 228, 229
   setgid, 118
   setpgrp, 118
   setuid, 118
   signal, 212–17
   stat, 62–70
   stime, 237
   sync, 233–34
   sys3b, 240
   time, 237
   times, 235–37
   to get IDs, 117
   ulimit, 227–28
   umask, 230
   umount, 239
   uname, 232–33
   unlink, 21, 44
   use of, 12–14
   ustat, 231–32
   utime, 61–62
   wait, 114–16, 214
   write (*See* Write system call)
System data, 5
System data segment, 5

System III, 156–57
System V, 157
   message system calls, 182–85
   process attributes, 242–44
   semaphores in, 188–90
   shared memory in, 193–98
Sys3b system call, 240

T

TAB3, 85
TCXONC, 85
Terminal I/O (input/output), 74–91
   ioctl system call, 82–88
   nonblocking, 178–82
   normal, 75–78
   portability, 90–91
   raw, 88–89
Termio structure, 83–84
Text busy, 54
Text file, 4
Time, 49–52
Time command, 236
Time member, 163
Timestart, 236–37
Timestop, 236–37
Times system call, 235–37
Time system call, 237
Tokens, 133–41
Trace flag, 9–10
Transaction, 203
Transaction-processing system, 157
TRUE, 139
Turnaround, 152, 153

U

Ulimit system call, 227–28
Umask system call, 230
Umount system call, 239
Uname system call, 232–33

Undo log, 203
Unlink system call, 21, 44
Unlock, 22–24
Updated, 99
Updating the environment, 95
User buffering, 32–37
User data segment, 5
User-ID, 7–9
Ustat system call, 231–32
Utime system call, 61–62

V

V, 186–90
Val, 96, 97
Victim selection, 204–5
Void, 14
Volume, 45

W

Waitfor, 144–45
Waitpid, 139

Waitsem, 191
Wait system call, 114–16, 214
Wall-clock time, 32
Write permission, 7, 8
Write system call:
  FIFOs and, 160
  ordinary files and, 28–31
  pipes and, 124, 125
  special files and, 45–46
  terminals and, 75, 78

X

XCASE, 85
Xenix 3:
  record locking in, 203–6
  semaphores in, 190–92
  shared memory in, 198–203

Z

Zombie process, 114